PLANET EARTH'S LEGACY

UNESCO WORLD HERITAGE SITES

DAVID J. PATTEN

David J. Patten

PATTENTED PRESS

ISBN-13:978-1720782971
ISBN-10:1720782970

On the cover:
NASA's photograph of Earth as seen from outer space

to JILL

A most congenial, adventurous,
and intrepid lady traveler

A stone stele displays UNESCO's World Heritage logo
at the entrance to Borobudur, Earth's largest Buddhist
monument, located in Central Java, Indonesia

FOREWORD

Why do people travel? If you ask a group of ten travelers, you will probably get ten, somewhat different answers.

Some travel to experience firsthand the food and drink of a destination. Examples are the tours specializing in wine-tasting and cooking courses. Others travel to see exotic animals in their native habitats, such as those going on African safaris. Others go to interact with people in exotic cultures and enjoy people-to-people tours. There are tours specializing in travel photography and tours to interact with local craftsmen. There are also those whose primary interests are in archaeological and historic sites.

I must admit that I traveled for decades thinking little about the conservation and preservation of the archaeological and historic sites I was visiting. I was usually unaware of the UNESCO World Heritage status of the historic sites on the tours I was taking. A mention of a location as being a World Heritage site would sometimes be seen in trip itineraries, or I might see the UNESCO World Heritage symbol displayed at a particular site while on a trip. But over time, I became more and more aware of the importance of the UNESCO World Heritage status of the places I visited. I found that, almost without exception, there were one or more aspects of a UNESCO site that usually made it one of the highlights of a trip. In recent years I would sometimes request extensions to tours to see specific UNESCO sites in which I was especially interested. On a trip to the south of India, I requested an extension to include the UNESCO site of Hampi. I requested a special extension to visit Copán located over the border into Honduras while on a tour of Guatemala. On a trip to Iran, I invested in a three-day extension of a tour to visit the Gonbad-e Qabus located in the northeastern section of the country.

Although I usually found a wealth of information on individual sites on the internet, I failed to find much literature that reviewed a group of UNESCO sites or that attempted to evaluate them from a traveler's point of view. Not finding much

The Lakshmi Narasimha Temple at Hampi, India. The Hindu deity, Narasimha, half lion, half human, and an avatar of Vishnu, sits on the seven-headed snake, Sesha.

interest in compiling a series of articles on UNESCO sites, I finally determined to write such a series of articles myself, with this book being the result.

This selection of fifty articles on specific UNESCO sites in thirty-four countries is obviously very arbitrary. The sites were selected primarily because of my interest in them and my wanting to learn more about them. Although the articles are heavily oriented towards ancient archaeological and historic sites, articles on historic Budapest, Tel Aviv's White City, the works of Antoni Gaudí, and Berlin's Museuminsel have been included. A few natural sites have been included such as those articles on Jordan's Wadi Rum, Kazakhstan's Tamgaly Park and Florida's Everglades. Such UNESCO ecological sites could easily be the subject and focus of another book.

In the writing of this book, I have relied heavily on the literature accessible on the internet. I have usually found internet sources to be more complete and more up-to-date than the information found in travel books or guidebooks. Guidebooks often devote more space to accommodations, places to eat, and in giving directions on how to get to destinations rather than on descriptions of the sights to be seen at a particular location.

The internet sources cited at the ends of articles are not only to give credit where credit is due but are given so more information might be found on the various sites than what could be given in the brief articles in this book.

All photographs accompanying the articles are those of the author unless otherwise indicated.

I have found travel to be very much a life-transforming experience. It has opened my eyes to a world that I did not know existed. I have become someone I would not have otherwise become.

Mark Twain said it best: "Travel is fatal to prejudice, bigotry and narrow-mindedness."

David J. Patten

ACKNOWLEDGMENTS

Two of my most faithful e-mail correspondents have requested that they remain anonymous, but they have been of unfailing assistance in the writing of this book. They have proofread nearly every one of the book's articles and have always responded quickly with corrections and comments.

As very much a world traveler, Jill Athey must be acknowledged for her support, advice and proofreading of many of the book's chapters. She has been a great source of inspiration and a most congenial travel companion on all seven trips we have taken together as singles.

Jackie Seal and Ruth Danielle, both members of local travel groups in Florida's Tampa Bay area, must be acknowledged for their expertise in the proofreading and editing of the book's text.

Carmen Gonzalez, sister of my very good friend and former colleague at the *Tampa Bay Times*, Sandra Gonzalez, must also to be acknowledged for her editing and proofreading expertise.

Ralph Hamblin, graphic artist, published writer, and former colleague at the *Saint Petersburg Times* (now the *Tampa Bay Times*) is also to be thanked for his feedback and his many constructive criticisms.

It must also be acknowledged that six of the articles in this collection were originally published in *International Travel News* (*ITN*), but most have been extensively revised and enlarged. David Tykol, editor of *ITN* has stated that republication of the articles first published in *ITN* is permitted by saying: "All materials submitted become the property of *ITN*, which has explicit reprint rights. However, authors still retain all rights."

The six articles originally published in *ITN* are as follows:

2009, November: "Tel Aviv's Bauhaus architecture," p. 13-14
2010, October: "Vietnam's Champa kingdom," p. 16-17
2011, July: "Captivating art: Gal Vihara, Sri Lanka," p. 44-45

2011, November: "Ethiopia's enigmatic stelae at Tiya,"
    p. 30-31
2014, April: "Timur's Summer Palace, Shakhrisabz," p. 33-35
2017, February: "Iran's Gonbad-e Qabus," p. 26-27

Thanks must also be extended to all those who have submitted reviews on Amazon.com of my earlier book on travel, *Wanderlust: Travel off the Tourist Track*. Having received so many favorable reviews on Amazon has been a great source of encouragement and inspiration.
                        David J. Patten

The author photographed by a local guide at the
Jantar Mantar, Jaipur, India, in May, 2004

ABOUT THE AUTHOR

David J. Patten is a writer, travel photographer, graphic designer, and world traveler based in Saint Petersburg, Florida.

David graduated with an undergraduate degree in art from the University of Nebraska, Omaha. He has a master's degree in art history from the State University of Iowa, Iowa City, and a master's degree in information science from the University of Michigan, Ann Arbor.

He has held professional staff positions at the University of Cincinnati; Washington University, St. Louis; and Oberlin College, Ohio. He worked for ten years as the editor of an art periodicals indexing service at a New York City publishing firm. He also held the position of index editor at an art indexing and abstracting service of the J. Paul Getty Trust based in Williamstown, Massachusetts.

Before retiring, he held the position of graphic designer at the *Saint Petersburg Times,* now the *Tampa Bay Times.*

David has traveled to a total of fifty-six countries, with forty-eight of them having been visited since retiring in 2003. While living in New York City, he traveled primarily in Europe and visited an additional eight countries.

His writing on travel includes twenty-three articles published in *International Travel News (ITN)*. His travel photographs have been published in *International Travel News* and the *Saint Petersburg Times* and have been exhibited at the Morean Arts Center, Saint Petersburg, Florida.

His earlier book on travel includes a series of thirty-six articles on offbeat sites entitled, *Wanderlust: Travel off the Tourist Track*, available on Amazon.com.

David may be contacted at: djpatten@tampabay.rr.com

UNESCO WORLD HERITAGE SITES VISITED

UNESCO's 1,073 World Heritage Sites are listed online at: https://whc.unesco.org/en/list/.

David Patten has visited most of the sites listed below on various trips starting in the mid-1980s until April of 2017. A total of 192 sites in 49 countries have been visited.

Sites with an asterisk have separate articles included in this book which can be found listed in the table of contents.

Algeria
Djémila
Timgad*
Tipasa
Kasbah of Algiers

Armenia
Cathedral and Churches of Echmiatsin
Monastery of Geghard

Austria
Historic Centre of Vienna

Azerbaijan
City of Baku with the Shirvanshah's Palace and Maiden Tower*

Belgium
La Grand-Place, Brussels

Cambodia
Angkor*

Chile
Rapa Nui National Park*
Historic Quarter of Valparaíso

China
Imperial Palaces of the Ming and Qing Dynasties in Beijing and Shenyang
Mogao Caves*
The Great Wall*
Summer Palace, an Imperial Garden in Beijing
Temple of Heaven. Beijing
Imperial Tombs of the Ming and Qing Dynasties
Xinjiang Tianshan

Croatia
Historical Complex of Split with the Palace of Diocletian*
Plitvice Lakes National Park

Cuba
Old Havana and its Fortification System
Trinidad and the Valley de los Ingenios
Urban Historic Centre of Cienfuegos

Egypt
Ancient Thebes with its Necropolis
Historic Cairo
Nubian Monuments from Abu Simbel to Philae*
The Pyramid Fields from Giza to Dahshur

Ethiopia
Rock-Hewn Churches, Lalibela*
Simien National Park
Aksum*
Tiya*

France
Chartres Cathedral
Mont-Saint-Michel and its Bay
Palace and Park of Versailles
Arles, Roman and Romanesque Monuments*
Pont du Gard*
Cathedral of Notre-Dame, Reims
Paris, Banks of the Seine
Historic Centre of Avignon: Papal Palace

Germany
Palaces and Parks of Potsdam and Berlin
Cologne Cathedral
Museumsinsel, Berlin*

Great Britain and Northern Ireland
Stonehenge
City of Bath
Tower of London
Canterbury Cathedral
Palace of Westminster and Westminster Abbey

Greece

Acropolis, Athens
Archaeological Site of Delphi
Metéora*
Archaeological Site of Olympia
Delos*
Archaeological Site of Mycenae

Guatemala

Antigua Guatemala
Tikal National Park
Archaeological Park and Ruins of Quirigua

Holy See

San Paolo Fuori le Mura
Vatican City

Honduras

Maya Site of Copán*

Hungary

Budapest, the Buda Castle Quarter and Andrássy Avenue*

India

Agra Fort
Ajanta Caves
Ellora Caves
Taj Mahal
Group of Monuments at Mahabalipuram
Fatehpur Sikri
Group of Monuments at Hampi
Khajuraho Group of Monuments
Elephanta Caves
Great Living Chola Temples
Humayun's Tomb, Delhi
Qutb Minar and its Monuments, Delhi
Red Fort Complex
The Jantar Mantar, Jaipur
Hill Forts of Rajasthan

Indonesia

Borobudur Temple Compounds*
Prambanan Temple Compounds*

Iran

Meidan Emam, Esfahan
Persepolis
Takht-e Soleyman
Pasargadae
Soltaniyeh
Bisotun
Shushtar Historical Hydraulic System
Shrine Ensemble in Ardabil
Tabriz Historic Bazaar Complex
Gonbad-e Qābus*
Masjed-e Jāmé of Isfahan
Golestan Palace
Susa
Historic City of Yazd

Israel

Masada
Old City of Acre
White City of Tel-Aviv – the Modern Movement*
Megiddo

Italy

Church of Santa Maria delle Grazie
Historic Centre of Florence
Piazza del Duomo, Pisa
Venice and its Lagoon
Historic Centre of Naples
Archaeological Areas of Pompei
Asissi, the Basilica of San Francexco
City of Verona
Villa d'Este, Tivoli
Syracuse
Mount Etna
Palermo & Cathedrals of Cefalú and Monreale*

Japan

Buddhist Monuments in the Horyu-ji Area*
Historic Monuments of Ancient Kyoto
Historic Monuments of Ancient Nara
Shrines and Temples of Nikko

SITES VISITED (continued)

Jerusalem (Site proposed by Jordan)

    Old City of Jerusalem and its Walls

Jordan

    Petra

    Quseir Amra*

    Wadi Rum Protected Area*

Kazakhstan

    Petroglyphs within the Archaeological Landscape of Tamgaly*

Korea, Republic of

    Seokguram Grotto and Bulguksa Temple

    Gyeongju Historic Areas*

    Haeinsa Temple Janggyeong Panjeon, the Depositories for the
        Tripitaka Koreana Woodblocks

Lao People's Democratic Republic

    Town of Luang Prabang

    Vat Phou and Associated Ancient Settlements*

Luxembourg

    City of Luxembourg: its Old Quarters and Fortifications

Malta

    City of Valletta

    Megalithic Temples of Malta*

Mexico

    Historic Centre of Mexico City and Xochimilco

    Historic Centre of Oaxaca and Archaeological Site of Monte Albán

    Historic Centre of Puebla

    National Park of Palenque*

    Pre-Hispanic City of Teotihuacan

    Pre-Hispanic City of Chichén-Itzá

    Pre-Hispanic Town of Uxmal*

Morocco

    Medina of Fez

    Medina of Marrakesh

    Historic City of Meknes

    Rabat

Netherlands

    Canal Ring Area of Amsterdam inside the Singelgracht

Palestine

Church of the Nativity, Bethlehem*

Peru

City of Cuzco
Historic Sanctuary of Machu Picchu
Historic Centre of Lima
Lines and Geoglyphs of Nasca and Palpa*

Portugal

Cultural Landscape of Sintra
Monastery of the Hieronymites and Tower of Belém in Lisbon

Russia

Historic Centre of Saint Petersburg
Kremlin and Red Square, Moscow

Spain

Alhambra, Generalife and Albayzín, Granada
Historic Centre of Cordoba
Monastery and Site of the Escurial, Madrid
Works of Antoni Gaudí *
Historic City of Toledo
Cathedral, Alcázar & Archivo de Indias. Seville*

Sri Lanka

Ancient City of Polonnaruwa*
Ancient City of Sigiriya
Sacred City of Anuradhapura
Old Town of Galle and its Fortifications
Sacred City of Kandy*
Golden Temple of Dambulla
Central Highlands of Sri Lanka

Thailand

Historic City of Ayutthaya*
Historic Town of Sukhothai*

Tunisia

Amphitheatre of El Jem*
Archaeological Site of Carthage
Medina of Tunis
Kairouan*
Dougga / Thugga

Turkey

Rock Sites of Cappadocia
Historic Areas of Istanbul
Nemrut Dağ*
Hierapolis-Pamukkale
Archaeological Site of Troy
Ephesus
Archaeological Site of Ani
Aphrodisias*
Bursa
Pergamon
Göbekli Tepe*

Turkmenistan

Historical and Cultural Park "Ancient Merv"

United States of America

Yellowstone National Park
Everglades National Park*
Grand Canyon National Park
San Juan National Historic Site in Puerto Rico
Statue of Liberty
Yosemite National Park

Uzbekistan

Itchan Kala
Historic Centre of Bukhara
Historic Centre of Shakhrisabz*
Samarkand – Crossroad of Cultures

Viet Nam

Complex of Hué Monuments
Ha Long Bay
Hoi, An Ancient Town
My Son Sanctuary*

TABLE OF CONTENTS

CONTENTS (continued)

UNESCO WORLD HERITAGE

In 1965 the White House Conference recommended a "World Heritage Trust" to preserve "the world's natural and scenic areas and historic sites for the present and future of the entire world citizenry." A similar proposal was drafted by the United Nation's Conference on the Human Environment in 1972 in Stockholm, Sweden.   At a UNESCO conference on 16 November, 1972, the Convention Concerning the Protection of the World Cultural and Natural Heritage was agreed upon at UNESCO's General Conference. Effective on 17 December, 1975, it was ratified by 193 states parties and by 189 UNESCO member states. Four countries have not ratified it: Liechtenstein, Nauru, Somalia, and Tuvalu.

As stated by UNESCO, it seeks to "encourage the identification, protection and preservation of cultural and natural heritage considered to be of outstanding value to humanity."

Its mission statement is as follows:

"Encourage countries to sign the World Heritage Convention and to ensure the protection of their natural and cultural heritage

"Encourage States Parties to the Convention to nominate sites within their national territory for inclusion on the World Heritage List

"Encourage States Parties to establish management plans and set up reporting systems on the state of conservation of their World Heritage sites

"Help States Parties safeguard World Heritage properties by providing technical assistance and professional training

"Provide emergency assistance for World Heritage sites in immediate danger

"Support States Parties' public awareness-building activities for World Heritage conservation

"Encourage participation of the local population in the preservation of their cultural and natural heritage"

"Encourage international cooperation in the conservation of our world's cultural and natural heritage."
(From: http://whc.unesco.org/en/about/)

Prior to 2005 UNESCO listed four criteria for natural heritage and six for cultural heritage. In 2005 the criteria were combined into one list of ten criteria which have been modified several times since then. Today, sites nominated for heritage status must evidence what UNESCO calls "outstanding universal value" and meet at least one of the following criteria:

"Represents a masterpiece of human creative genius and cultural significance

"Exhibits an important interchange of human values, over a span of time, or within a cultural area of the world, on developments in architecture or technology, monumental arts, town-planning, or landscape design

"To bear a unique or at least exceptional testimony to a cultural tradition or to a civilization which is living or which has disappeared

"Is an outstanding example of a type of building, architectural, or technological ensemble or landscape which illustrates a significant stage in human history

"Is an outstanding example of a traditional human settlement, land-use, or sea-use which is representative of a culture, or human interaction with the environment especially when it has become vulnerable under the impact of irreversible change

"Is directly or tangibly associated with events or living traditions, with ideas, or with beliefs, with artistic and literary works of outstanding universal significance

"Contains superlative natural phenomena or areas of exceptional natural beauty and aesthetic importance

"Is an outstanding example representing major stages of Earth's history, including the record of life, significant on-going geological processes in the development of landforms, or significant geomorphic or physiographic features

"Is an outstanding example representing significant on-going ecological and biological processes in the evolution and development of terrestrial, fresh water, coastal and marine ecosystems, and communities of plants and animals

"Contains the most important and significant natural habitats for in-situ conservation of biological diversity, including those containing threatened species of outstanding universal value from the point of view of science or conservation"

(From: https://en.wikipedia.org/wiki/World_Heritage_Site)

World Heritage designation protects sites under the Geneva Convention's Law of War. Prohibited are committing of any "acts of hostility" against cited monuments, the use of sites for a "military effort," or using them as "objects of reprisal."

For a site to be accepted as a World Heritage Site, it must first be listed as a protected site by the country proposing it for UNESCO status and then included in a tentative list. After being selected from a nominating file, it must be recommended to the World Heritage Committee, which meets once a year and votes to accept the site for designation or may defer or deny the decision for inclusion.

The process for gaining acceptance as a UNESCO site can be a long and costly one, and UNESCO has been criticized for its underrepresentation of sites in non-European countries. Especially since UNESCO status has the potential to increase tourism as well as revenue from visitors to the site, lobbying for inclusion has been growing. As a result, smaller and poorer countries are often placed at a disadvantage in the selection process.

As of June, 2018, 1,073 sites located in 167 countries have been designated as World Heritage Sites. 832 sites have been inscribed as being of cultural importance, while 206 sites have been listed as being important as natural heritage. Thirty-five sites have been listed as being a mixture of both. World Heritage

Sites are classified in five separate world regions: Africa, Arab States, Asia, and the Americas, including the Caribbean. Of the 1,073 listed sites as of July, 2017, Italy has the highest number of 53. Other countries with high numbers are: China (52), Spain (46), France (43), Germany (42), India (36), and Mexico (34). The United States has 23 UNESCO sites, with one listed as being endangered, the Florida Everglades.

Changes in the status of sites may include boundary extensions, reductions of protected areas, or minor boundary changes. If a change has a significant impact on the site or is a name change, it must be returned to the World Heritage Committee.

Since inscribed sites are evaluated annually, the Committee may list a site as endangered or may delete it from the list. So far, only two sites have been deleted: the Arabian Oryx Sanctuary, resulting from its protected area being reduced by ninety percent, and the Dresden Elbe Valley, for its construction of the Waldschlösschen Bridge, which seriously impacted the area.

A site may also be added to the List of World Heritage in Danger if threatened by wars, pollution, and human development. At present, fifty-four sites have been listed as endangered.

A recent assessment of natural heritage sites revealed that sixty-three percent of the sites have been impacted by human settlements, roads, and land being used for agriculture. For sites containing forests, ninety-one were found to have suffered losses since 2000. Many natural heritage sites are now thought to require conservation measures, since they were found to have been much more seriously affected than originally thought.

Adapted from:
https://whc.unesco.org/en/list/

UNESCO AND THE USA

The relationship of the United States with UNESCO has been on-again and off-again.

The concept of an organization similar to UNESCO was initiated in 1965 at the White House Conference that proposed the formation of a "World Heritage Trust." The United States then ratified the Convention Concerning the Protection of the World Cultural and Natural Heritage that was agreed upon at UNESCO's General Conference and became effective on 17 December, 1975.

In 1984, during the administration of Ronald Reagan, the USA withdrew from UNESCO citing what it saw as corruption, a pro-Soviet Union bias, and its criticism of Israel. In 2002, during the George W. Bush administration, the USA rejoined UNESCO in what was described as a desire for international cooperation, but was also seen as a means of gaining multinational support for its war with Iraq.

When the State of Palestine was admitted as a full UNESCO member in 2011, the United States stopped funding UNESCO but continued to maintain an office in UNESCO's headquarters in Paris. In accordance with an amendment ratified fifteen years earlier, the USA was found to be prohibited from funding any organization recognizing Palestine as a state.

According to an announcement made on 12 October, 2017, by the Trump administration, the USA will be again pulling out of UNESCO which is to be effective as of 31 December, 2018. Cited as one of the reasons for withdrawal from UNESCO was its anti-Israel bias. There has been a long-standing belief that UNESCO has had a bias against Israel, partly caused by the fact that it is far outnumbered by Arab UNESCO members.

The Trump administration has delegated no funds for UNESCO in its budget for the next fiscal year and has informed some diplomats that their jobs are on hold and that they best start seeking other jobs. UNESCO has also been recently denounced by various American officials and especially by the

American ambassador to UNESCO, Nikki R. Haley. Haley has called UNESCO's politicization a "chronic embarrassment" and that "U.S. taxpayers should no longer be on the book to pay for policies that are hostile to our values and are a mockery of justice and common sense."

Israel's prime minister, Benjamin Netanyahu, labeled the USA's decision to leave UNESCO "brave" and "moral" and called UNESCO a "theater of the absurd" and that "instead of preserving history, it distorts it." He has stated that Israel will also withdraw from UNESCO.

Meanwhile, UNESCO's director-general, Irina Bokova, expressed regret at the decision of the USA and called it a "loss for multilateralism."

The USA has already lost its vote on issues relating to UNESCO as a result of nonpayment of its membership dues since 2013, but it says it will remain as a nonmember observer and will continue to participate in debates and discussions about UNESCO's activities. The USA is already in debt to UNESCO by about USD $550 million, which will increase to over $600 million at the end of 2018 and will continue to make the funding of UNESCO a problem, since the USA is responsible for approximately 22% of UNESCO's annual budget.

The rift between UNESCO and the USA and Israel has also been exacerbated by UNESCO's declaring the ancient, old city section of Hebron and its Tomb of the Patriarchs, also called the Ibrahimi Mosque, a UNESCO heritage site. This decision, as well as the recognition of the Church of the Nativity in Bethlehem, is cited as exhibiting anti-Israel bias, since both sit on Palestine's West Bank.

UNESCO has also criticized Israel for mishandling sites in Jerusalem and prohibiting freedom of worship. In 2016, a resolution condemned Israel for "escalating aggressions" relating to Jerusalem's holy site, known to Jews and Christians as the Temple Mount and to Muslims as the "holy sanctuary," the al-Haram al-Sharif.

The designation of the ancient city of Hebron as a UNESCO site has been especially contentious.

Inscribed by UNESCO as a heritage site in danger in 2017 (no. 1565) under the title, "Hebron/Al-Khalil Old Town," it is primarily a city of Palestinians whose old city is under full Israeli control. It is also the home of hundreds of Jewish settlers. Since the recognition of Hebron as a heritage site was fast tracked, it is subject to UNESCO's annual review.

In opposing the designation of Hebron as a heritage site, the American ambassador, Nikki Haley, called it "an affront to history" and that "it undermines the trust that is needed for the Israeli-Palestinian peace process to be successful." She also added, "It further discredits an already highly questionable U.N. agency."

Hebron has seen much Palestinian-Jewish conflict. In 1929, sixty-nine Jews were killed in Hebron. In 1980, six Jewish settlers were killed on their way home from prayers, and in 1983 three students at Hebron's Islamic College were killed by the Jewish Underground.

More recently, in 1994, an American-Israeli physician and member of the Israeli Kach movement, Baruch Goldstein, gunned down Muslims praying in the Ibrahimi Mosque, which includes the Cave of the Patriarchs, venerated by Jews, Christians and Muslims as the location of the burials of the Biblical patriarchs and matriarchs. Called by the Muslim name, Ibrahim, for Abraham, the site is believed to be the place bought by Abraham, regarded by Muslims as a saint, for the burial of himself and his wife, Sarah, as recorded in the Christian Bible,

On the day celebrated as the Jewish Purim and during the Muslim holy month of Ramadan, Goldstein fired upon eight hundred Muslims at the Fajr, the first of five daily prayers required of Muslims, killing twenty-nine people and wounding 125 others. Jewish settlers in Hebron praised Goldstein as a hero and declared him a martyr when he died later,.

As a result, today the holy site is divided into separate sections, administered separately by Jews and Palestinians and with separate entrances for Jewish and Palestinian worshippers.

Hebron also figures in Israeli prime minister Netanyahu's plans to build a Jewish People's Heritage museum in the predominantly Palestinian city. To do so, he says he will reduce Israel's contribution to UNESCO by one million dollars annually.

With the controversial announcement by the Trump administration that the USA will be moving its embassy from Tel Aviv to Jerusalem, it appears that the positions of both sides of the many issues relating to Israel and the State of Palestine will only continue to solidify and escalate.

Adapted from:

https://www.fastcompany.com/40480569/3-things-to-know-about-the-united-states-leaving-unesco

http://time.com/4979411/unesco-united-states-withdrawal/

https://www.nytimes.com/2017/10/12/us/politics/trump-unesco-withdrawal.html

https://www.theguardian.com/world/2017/oct/12/us-withdraw-unesco-december-united-nations

https://www.theguardian.com/world/2017/jul/07/unesco-recognises-hebron-as-palestinian-world-heritage-site

https://www.nytimes.com/.../unesco-hebron-world-heritage-site-israel-palestinians.html

UNESCO HERITAGE SITES IN THE USA

The USA's twenty-three UNESCO World Heritage Sites, along with their dates of inscription, are as follows:

Cultural (10)

Cahokia Mounds State Historic Site (1982)
Chaco Culture (1987)
Independence Hall (1979)
La Fortaleza and San Juan National Historic Site in Puerto
    Rico (1983)
Mesa Verde National Park (1978)
Monticello and the University of Virginia in Charlottesville
    (1987)
Monumental Earthworks of Poverty Point (2014)
San Antonio Missions (2015)
Statue of Liberty (1984)
Taos Pueblo (1992)

Natural (12)

Carlsbad Caverns National Park (1995)
Everglades National Park (1979)
Grand Canyon National Park (1979)
Great Smoky Mountains National Park (1983)
Hawaii Volcanoes National Park (1987)
Kluane/Wrangell-St. Elias/Glacier Bay/Tatshenshini-
    Alsek (1979,1992, 1994)
Mammoth Cave National Park (1981)
Olympic National Park (1981)
Redwood National and State Parks (1980)
Waterton Glacier International Peace Park (1995)
Yellowstone National Park (1978)
Yosemite National Park (1984)

Mixed (1)

Papahānaumokuākea (2010)

(From: http://whc.unesco.org/en/statesparties/us)

DESTROYED BY THE TALIBAN: BAMIYAN, AFGHANISTAN

Country name: Islamic Republic of **Afghanistan**

Site name: Cultural Landscape and Archaeological Remains of the Bamiyan Valley

Location: Bamiyan Province, Bamiyan District, Hazaraiat region, 230 km (140 miles) northwest of Kabul, central Afghanistan

UNESCO World Heritage Site: Inscribed 2003, no. 208

As early as 1997, the Taliban leader, Abdul Wahed, had expressed his intentions to destroy the colossal images of the Buddha located at the UNESCO World Heritage Site of Bamiyan in Afghanistan. Once the valley was finally under his control, he launched his plan to drill holes in the heads of the images for explosives but was prevented from doing so by the area's local governor and by the Taliban leader, Mullah Mohammed Omar. In July of 1999, Omar issued an order in favor of preserving the images based on the fact that Buddhism was no longer practiced in Afghanistan and that the images were a source of income from tourism. In 2000 the Taliban had asked the UN for funds to rebuild ditches for drainage around the tops of the niches where the images were located as a means for preserving them. But tenets of radical Islam were initiating a program against what they saw as non-Muslim elements infiltrating Afghan society and succeeded in banning all forms of imagery in accordance with a strict form of Sharia.

As a result, in March of 2001, Bamiyan's two colossal images were destroyed by decree of the Taliban's supreme commander, Mullah Mohammad Omar. His reason, given in an interview, was that he had been angered that foreign aid was being offered to save the images while thousands of the Afghan people were dying of hunger. On the other hand, the Taliban's Information and Culture Minister, Qadratullah Jamal, stated in an interview with the Associated Press that four hundred Islamic clerics had determined that the images were idolatrous and not in accord with the teachings of Islam. The Taliban's ministry of religious affairs also stated that the destruction of the images was mandated by Islamic law. It was stated that their destruction had also been ordered by Abdul Wali, minister for the Propagation of Virtue and the Prevention of Vice.

After the destruction of the images, Omar was quoted as saying that "Muslims should be proud of smashing idols. It has given praise to Allah that we have destroyed them." Wakil Ahmad Mutawakel, Afghan's foreign minister, also stated that "we are destroying the statues in accordance with Islamic law, and it is merely a religious issue."

Beginning on 2 March of 2001, the images were destroyed in several stages. They were first attacked by artillery and anti-aircraft guns that succeeded in only damaging them and not totally destroying them. Anti-tank mines were then set out at the bottom of the niches holding the images, and Taliban members were lowered down the face of the cliffs to set explosives drilled into holes drilled into the Buddhist images. Finally, not finding it possible to completely destroy the face of one of the Buddhas, a rocket was launched leaving a hole in the image's colossal head.

The two monumental statues of the standing Buddha, examples of the region's Gandhara style, had been carved into a sandstone cliff in the Bamiyan Valley. The larger image, measuring 53m in height, has been dated to 554 CE. The smaller image, measuring 35m in height, has been dated to 507 CE. With the images' details being worked in mud mixed with straw and then finished with stucco, the larger image had been painted in carmine red, while the smaller images had been painted in a combination of colors. Identified by their hand gestures or *mudras*, the statues represented the Buddhas Variocana and Sakyamuni. The larger image was often called "Solsol," while the smaller was called "Shahmama." Until their destruction in 2001, they were the world's largest images of the standing Buddha.

From the 2nd to the 7th centuries, the Hindu Kush mountain region of Afghanistan had been part of Central Asia's Silk Road that united China with the West. The area became the center of numerous Buddhist monasteries and an active center for philosophy, art, and religion. Hermits living in small caves within the monastic communities often embellished the caves with Buddhist images and brightly painted frescos. Starting with the invasions of the Muslims in the seventh century, Buddhist and Gandharan culture in the region came to an end when it was conquered by the Safavids in the ninth century.

Until their destruction by the Taliban, the two images had survived the invasion of Genghis Khan and the efforts of the Mughal emperor Aurangazeb to destroy them. They had also survived being fired at by the canons of the Persian king, Nader Afshar, in the 18th century.

In 2002, funds from foreign sources began the stabilization and recovery of the statues, and in 2009 the International Council on Monuments and Sites (ICOMOS) erected scaffolding inside one of the niches to conserve what was left of its image. In 2006, Afghan officials decided to attempt the reconstruction of the images, and in 2008, the World Monuments Fund cited Bamiyan on the World Watch List of the 100 Most Endangered Sites. In 2011, the UNESCO Expert Working Group on Afghanistan discussed what should be done at Bamiyan. Thirty-nine recommendations for conserving the site were drafted at the conference, with one solution suggesting the reconstruction of the smaller image but leaving the larger empty niche as a memorial of Taliban fanaticism. The Afghan regional governor has advocated the rebuilding of the statues as a means of increasing tourism, but others have advocated that money would be better spent on supplying housing and electricity for the local residents.

Activity at Bamiyan continues, with archaeologists making the remarkable discovery in September, 2008, of the remains of an unknown image of a reclining Buddha symbolizing the death or *parinirvana* of the Buddha. Then in July of 2015, a Chinese couple used 3D laser light projections to fill the empty niches with images of the destroyed Buddhas. Approved by UNESCO and Afghan officials, the use of holograms of the images to fill the empty niches attracted approximately 150 local residents on 7 June, 2015.

UNESCO has developed a three-phase program of safeguarding and de-mining the site, and in March, 2011, at the meeting of the 9th Bamiyan Expert Working Group, it was decided that Bamiyan was eligible for being deleted from the List of World Heritage in Danger by 2013.

Eight guards are said to be stationed and on duty at Bamiyan to prevent any further looting and vandalism, and that a dedicated police force for the protection of cultural property has been formed by the Afghan Ministry of the Interior.

Regardless of whatever transpires in the future, the original colossal images of the Buddha at Bamiyan have been lost to posterity forever.

Adapted from:

https://whc.unesco.org/en/list/208
https://en.wikipedia.org/wiki/Buddhas_of_Bamiyan

ANCIENT SITES DAMAGED BY ISIS

Islamist militants in Iraq and Syria continue their war on the region's cultural heritage, attacking archaeological sites with bulldozers and explosives.

The Islamic State (ISIS) released a video that shocked the world by showing the fiery destruction of the Temple of Baalshamin, one of the best-preserved ruins at the Syrian site of Palmyra. Explosions have been reported at another Palmyra temple, dedicated to the ancient god Baal. A United Nation agency has said that satellite images show that the larger of the temples has largely been destroyed.

The destruction is part of a propaganda campaign that includes videos of militants rampaging through Iraq's Mosul Museum with pickaxes and sledgehammers and the dynamiting of centuries-old Christian and Muslim shrines.

ISIS has controlled large stretches of Syria, along with northern and western Iraq, so there is little to stop its militants from plundering and destroying sites under its control in a region known as the cradle of civilization. The militant group is just one of many factions fighting for control of Syria, where a civil war has left more than 230,000 dead and millions more homeless.

The group claims the destruction of ancient sites is religiously motivated. Its militants have targeted well-known ancient sites along with more modern graves and shrines belonging to other Muslim sects, citing idol worship to justify their actions. At the same time, ISIS has used looting as a moneymaking venture to finance its military operations.

"It's both propagandistic and sincere," says Columbia University historian Christopher Jones, who has chronicled the damage on his blog. "They see themselves as recapitulating the early history of Islam."

The following are sites that ISIS has damaged or destroyed:

SYRIA

Palmyra

Palmyra thrived for centuries in the desert east of Damascus as an oasis and stop for caravans on the Silk Road. As part of the Roman Empire, it was a thriving, wealthy metropolis. The city-state reached its peak in the late 3rd century, when it was ruled by Queen Zenobia and briefly rebelled against Rome.

Zenobia failed, and Palmyra was re-conquered and destroyed by Roman armies in A.D. 273. Its colonnaded avenues and impressive temples were preserved by the desert climate, and in the 20th century the city had become one of Syria's biggest tourist destinations.

When ISIS seized the modern town of Palmyra and the ancient ruins nearby, the militants initially promised to leave the site's columns and temples untouched, but those promises were empty. They proceeded to publicly execute Khaled al-Asaad, a Syrian archaeologist, who oversaw excavations at the site for decades, and hung his headless body from a column.

The group released photos of militants rigging the 1,900-year-old Temple of Baalshamin with explosives and blowing it up. It was one of Palmyra's best-preserved buildings, originally dedicated to a Phoenician storm god. Now it is only rubble.

Just days later, explosions were reported at the Temple of Baal, a nearby structure that was one of the site's largest, and a United Nations agency says the building was flattened.

Mar Elian Monastery

The Christian monastery was captured when ISIS militants captured the Syrian town of al-Qaryatain near Palmyra. Dedicated to a 4th-century saint, it was an important pilgrimage site and sheltered hundreds of Syrian Christians. Bulldozers were reportedly used to topple its walls, and ISIS posted pictures of the destruction on Twitter.

Apamea

A rich Roman-era trading city, Apamea has been badly looted since the beginning of Syria's civil war and even before ISIS appeared. Satellite imagery shows dozens of pits dug across the site; previously unknown Roman mosaics have reportedly been excavated and removed for sale. ISIS is said to take a cut from sales of ancient artifacts, generating tens of millions of dollars to fund their operations.

Dura-Europos

A Greek settlement on the Euphrates not far from Syria's border with Iraq, Dura-Europos later became one of Rome's easternmost outposts. It housed the world's oldest known Christian church, a beautifully decorated synagogue, and many other temples and Roman-era buildings. Satellite imagery shows a cratered landscape inside the city's mud-brick walls and evidence of widespread destruction by looters.

Mari

Mari flourished in the Bronze Age, between 3000 and 1600 BCE. Archaeologists have discovered palaces, temples, and extensive archives written on clay tablets that shed light on the early days of civilization in the region. According to reports from locals and satellite imagery, the site, especially the royal palace, is being systematically looted.

IRAQ

Hatra

Built in the third century BCE, Hatra was the capital of an independent kingdom on the outskirts of the Roman Empire. Its combination of Greek and Roman-influenced architecture and Eastern features testify to its prominence as a trading center on the Silk Road. Hatra was named a UNESCO World Heritage site in 1985.

In 2014, Hatra was taken over by ISIS and reportedly used as an ammo dump and training camp. A video released by ISIS in April, 2015, showed soldiers using sledgehammers and automatic weapons to destroy sculptures in several of the site's largest buildings. "The destruction of Hatra marks a turning point in the appalling strategy of cultural cleansing underway in Iraq," UNESCO's head, Irina Bokova, said at the time.

Nineveh

Ancient Assyria was one of the first true empires, expanding aggressively across the Middle East and controlling a vast stretch of the ancient world between 900 and 600 BCE. The Assyrian kings ruled their realm from a series of capitals in what is today northern Iraq. Nineveh was one of their capitals, and it flourished under the Assyrian emperor Sennacherib in about 700 BCE. At one point, Nineveh was the largest city in the world.

Its location on the outskirts of Mosul, now part of the modern city built over Nineveh's ruins, put it in ISIS's crosshairs when the group took over the city in 2014. Many of the site's sculptures were housed in the Mosul Museum, and many were damaged during the rampage through the museum that was documented on a video. Men were shown smashing half-human, half-animal guardian statues called lamassus on Nineveh's ancient Nirgal Gate. It is said there's not much left to destroy in Mosul that is part of Iraq's ancient history.

Mosul Museum and Libraries

Reports of looting at Mosul's libraries and universities began to surface almost as soon as ISIS occupied the city. Centuries-old manuscripts were stolen, and thousands of books disappeared into the shadowy international art market. Mosul University's library was also burned. Later, ISIS's campaign of destruction escalated. Mosul's central public library, a landmark built in 1921, was rigged with explosives and razed, together with thousands of manuscripts and instruments used by Arab scientists.

The book burning coincided with the release of a video showing ISIS fighters rampaging through the Mosul Museum, toppling statues and smashing others with hammers. The museum was Iraq's second largest, after the Iraq Museum in Baghdad. Statues included masterpieces from Hatra and Nineveh.

Margarete van Ess, head of the German Archaeological Institute's Iraq field office, says that a trained eye could tell that about half of the artifacts destroyed in the video were copies, while many of the originals were in the Iraq Museum.

Nimrud

Nimrud was the first Assyrian capital, founded 3,200 years ago. Its rich decoration reflected the empire's power and wealth. The site was excavated beginning in the 1840s by British archaeologists who sent dozens of its massive stone sculptures to museums around the world. Antiquities were sent to New York's Metropolitan Museum of Art and the British Museum in London, but many originals remained in Iraq.

The site itself is massive and includes an earthen wall surrounding 890 acres. The Iraqi Ministry of Tourism and Antiquities says ISIS bulldozed parts of the site, but the extent of the damage is not entirely known. Some of the city was never excavated, remains underground, and protected as a result.

Khorsabad

Khorsabad is another ancient Assyrian capital located a few miles from Mosul. The palace was built between 717 and 706 BCE by Assyria's King Sargon II. Its reliefs and statues were remarkably well preserved with traces of the original paint still decorating depictions of Assyrian victories and royal processions.

Most of the reliefs and many of the statues were removed during French excavations in the mid-1800s and by teams from Chicago's

Oriental Institute in the 1920s and 1930s. Some are now in the Iraq Museum in Baghdad, as well as in Chicago and the Louvre in Paris.

It remains unclear as to what part of the site ISIS targeted. No photographs have been seen showing how extensive the damage might be. There has been only information coming from local people and the Iraqi antiquities ministry.

Mar Behnam Monastery

Established in the 4th century, the monastery was dedicated to an early Christian saint. The holy site, maintained since the late 1800s by Syriac Catholic monks, survived the Mongol hordes in the 1200s but fell to ISIS. The extremists used explosives to destroy the saint's tomb and its elaborate carvings and decorations.

Mosque of the Prophet Yunus

Mosul's Mosque of the Prophet Yunus was dedicated to the Biblical figure Jonah, who is considered a prophet by many Muslims. But since ISIS adheres to an extreme interpretation of Islam that sees veneration of prophets such as Jonah as forbidden, ISIS fighters evacuated the mosque and demolished it with explosives.

As with many of Iraq's sites, the mosque contains layers of history and was built atop a Christian church that, in turn, had been built on a mound that made up the Assyrian city of Nineveh.

Imam Dur Mausoleum

ISIS succeeded in blowing up the Imam Dur Mausoleum, a magnificent specimen of medieval Islamic architecture and decoration not far from the city of Samarra.

Adapted from:

http://news.nationalgeographic.com/2015/09/150901-isis-destruction-looting-ancient-sites-iraq-syria-archaeology/

STUDIES AND SURVEYS

A number of studies and surveys have been conducted to ascertain why people travel and to ask their opinions about UNESCO World Heritage Sites. There is also a significant amount of literature about the historic preservation and ecological conservation of travel destinations.

The National Geographic study on travelers' attitudes regarding travel is especially instructive. While much is revealed in the studies located online, more studies and more up-to-date surveys are needed.

NATIONAL GEOGRAPHIC STUDIES

The "Geotourism Study," conducted by the Travel Industry Association of America (TIA) is especially relevant as to why people travel. It has been called the first study of its kind and was undertaken in cooperation with *National Geographic Traveler* magazine. The study was an attempt to ascertain the attitudes of Americans towards travel and their concerns regarding historic preservation and environmental conservation.

The survey was composed of 150 questions and received 3,300 responses from Americans, who had traveled in the past three years. Those preferring guided group tours represented twenty-seven percent of those responding. Seventy-one percent believed that travel should not damage the environment. Sixty-one percent believed their travel experiences were better when historic, cultural and natural aspects of sites had been preserved. Fifty-four percent believed that fewer such well-preserved sites still exist.

At the conclusion of the survey, respondents were classified into the following eight groups based on the frequency of their travel:

• Wishful thinkers - This was the largest and least-traveled group. They are those wanting to travel more if only they had the time and money.

- Traditionals - These include many older people and women who travel conservatively. They are not all that wealthy, but they take an occasional trip.
- Apathetics - These are travelers not really interested in travel but may do so occasionally, especially if encouraged by a spouse, friends or relatives.
- Outdoor sportsmen - They travel primarily to domestic destinations and enjoy such activities as hunting and fishing rather than cultural activities.
- Good citizens - They are well-educated and civic-minded but generally haven't thought much about conservation when traveling.
- Self-indulgents - These are well-to-do travelers who expect to be pampered and are not all that concerned about travel destinations. They generally believe natural resources are there to be exploited by humans.
- Urban sophisticates - This is the wealthiest group. They are environmentally conscious and are concerned about receiving a full cultural experience when traveling.
- Geo-savvys - They are much like the urban sophisticates but are less wealthy and are very environmentally conscious.

Survey respondents were also asked whether or not they would travel with companies or organizations supporting ecotourism even if their trips were to cost more. Over half of the urban sophisticates and geo-savvy traveler replied "yes," with the good citizens and traditionalists close behind. Even a fifth of the self-indulgent travelers were in agreement.

Adapted from:
  https://news.nationalgeographic.com/news/2003/10/1024_031024_travelsurvey_2.html

National Geographic experts conducted a study from 2004 to 2010 to rate various sites on "cultural factors, built heritage, aesthetics, and tourism management." While most of the sites evaluated were of the natural environment type, a few were what the study would call "built heritage."

While no site received an "A" grade, Austria's Wachau/Melk Abbey receiving an "A-."

The sites receiving a "B+" grade were: Austria's Graz, Belgium's Historic center of Ghent, France's Aix-en-Provence, France's Dijon and Bourgogne region, France's Vézelay, Japan's Nikko historic area, and Stockholm, Sweden's Gamia Stan.

Listed among the sites "in trouble" were: the Dominican Republic's north coast, Egypt's northern Red Sea coast, India's Goa, Israel/Jordon's Dead Sea, Portugal's Algarve, Vietnam's Ha Long Bay, and in the USA, South Carolina's Myrtle Beach and region and Maryland/Virginia's Chesapeake Bay.

Adapted from:

http://destinationcenter.org/

THE WORLD WILDLIFE FEDERATION

Founded in 1961, the World Wildlife Federation (WWF) is a non-governmental, international organization concerned with environmental preservation. Formerly, it was known as the World Wildlife Fund, which is still its official name in Canada and the United States. It has published a "Living Planet Report" every two years since 1998. The report is said to be based on a "Living Planet Index" and what is called an "ecological footprint calculation."

In a recent report, the WWF has stated that 114 out of the 229 UNESCO Heritage Sites classified as natural and cultural sites have been placed in danger by industrialization. Among the factors seen as creating the threatened status of the various sites were oil extraction and mining activities, water management, logging, and the construction of railroads, roads, shipping lanes and power lines. While tourism was not specifically considered, it was noted that the construction of the infrastructure needed to support tourism was often a factor in site degradation.

Cited as being affected by water management issues were: Croatia's Plitvice Lakes National Park, Japan's Shiretoko National Park, Zimbabwe's Victoria Falls, and the Iguazú Falls located between Brazil and Argentina. Logging was cited as affecting Sri Lanka's Sinharaja Forest Reserve and Peru's Machu Picchu. Construction of railways and roads has affected Russia's Volcanoes of Kamchakra, Yemen's Socotra Archipelago, and Sumatra's tropical rainforests. Shipping lanes have affected the barrier reefs of Belize and Australia.

Classified by world areas, sub-Sahara African sites were found to be the most adversely affected, followed by those in south Asia, east Asia, the Pacific, and Latin America.

Among the sites cited by the WWF as not being affected by industrialization were Turkey's Cappadocia, Vietnam's Ha Long Bay, Jordan's Wadi Rum, Kenya's Mount Kenya National Park and Ecuador's Galapagos Islands. Both the United Kingdom and Tanzania were cited as having no industrialization affecting any of their natural heritage sites.

Adapted from

www.worldwildlife.org/pubications/protecting-people-through-nature

http://en.wikipedia.org/wiki/World_Wide_Fund_for_Nature

A SMALL OPINION SURVEY

Several years ago, I conducted a small, informal survey of friends whom I knew were world travelers. Below are four of the questions listed on the questionnaire, along with a tally of the responses. Also included are a number of the comments that were received.

Since I received only twenty-two responses to the questionnaire, the sampling of opinions about UNESCO World Heritage Sites may be regarded as far too small to reflect what might have been found if a much broader survey could have been conducted.

Nevertheless, it is instructive to see the differing opinions of the various travelers that were surveyed. It is especially interesting that the most comments received were concerned with how a UNESCO designation might impact a site.

1. Are you influenced by whether or not a site is a UNESCO site when planning a trip?

Yes -12   No - 10   Undecided/Don't Know - 0

Comments:

• No, but I have added some places to my "bucket list" after learning about them via UNESCO.

• Sometimes.

• Not really, but when we note that a tour includes UNESCO sites, we're pleased.

2. Do you think that UNESCO designations increase tourism and pose a threat to the sites?

Yes - 11   No - 4   Undecided/Don't Know - 7

Comments:

• Yes, in some cases due to increased pollution, damage, and people taking souvenirs from places, i.e., chipping off stone, etc.

• I think that the designation may increase tourism, but I have not seen evidence that it poses a threat to the sites.

• Yes, unfortunately, I think it can. For example, they've closed some sites due to the risk of negative impact from tourism.

• Yes, increased tourism. Do not pose a threat to the site.

• This is a problem. Too many visit just to say they did it or as part of package deals.

• I believe that the UNESCO designation does increase tourism. Regarding threats to the sites, it depends on the type of site and how well it's managed by the host country.

• Increase tourism? I don't know. Threat to the site? No. They are already in danger by the time UNESCO recognizes them. The whole planet is in danger. In fact, UNESCO recognition may help to save some sites before it is too late.

- Increase tourism: Yes. Pose a threat to the site: No.
- Yes, to the first part. As far as damaging the sites, that is a challenge to local management to prevent that from happening.
- Maybe somewhat, but overall they are usually watched and cared for.

3. Do you remember specific UNESCO sites you've visited?

Yes -20   No - 1   Undecided/Don't Know - 1

Comments:

- Don't know, because I was somehow unaware of the UNESCO designations until a few years ago.
- Yes, many of them, here and abroad.
- Yes, all of them. They were and are very special to me; in many ways, the best of the best.
- Some. I would have to review trip notes, if I can find them.

4. Did they meet your expectations?

Yes -21   No - 1   Undecided/Don't Know - 0

Comments:

- Yes, for the most part.
- Yes, almost always.
- Yes. They've almost always exceeded expectations.
- Some yes, some no.
- Most, but not because of World Heritage status.

If a travel magazine or organization were to initiate a survey of travelers' opinions of UNESCO World Heritage Sites, the results might serve to be much more useful. *National Geographic Traveler* and *International Travel News (ITN)* might be travel publications that could survey a much larger group of travelers, while the American Society of Travel Agents (ASTA) might find it to be worthwhile as a marketing research tool. Such glossy travel magazines as *Travel+Leisure* and *Condé Nast Traveler* appear less likely to conduct such a survey, since their emphasis seems more focused on travelers who are less interested in archaeology, historic conservation, and ecotourism.

Above all, it appears that UNESCO would benefit the most from such a survey to promote its activities and to rally the support of its member nations in the restoration and conservation of their designated sites.

Unfortunately, so far it appears that no definitive or large-scale survey of travelers' views about UNESCO sites has been conducted, nor has any been planned.

ALGERIA

Country name: People's Democratic Republic of Algeria
  (Arabic: al-Jaza'ir; French: Algérie)
Site name: Timgad; ancient Berber name: Thamugas or
  Thamugadi; full Roman name: Colonia Marciana Ulpia
  Trajana Thamugadi
Location: Northern slopes of the Aurès Mountains; 480 km
southeast of Algiers;
  110 km south of Constantine; 35 km east of Batna
UNESCO World Heritage Site: Inscribed 1982; no. 194
Date of Visit: 5 October 2014

A ROMAN CITY PLANNING EXEMPLAR: TIMGAD

The ancient, Roman city of Thamugadi, now called Timgad, is reputed to be the largest city built by the Romans in North Africa. Originally founded as a military colony, the city is regarded as one of the finest extant examples of the grid plan used by the ancient Romans when planning the layout of a city. Founded by the emperor Trajan in about 100 CE, the perfectly square city originally measured 355 meters on each side. Planned for a population of 15,000 residents, the city was bisected from east to west, as was typical, by a Roman street called the *decumanus maximus* and by a north/south street called the *cardo*.

The planning and layout of the city is considered to be remarkable for its precision and is regarded as an example of Roman city planning at its finest.

By the second century, the city had outgrown its original boundaries, and such public buildings as the Capitalium, various other temples, markets, and baths had been constructed outside the confines of the original city. The Severan period is regarded as being the golden age of Timgad and a time when lavish private residences, decorated with fine mosaics and expensive marbles were built.

The Arch of Trajan, dated to the late 2nd
to early 3rd centuries CE, Timgad, Algeria

Called Thamugas or Thamugadi in the Berber language, the complete Roman city's name was Colonia Masrcuana Ulpia Trajana Thamugadi. It commemorated the emperor's father, Marcus Ulpius Trajanus, his mother, Marcia, and his sister, Marcia. "Thamugadi," was added as the Berber name of the site.

The original city was walled, but not fortified. It quickly grew well beyond its walls and eventually grew into a city four times its original size. It was intended as a defense against the Berbers in the nearby Aurès Mountains, and its original inhabitants were Parthian veterans from within the Roman army who were given lands in return for their military service.

During the second and third centuries, the city's location gave the Romans control over one of the major passes through the Aurès Mountains which was used to give access to the Sahara beyond. While Timgad served as a defense against the

Berbers in the nearby mountains, it also assimilated many of the local North Africans, as evidenced by funerary stelae that have been discovered decorated with local deities, as well as Roman ones.

Beginning in the third century, Timgad became a center of Donatism. By the end of the fourth century, Optat, its bishop, had become the spokesman for the Donatist movement. It also had two later, notable bishops, the Donatist Gaudentius and the Catholic Faustinus.

In the fifth century, Timgad was invaded by the Vandals and was also sacked by the Berbers. In the sixth century the city experienced a revival during the reign of the Byzantine emperor Justinian only to be invaded by Muslims in the seventh century. Abandoned in the eighth century, the city remained remarkably well preserved and largely hidden under the encroaching sands of the Sahara for centuries, until excavations were undertaken in 1881.

Among the many notable structures identified within the ruins of Timgad are the following:

A well-preserved theater seating 35,000 which is sometimes used for modern theatrical productions.

A large Capitoline Temple dedicated to Jupiter, with dimensions that have been compared to that of the Pantheon in Rome.

A library, said to have been the gift of Julius Quintianus Flavius Rogatianus, possibly dating from the late third to fourth centuries. It is thought to have contained a reading room with freestanding bookcases, a lecture hall, and a book stack room with wooden shelves.

At the western end of the *decumanus maximus* stands Timgad's most spectacular structure, the Arch of Trajan. Standing 12 meters high and constructed primarily of sandstone, it is of the Corinthian order and has three arches, the central one having a span of 11 feet.

Other structures of note are a basilica and four baths. There are also such later buildings as a seventh century church with a semi-circular apse and a large Byzantine citadel located southeast of the main city.

A Scotsman, James Brucc, is credited with having discovered ancient Timgad in 1765, but it was not until over a century later that excavations were underway at the site in 1881. They were conducted at Timgad almost continuously from 1881 to 1980. Today the site, in addition to its UNESCO World Heritage designation, is protected by a "Protection and Presentation Plan" and is managed by the Office of Cultural Properties Management and Exploitation.

Today, the extensive ruins of Timgad appear to be seldom visited by either the local people or by foreign visitors. When Timgad was visited in 2014, our small group had the city almost exclusively to ourselves except for the guards, who always accompanied us on the tour when we were outside of our hotels. It appeared that little, if anything, had been accomplished at such an archaeological site since the French were expelled from the country. The immense city appeared very empty and forlorn, with only its extensive, majestic ruins serving to tell of its former glory as one of the most magnificent Roman cities of North Africa.

Adapted from:

http://whc.unesco.org/en/list/194

https://en.wikipedia.org/wiki/Timgad

http://www.amusingplanet.com/2015/10/timgad-ancient-roman-city-with-very.html

http://www.telegraph.co.uk/travel/destinations/africa/algeria/articles/Timgad-Algeria-Tales-of-the-Unexpected/

AZERBAIJAN

Country name: Republic of Azerbaijan (**Azerbaijani:** Azərbaycan Respublikası)

Site name: Walled City of Baku with the Shirvanshah's Palace and Maiden Tower

Location: Baku (also spelled Baki or Bakou), southern shore of the Absheron Peninsula, western shore of the Caspian Sea

UNESCO World Heritage Site: Inscribed 2000; no. 958

Date of Visit: 25-26 September 2011

AZERBAIJAN'S OLD CITY OF BAKU

Baku is Azerbaijan's capital and is its largest city. It is also the largest city in the Caucasus region and the largest city situated on the Caspian Sea. The Baku International Sea Trade Port is one of the region's busiest seaports, handling millions of tons of cargo each year. It has also become a major tourist destination, with its hotels grossing over seven million euros in 2009.

In 2000, Baku's Old City was inscribed as Azerbaijan's first UNESCO World Heritage Site. In 2003 it was placed on the endangered list, partly as a result of damage caused by an earthquake in November of 2000. Also cited were overdevelopment in the inscribed area and the illegal demolition of buildings. Fortunately, corrective measures were taken, and the endangered listing was lifted in 2009.

It is Baku's inner or Old City that has received the UNESCO designation. Following the boundaries of the city's ancient walls, the Old City has been cited by UNESCO as an urban unit displaying many diverse influences, such as those deriving from Zoroastrian, Sassanian, Arabic, Persian, Ottoman, and Russian sources.

Divided into two basic sections, the inner or Old City was called the Ichari Shahar, while the outer city was called the Bayir Shahar. Residents of the inner city were regard as the

The ornate entrance to the Mausoleum of
the Shirvanshahs, Baku, Azerbaijan

city's natives and thought of themselves as superior to what they called the "barefoot people" of the outer city.

The Maiden Tower

(Azerbaijani: Qiz Qalasi, also transliterated as Gyz Galasy)

The Maiden Tower is Baku's most famous and iconic ancient monument. Located in the southeastern part of the Old City and rising to a height of 29.5m (97 feet), the eight-story cylindrical tower has a base 5m thick (16 feet), tapering to 4.5m (15 feet) at its top. It has been dated to the twelfth century CE by some archaeologists and to a much earlier eighth to seventh centuries BCE date by others. Those giving it the earlier date believe that it is an example of pre-Islamic and Zoroastrian architecture and believe its construction was originally that of a Zoroastrian fire temple, later finished in the 12th century. Some believe it may have been used as an astronomical observatory and that thirty protuberances on the lower section of the tower may be linked with a stone belt around the tower and with thirty-one additional protuberances on the tower's upper level, all of which can be correlated with the days of the months.

Another of the tower's features, discovered in the second floor of the tower, is a well measuring .7m (2.3 feet) in diameter and 21m (69 feet) deep. It has been also interpreted as being a cistern and as a means of collecting rainwater.

Up to twenty different legends have been associated with the tower. One legend, based on Zoroastrian beliefs, states that the maiden associated with the tower, a fire-haired virgin, had saved Baku's people from slavery. Another legend tells of a king who insisted that his daughter marry a man she does not love. Seeking to escape from such a marriage, she asked the king to construct a tower for her. When finished, she succeeded in committing suicide by leaping from the tower's top. In 1940, one of the legends became the basis for a ballet entitled "Maiden Tower" by Afrasiyyab Badalbayli performed in Baku's Opera and Ballet Theater. Another version of the ballet was performed in 1999.

Evidence of the tower's iconic status is its depiction on Azerbaijan's 250 *manat* and 10 *manat* banknotes. It also has been represented on Azerbaijan's 5 *qapik* coins.

Strengthened in 1806 during the Soviet era, the massive tower remains one of Baku's major tourist attractions. For a small fee, the tower's museum and gift shops can be visited, and its spiral stairways can be climbed to the tower's top for panoramic views of the city.

The Shirvanshah Palace

(Azerbaijani: Sirvasahlar Sarayı)

The Palace of the Shirvanshahs, dated to the fifteenth century, has been described as being one of the "pearls" of Azerbaijani architecture. Since it was cited as a museum in 1964, extensive renovations on the Shirvanshah's Palace complex were conducted in 2001 and 2002. Among the various parts of the palace are the following:

The main palace building, built by Shirvansha Sheykh Ibrahim I, is dated to 1411 CE.

The Divankhana is a small, octagonal pavilion located in an arcaded courtyard.

The Keygubad Mosque contains, in its southern section, the Dervish's Tomb constructed by Farrukh Yasar.

Built for the mother and son of Khalilullah I, the Mausoleum of the Shirvanshahs is a rectangular structure topped with a hexahedral cupola.

Located in the lower portion of the complex is the Palace Mosque dated to the 1430s.

The mausoleum of Seyid Yahyah Bakuvi, a scholar in the court of Shirvanshah Khalilullah, is in the southern section of the complex.

Also of note is the gate of Sultan Murad, constructed during the Ottoman era and dated to 1585.

Discovered in 1939 and dated to the 17th century is the complex's bathhouse containing twenty-six rooms.

The ancient, walled city of Baku is protected as a National Monument. It is also covered under the protection of the Presidential Decrees of 2005 and 2007 and is included in the State-Historical Architectural Reserve "Icherisheher (SHAHAR), which is funded and staffed by Azerbaijan's government. In addition, along with a conservation master plan, an Integrated Area Management Action Plan has been created.

During Soviet rule and during the 19th and 20th centuries, much has changed in Baku with many buildings being built in many different Western styles. Today, its promenade along the Caspian Sea is an especially lively scene with many very modern buildings. Modern shopping areas contain many high-end shops bordering broad pedestrian streets. Typifying the modern aspects of today's Baku are the SOCAR Tower and the Flame Towers. The latter is a group of flame-shaped glass towers built atop one of Baku's hills as a reminder of Azerbaijan's Zoroastrian heritage. It is obvious that much of Baku's modernity and prosperity has been due to its location within an oil rich region.

In marked contrast to other parts of our tour of the Caucasus, our time spent in Baku was made especially enjoyable, largely due to our lively, very idiosyncratic and personable local guide.

Adapted from:

en.wikipedia.org/wiki/Baku
https://en.wikipedia.org/wiki/Old_City_(Baku)
https://en.wikipedia.org/wiki/Maiden_Tower_(Baku)
http://whc.unesco.org/en/list/958

CAMBODIA

Country name: Kingdom of **Cambodia** (Khmer: Kampuchea)

Site name: Banteay Srei, Angkor

Location: Near the hill of Phnom Dei, 32 km northwest of Siem Reap and 25 km (16 miles) northeast of Angkor's main temple groups

UNESCO World Heritage Site: Inscribed 1992; no. 668

Dates of Visits: 12-27 December 2005; 13-22 December 2009

A JEWEL OF KHMER ARCHITECTURE: ANGKOR'S BANTEAY SREI

The ancient site of Angkor, in today's Cambodia, is one of the world's largest archaeological sites and is regarded as one of the most important sites in all of Southeast Asia. Stretching over approximately 400 square kilometers, the Angkor Archaeological Park contains the ruins of the various capitals of the vast Khmer Empire that dominated much of Southeast Asia from the ninth to fifteenth centuries.

The site includes what are considered by many as architectural masterworks, such as the site's main temple, Angkor Wat, the Bayon, and the small, elegant temple of Banteay Srei.

Banteay Srei, meaning "citadel of the woman" or "citadel of beauty," has been so named because it was believed that its very elaborate, delicate, and elegant decoration could not have been created by men. Carved from a pink sandstone, its refined, filigree reliefs, which decorate almost every surface of its various structures, are often cited as being some of the world's finest. It is regarded as being a small temple, especially in comparison to many of Angkor's other much larger temples. The temple's pediments and lintels possess some of the most highly detailed and deeply carved scenes seen on the various temple buildings.

Façade of one of the red sandstone libraries of
Banteay Srei, Angkor, Cambodia

According to an inscription found in 1936 on a foundation stone at the site, Banteay Srei was dedicated on 22 April, 967 CE. The temple had previously been dated to the thirteenth to fourteenth centuries because it was believed that the refinement of its sculptures was evidence of a later date. The inscription credits a Brahman priest, Vishnukumara, a counselor to King Rajendravarman II, and his brother, Yajnavaraha, with commissioning the temple and praises the reigning king, Jayavarman V. The temple complex was later expanded and partially rebuilt in the 11th century. It also appears that the temple was also given over to a priest, Divakarapandita, and was rededicated to Shiva. It is thought that the temple remained in use until the 14th century.

Surrounded by the town of Isvarapura, Bantaey Srei was discovered by the West in 1914, and ten years later the site was cleared. Banteay Srei was the site of some of the earliest restoration work undertaken at Angkor, with Henri Marchal, a French conservator, working at the site in the 1930s. His restoration methods became a model for much of the later restoration work at Angkor. Use of the anastylosis method meant that as much of the existing, original stonework of the temple as possible was used in the restoration work.

Unfortunately, some reliefs have been taken from the temple complex, with some of its sculptures now being housed in the Musée Guimet in Paris. André Malraux is known to have stolen four sculptures from the site but was arrested and returned the sculptures. The Cambodian-Swiss Conservation Project installed a drainage system in 2000 to 2003,, and measures have been taken to prevent damage to buildings from trees. Some of the temple's original sculptures were replaced by concrete copies in the late twentieth century, but even the replicas have been known to have been vandalized.

The site has recently been improved with the addition of a larger parking area, as well as shopping and dining areas. Boat trips are also available on a reservoir behind the temple complex.

Banteay Srei is composed of four enclosures. The outermost one has a processional walkway bordered by galleries leading to an entrance on the east. Lintels and pediments of the galleries contain scenes from the Hindu epic, the Ramayana, such as the abduction of Sita. Other scenes include Indra riding a three-headed elephant and an image of Varuna, god of the oceans.

The temple's third enclosure has a 100m wall and is now a dry moat. A causeway crossing the area leads to the eastern and western gateways guarded by statues of lions.

The second enclosure measuring 38m by 42m contains two library buildings composed of brick, laterite and sandstone. The south library has pediments with images of Shiva and of Ravana shaking Mt. Kailash, as well as of Kama, god of love, shooting an arrow at Shiva. On the north library, Indra puts out a forest fire started by Agni, and Krishna kills Kamsa, his uncle.

The temple complex's main temple or sanctuary stands on a one-meter-high platform. It is entered on the east though a doorway measuring only 1.08m in height. A *mandapa* or porch-like chamber stands in front of the towers of the sanctuary, a feature first seen at Angkor at Banteay Srei. The central tower, standing 10m in height, and two flanking shorter towers, are decorated with legendary scenes of the Ramayana. According to the foundation stone discovered in 1936, the sanctuary's central chamber housed a lingam dedicated to Shiva, called Sri Tribhuvanamahesvara, meaning "great lord of the threefold world."

Because of its distance from other major temples at Angkor, Banteay Srei is often not included in many of the itineraries that include only a one-day tour of Angkor. Fortunately, on my tour of Southeast Asia in December of 2009, the tour allowed for several days at Angkor. Being disappointed at missing seeing the temple on an earlier trip, I informed my local guide that seeing Banteay Srei was one of my top priorities. He responded by saying that he had planned Banteay Srei as the first temple we'd be the visiting on his tour.

Adapted from:

https://en.wikipedia.org/wiki/Banteay_Srei

http://www.sacred-destinations.com/cambodia/angkor-banteay-srei

http://www.tourismcambodia.com/attractions/angkor/banteay-srei.htm

https://www.renown-travel.com/cambodia/angkor/banteay-srei.html

http://whc.unesco.org/en/list/668

In the background, the moai at Ahu Tahai with its
restored white coral and obsidian eyes, Easter Island

CHILE - RAPA NUI (EASTER ISLAND)

Country name: Republic of Chile (Spanish: República de Chile) - Rapa Nui was annexed by Chile in 1888.

Site name: Rapa Nui, also known as Easter Island; Spanish: Isla de Pascua

Location: The Pacific Ocean, over 2,000 miles west of Chile

UNESCO World Heritage Site: Inscribed as Rapa Nui National Park in 1995; no. 715

Tour Dates: 2-9 January 2009

THE WORLD'S MOST REMOTE, INHABITED ISLAND: RAPA NUI

Hundreds of the ancient effigies, the moai, sit like unseeing sentinels on the Pacific Ocean's remote island of Easter Island. Called Rapa Nui in the islanders' native language, it was discovered by Dutch explorers on Easter Sunday in 1722.

Formed by volcanic action, the island possesses three prominent extinct volcanos and measures only fourteen miles long and seven miles wide. It sits out in the vast Pacific Ocean, located 2,300 miles from mainland Chile and 2,500 miles from Tahiti. Annexed by Chile in 1888, the island was given UNESCO World Heritage Site status as Rapa Nui National Park in 1995.

Ironically, Rapa Nui is a name given to the island by Tahitian fishermen. Thinking the island as being similar to one of their nearby islands called "Rapa," they added "nui," meaning "big," since Easter Island was larger than Rapa. It is now thought that the ancient islanders called their island "Te Pito o Te Henua," meaning "the navel of the world."

The Colonization of Rapa Nui

Recent DNA analyses have shown quite conclusively that the ancient Easter Islanders were Polynesians, probably coming from the Marquise Islands or, more likely, from Mangareva, now the Gambier archipelago. It is conjectured that the island was colonized in about 400 CE.

Ancient legends tell of Hotu Matu'a, a great "ariki henua," or chieftain, coming from a place, now unknown, called Hiva, located somewhere in Polynesia. Forced to leave Hiva by a rival chieftain, Hotu Matu'a, having been told by his tattooist of a dream about a faraway island with beaches and craters that was awaiting him, sent a reconnaissance team. Hotu Matu'a followed later with his family and other colonists. By planting seeds brought with them and living for a time on the fish from the Pacific, the islanders eventually were able to feast on the taros, yams, bananas, and sugarcane they had raised. Chickens and rats, brought by the ancient colonists, also flourished on the island. Eventually, eight separate clans were formed, each clan having its own "tangata honui," or great leader.

Rapa Nui History

After the island's discovery in 1722, a Spanish expedition visited Easter Island in 1770. A survey of the island revealed that none of the huge, stone figures, the moai, had been destroyed. In 1774, Captain Cook visited Easter Island and found many overturned moai. In 1868, an English doctor reported that no moai were still standing.

In 1805, Easter Island was invaded by slave traders. Between 1862 and 1864 Peruvians attacked the island and captured over 2,500 islanders to work in the Peruvian guano mines. After Tepano Jaussen, bishop of Tahiti, finally persuaded the Peruvians to return the islanders to their island, only sixteen survived on the return trip. Tragically, the returning islanders brought smallpox and tuberculosis, and the resulting epidemic reduced the island population to only a few more than 100.

Disease is thought to have caused the greatest loss of indigenous island culture with the last "ariki henua" (chieftains), moari (keepers of the sacred knowledge) and "tangata rongo rongo" (readers of the ancient script) being among the many who perished.

In 1864, the first missionary, Eugéne Eyaud, brought Christianity to the island and in four years had converted the population. Soon thereafter, a French plantation owner bought large land tracts and ran the island as his personal ranch. In 1877, the autocratic rule of the land owner ended with his assassination at the hands of the oppressed islanders. The government of Chile then proceeded to take control of the island, leaving only the small village of Hanga Roa to the islanders.

On September 9, 1888, Chile officially annexed the island. Chile then leased the island to a British wool-trading company which ran the island primarily as a sheep farm. In 1953, the company's lease was revoked, and the Chilean navy took command. In 1964, islanders were allowed outside of Hanga Roa and were granted citizenship and the right to vote.

Ecological Disaster and Civil War

One of the major causes for the collapse of Rapa Nui culture may have been the cult of the moai. As stated by the noted Norwegian archaeologist, William Mulloy, "[statue carving] came to take up so much of the focus of the culture that such important activities as farming and fishing were neglected. The common people didn't have enough to eat, and it seems that the delicate balance between food distribution and statue-carving was destroyed."

The growing scarcity of food may also have been brought about by overpopulation. There was also the probable deforestation of the island resulting from centuries of logging for boat-building, fuel consumption, cremation, transportation of the moai, and for erecting the moai on their ahu.

When Europeans arrived in the eighteenth century, there was hardly a single tree left on the island. The large palm tree, indigenous to the island, had become extinct. Islanders probably had more and more difficulty in feeding themselves and providing for other basic necessities such as housing. Deep sea fishing may have declined due to the lack of wood available for boat building. Land cultivation may also have declined due to soil erosion caused by deforestation. A combination of such factors may well have caused the entire ancient culture to collapse. Much of the ancient island civilization appears to have ended in anarchy, leading to the abandoning of the moai and the toppling of those which had been erected on the ahu.

Warfare between rival clans and social groups also probably contributed to the collapse of the ancient culture. The legend of the "short ears" versus the "long ears" supports such a theory. The "long ears" may have been an aristocratic group noted for their long earlobes created by their wearing ear plugs, while the commoners were prohibited from such a practice. On the other hand, the "long" and "short ears" legend seems more likely the result of a mistranslation. The words in the Rapa Nui language for "ear" and "people" are very similar. Most probably there was a conflict between the "short and stocky people" and the "tall and slim people." The "long ears," the more aristocratic, ruling class, are said to have forced the "short ears" to clear the land of rocks for cultivation. In a revolt of the "short ears," the "long ears" are said to have been exterminated in a surprise raid by being driven into a ditch filled with brush that was set ablaze. Ironically, the ditch had been built on a section of the island by the "long ears" to imprison the "short ears."

The Moai

Two hundred and seventy-two ahu, or platforms, have been located on Easter Island, but few held more than one statue. Most ahu were built near the island's coasts with the statues looking inland. Only twenty-five ahu have been located inland. The earliest ahu are thought to have measured only 20 meters in length. Later they measured more than 100 meters in length and held upwards of ten moai. Since the 1960s, only thirty-five moai on ahu have been been reset upright. The rest remain in some form of toppled condition.

Four routes have been discovered over which the moai traveled to their destinations. How the moai were moved is still a matter of dispute. Oral tradition states they "walked" to their destinations, possibly meaning they were transported while standing upright.

Finish work on the moai appears to have been completed only after the moai were at their final destination. It is thought that one of the last features to be finished were the eyes. It was during the restoration of Ahu Nau Nau that the archaeologist Sergio Rapu discovered that the moai had been given eyes. The eyes were made of a polished, almond-shaped coral in the center of which was added a black obsidian or red tufa disc to resemble a pupil. Only one moai on the island has had its eyes restored.

The pukao, the headdresses or topknots located atop some of the moai were quarried at a separate site at Puna Pau. The pukao may have been indicative of a very important and very powerful chieftain.

The moai are thought to have represented protective ancestors which stood with their backs to the sea in order to protect the island clans, using their powers called "mana." Bones of dignitaries have been found buried at the base in front of the moai, while the bodies of commoners were cremated and buried behind the ahu.

Ranu Rarku

Rapa Nui's Rano Raraku is the site of the largest number of the island's moai. It is the island's primary quarry where the tuff, a stone of compressed volcanic ash, was used for the creation of an estimated 95% of all the large ancestral figures found on the island. It is thought that the quarry was used for some five hundred years, until the early eighteenth century, as the island's major source of stone for its famous images.

Rano Raraku's ancient name is thought to have been *Maunga Eo*, meaning "fragrant hill." An aromatic plant is said to have grown on the sides of the extinct volcano and to have permeated the air with its sweet fragrance.

Rano Raraku is one of seven primary archaeological sites on the small island. I had visited the site with a local guide earlier, but the tour had been cut short by a rainstorm that had suddenly blown in from the Pacific Ocean. With the assistance of helpful staff members at the small hotel in the village of Hanga Roa where I was staying, I was able to hire a driver to take me out to the quarry site for another visit on my own. It was on the second visit to Rano Raraku that I discovered many of the island's moai which many other island visitors are usually not given an opportunity to see.

When I visited Easter Island in 2009, an admission fee was required only at the site of Orongo, but I understand that now there is also a ranger station at Rano Raraku where an entrance fee is collected.

On the earlier tour, the guide had pointed to a stony path leading up a steep incline to the interior crater of Rano Raraku's extinct volcano. After coming over the rim of the volcano, I saw at least seventy more of the large statues sitting on the slopes of the caldera leading down to a fresh water lake inside the volcano.

Only when inside the crater could I appreciate its size, some 650m in diameter. In its center was a lake measuring from five to seven meters in depth and surrounded by totora reeds, called *nga'tu* by the islanders. The reeds, originally thought to evidence contact with South America, are now known to have been growing on the island for at least thirty millennia. Inside the crater I also discovered a herd of horses. Found running freely elsewhere on the island, horses are often rented to island visitors to tour the island on horseback.

Later I discovered that Rano Raraku is the site of an annual sporting event, the *Tau'a*, an Easter Island triathlon. Contestants must first cross the lake in a canoe, then run halfway around it, and finally recross the lake by swimming on a reed board.

Both inside and outside the extinct volcano, the moai sit scattered about on its slopes, looking as though the ancient islanders had just walked away from the site. Carved face side up, many of the images appear unfinished with many being half buried in the hillsides. Characteristic of the figures are their large heads, being about a third the height of the entire figure. Carved with prominent noses and recesses for eyes, the figures have spindly arms with long fingers clasped to their sides.

Since none of the moai at Rano Raraku ever reached their ahu, or platforms, located around the island for which they were intended, none have their eyes of coral and obsidian inserted into them. Only when on their ahu and with the eyes inserted were the images thought to be imbued with the spiritual power, or "mana," of the ancestors. Most of the moai at the site have smooth backs and no special carvings on them except for one moai, which has a ship with three square sails carved on its torso.

Rano Raraku is also the site of "El Gigante," meaning "the giant," a huge stone figure still lying unfinished in its site in the rock. If the image had been finished, it would have stood seventy-two feet high and would have weighed over 160 metric tons.

The most unusual figure at Rano Raraku is the"Tukuturi" or "kneeling moai." Excavated by Thor Heyerdahl in 1955, the figure astonished even the islanders since they had not known of its existence. The bearded figure is tilted backwards and kneels with its hands on its knees in a posture called "tuku turi," a pose used by singers in a ritual performed by the "tangata manu" cult. It is now thought it may have been one of the last moai to have been carved.

The Birdman Cult

The Birdman cult, which replaced the cult of the moai, is thought to have been based on earlier beliefs. The cult involved an annual competition held in September at the time of the summer equinox at the ceremonial site of Orongo. The island's chieftains, gathered at the site, would appoint young men to represent each of the various clans. Swimming out to Motu Nui, the furthest of three small islands, opposite the site, the competitors were required to wait until they could retrieve an egg of the sooty tern, a migratory bird, and bring it back to the main island. The chief of the victorious swimmer, then was designated the "tangata manu," or the Birdman. The new Birdman would have all his hair shaved and would be taken, along with the sacred egg, to a house at the foot of the volcanic crater of Rano Raraku. There he would live in seclusion for the year. He could eat only certain foods and was forbidden to bathe or cut his nails. Meanwhile, his clan possessed a special, high status and could rule over other rival clans. At year's end, the powers of the sacred egg disappeared, and another competition was held to select a new Birdman for the next year.

The Rongo Rongo Script

The ancient writing of the islanders remains a mystery. The writing is preserved on only twenty-nine of the wooden tablets located in various museums around the world.

The glyphs contain about one hundred and twenty basic elements which are combined to form between 1500 and 2000 compound signs. Many of the glyphs are seen in the island's petroglyphs, but few have been found on any of the moai or ahu. The texts are written in a form known as boustrophedon, meaning "as the ox ploughs." Starting at one side, the line is read to the end. Then the tablet must be turned over to read the next line, resulting in reading the next line in the opposite direction.

It is generally believed that the glyphs are a form of phonetic writing, in which pictographs are used to express ideas as well as objects. The glyphs probably do not represent an alphabet or syllables but may be mnemonic devices or memory aids for words, ideas, or events taking place in the legends.

In 1995, Steven Fischer claimed to have deciphered the script, but his findings have been rejected by almost all other epigraphers. Parallels have been cited between the Easter Island writing and various ancient South American and many different Polynesian scripts. Similarities have also been seen between the Easter Island script and the 4,500 year old writing of Mohenjo-Daro and Harappa, located in the Indus Valley of western India.

Rapa Nui Today

Due to much intermarriage with outsiders, there are probably few remaining pure-blooded indigenous Rapa Nui people. Today, many islanders still have fine-boned Polynesian features and speak their own Polynesian-based language, called Rapa Nui, in addition to Spanish.

Almost the entire island population still lives in the island's single, small town, Hanga Roa. Today, almost all islanders make their living from tourism, which has been growing steadily ever since the airstrip at the Mataveri Airport was built in 1968. Prior to the building of the airport, the island's only contact with the outside world was a yearly visit by a Chilean ship, bringing mail and provisions.

The island's educational system is now bilingual, with the teaching of both Spanish and the native Rapa Nui language. Recently, the islanders have been given control of many more of their local affairs.

I found Easter Island to be one of the most fascinating sites visited in fifteen years of travel. It is so remote. It is so enigmatic. It is an island so shrouded in mystery that I believe we will never know all of its many secrets.

Adapted from:

http://ourworld.compuserve.com/homepages/dp5/easter3.htm

http://www.suite101.com/article.cfm/archaeology/37245/

https://en.wikipedia.org/wiki/Easter_Island

http://whc.unesco.org/en/list/715

https://en.wikipedia.org/wiki/Rano_Raraku

http://imaginaisladepascua.com/en/easter-island-sightseeing/easter-island-volcanoes/rano-raraku/

CHINA

Country name: People's Republic of China
Site name: The Great Wall
Location: Xinjiang Uyghur Autonomous Region
UNESCO World Heritage Site: *Inscribed 1987; no. 438*
Dates of Visits: 19 September 2002; 25 April 2016

CHINA'S GREAT WALL

China's Great Wall is regarded as one of history's most impressive architectural accomplishments.

It has been known by various names during its long history. Evolving from being called the "Chinese Wall," during the 19th century, it has come to be called the "Great Wall," although in some European countries it is still known as the "Chinese Wall." One of its names in Chinese, the "Wanli Changcheng," meaning the "Ten Thousand Li Wall," is thought not to refer to its actual length but to signify that it is unmeasurable or of indeterminate length.

The beginnings of the Wall go far back into antiquity with what are believed to be walls built as early at the 7th century BCE. What exists of the Wall today dates primarily from the 14th through the 17th centuries and from the Ming dynasty (1368-1644), with evidence existing that Ming dynasty construction began in 1474.

Although built primarily for defensive purposes, the Wall also served as a border control, regulating the movement of goods along the ancient Silk Road and controlling trade, immigration and emigration. Some fortified stations served as custom houses, imposing taxes and duties on the goods being transported along the ancient trade routes.

The Wall appears not to have actually been visited by any of the early Westerners traveling in China or Mongolia during the Yuan dynasty. A traveler from North Africa, Ibn Battuta, visiting China around 1346, appears to be one of the first to recognize its

existence. In 1563 it is mentioned by Joao de Barros, and then in
1559, it was described by Bishop Juan Gonzalez de Mendoza.

It was after the First and Second Opium Wars, when China
was opened to foreign visitors, that the Wall became the tourist
attraction it is today. Nineteenth century travelers started
describing it in hyperbolic terms and initiated many of the
erroneous myths that still surround it.

Unfortunately, the Wall was constructed at great human cost. Built by soldiers, convicts, and commoners drafted into servitude, the Wall is reputed to have taken the lives of up to 400,000 workers. Others say that up to a million workers perished while building the Wall of Emperor Qin. Many of those who died are said to be buried inside the wall they were constructing.

On my first trip to China in 2002, I could immediately see that the Great Wall was one of China's most popular tourist attractions. It was packed with many other tourists in spite of it being a chilly, overcast day.

Our tour group had been taken to the Badaling section of the Wall, located 70m (43 miles) northwest of Beijing. Largely rebuilt in the 1950s, it is the section of the Wall that is visited by thousands of the local Chinese and foreigners every day. Starting from a base measuring 15 to 20 feet in width, the reconstructed Wall often rises to a height of fifteen to thirty feet. Topped by ramparts of twelve feet or higher, it is a section built of stone and bricks rather than rammed earth. Built at intervals along the Wall are examples of some 25,000 watchtowers estimated to have been built along its length. The towers not only housed soldiers and guards but enabled communication among the various towers' locations through fire and smoke signals

Our local guide informed us that the wall extending to our left was the easier climb, while that to the right was the more difficult. Seeing that the wall to the right was almost free of other tourists, that was the section of the Wall I chose to explore.

The climb was difficult but exhilarating. The views of the Wall, as it twisted and turned over the mountainous terrain, were awe inspiring. Almost before I realized it, the Wall came to an abrupt end. As I peered over the ramparts at the Wall's end, I was amazed to see what were only ruins. Often there were only the low outlines of the remains of the Wall. Only then did I realize that what I'd seen up to that point had been largely renovated or entirely reconstructed.

At the Wall's end was a lone merchant selling plaques with drawings of the Wall etched on them. I couldn't help but wonder if he would be selling anything that day due to the very few tourists I'd encountered on my trek along the Wall. I ultimately decided that I not only needed to give him at least one sale for the day, but that one of his plaques of a shiny black material would make a fitting souvenir of my visit to the Wall. As a result, I still have the souvenir engraved with the date of my visit, 19-9-2002, i.e., 19 September, 2002.

Fourteen years later in 2016, while on the second trip to China, I looked forward to seeing the other end of China's Great Wall, the western end. We were traveling in China's Xinjiang Uygur Autonomous Region when we were taken to the site of the Wall's western end marked with a boulder inscribed with UNESCO's logo. It was initially disappointing to see that very little remained to be seen so far out at the Wall's western end. Only very broken sections of the Wall remained, jutting up above the shifting sands that continue to threaten to obliterate them.

Not made of bricks or stone as found on the Wall's eastern end, the Wall had been made of the local yellow, sandy soil sandwiched between layers of jarrah branches. The overall effect of the Wall that remains seems best described as being made of sections of a layer cake. Later I learned that, unlike what I'd seen in 2002, much of the Wall had been built of a clay-rich soil called "loess" in a technique using rammed earth called *hangtu*.

Only later did I understand the true significance of the section of wall we had seen in 2016. It is now believed that the Wall extends 500 km further to the west than originally thought. Rather than ending at Jiayu Pass in Gansu Province, it is believed that Emperor Wudi of the Han dynasty extended the Wall from Dunhuang to Yanze, present-day Lop Nur. It must have been the Han dynasty extension of the Wall which we saw on our trip in 2016. Scenes of the Han dynasty construction project are said to be represented in frescoes in the Mogao Grottoes outside Dunhuang, a site also visited on the trip.

In addition to the newly discovered Han dynasty section of the Wall, it is now believed to have possibly extended even further to Kashi in the southeastern part of the Xinjiang territory.

Another site that was visited near the Wall was the so-called Small Fangpan Castle. This massive, rammed earth fortification sat forlornly on a flat, desolate plain. What was especially impressive was the massiveness of the earthen walls in sharp contrast to the small and cramped interior space. Looking like a huge cube, the massive ruin looked out over the desert landscape, with a salt lake in the foreground and sand hills that seemed to stretch out into infinity in the distance. Described by the local guide as a "customs house," this huge fortification must also have been created for the protection of China's vast western frontier.

One myth about China's Great Wall that needs to be dismissed dates from as early as 1754. It claims that the Wall can be seen from the Moon. Then in 1932 the myth appeared in Ripley's "Believe It or Not." It has been shown that the Wall, even at a maximum width of 9m, would appear like a human hair when seen from a distance of 3 km.

Whether or not the Wall can be seen from a low Earth orbit is more controversial. NASA claims that it would be barely visible at an altitude of 160 km and then only in the most ideal conditions. It is also said that it would be impossible to see the Wall with the naked eye unless the observer had a visual acuity seven times greater than normal.

Today, most of the Wall is in a sad state of repair. Local people have often used its stones and bricks to build homes and roads. Parts of it have been subjected to vandalism and graffiti. Much of the Wall has vanished due to weathering and, in its western sections, it has been subjected to erosion from sandstorms. Sections of the Wall are reported to have been reduced in height by up to ten feet. Poor restoration work has also taken its toll, as evidenced by the repair of one section of the Wall with concrete.

Even in its most ruinous condition, China's Great Wall impresses. It is not only recognized as one of China's most iconic monuments, but it is also one of the largest constructions ever built by human beings.

Adapted from:

https://en.wikipedia.org/wiki/Great_Wall_of_China
http://whc.unesco.org/en/list/438
http://www.china.org.cn/english/2001/Feb/7996.htm
https://www.travelchinaguide.com/china_great_wall/
https://www.britannica.com/topic/Great-Wall-of-China

The seven-story pagoda on the façade of Cave 96
at the Mogao Caves, Xinjiang Province, China

CHINA

Country name: People's Republic of China

Site name: Mogao Caves

Location: Above the Dachuan River, eastern foot of Mount Mingsha, Dunhuang County, Gansu Province. 25 km southeast of Dunhuang

UNESCO World Heritage Site: Inscribed 1987; no. 440

Date of Visit: 25 April 2016

ONE THOUSAND YEARS OF BUDDHIST ART: WESTERN CHINA'S MOGAO CAVES

The Mogao Caves are also often called the Mogao Grottoes. In Chinese they are called *Mogao ku*, meaning "peerless caves." They are considered as being among the greatest artistic and religious wonders of the world and as the world's largest collection of Buddhist art, spanning one thousand years of Chinese art.

An ancient legend states that, in 366 CE a monk, Lè Zun, had a vision of one thousand Buddhas surrounded by a radiant light on the site's cliff. He became so inspired that he started the excavation of a cave. He was joined by another monk, Faliang, and then by others as the site grew. The legend has given rise to another of the caves' names, the Caves of a Thousand Buddhas (pin yin: qian fó dóng). Originally a place of meditation for hermit monks, the caves became a place of worship and pilgrimage by the Sui and Tang dynasties.

From 100 BCE to 1400 CE, the caves were a major center located near a fork in the ancient Silk Road. Evidence points to its being a melting pot of cultures dating from the Northern Wei Dynasty (386-534 CE) to the Yuan Dynasty (1276-1386 CE). By 1400 CE, trade had become concentrated in sea routes, and the caves became deserted and were reclaimed by the desert.

A total of 735 caves have been found, carved into the relatively soft gravel conglomerate of the cliff. The 487 caves in the southern section were places of worship and pilgrimage and are the caves visited by tourists today. To the north are 248 additional caves that are mostly devoid of decoration and were living quarters, meditation chambers, and burial sites.

Cut into a cliff measuring nearly two km in length, the caves are estimated to contain 45,000 square meters (490,000 square feet) of paintings, with many of the caves totally covered in elaborate and detailed murals. Approximately 2,400 sculptures are estimated to have survived. In many of the caves, the central figure of the Buddha has been surrounded by bodhisattvas, devas, apsaras, yaksas, and various mythological figures. The sculptures usually had a stone core and wood armatures that were padded with reeds, modeled in clay stucco, and finally painted in what were often bright colors.

The site's largest sculpture, an image of the standing Buddha, was built in 695 CE at the order of the Tang dynasty empress, Wu Zetian. It is marked on its exterior cliff face by a multi-tiered pagoda built against the cliff. Another image, in what is called the "Nirvana Cave," is the image of a reclining Buddha measuring 15.6m in length.

Cave 17: The Library Cave

The discovery of what has been called the "Library Cave" is regarded as one of the greatest discoveries in the field of ancient Asian culture. It was discovered in 1900 by a Taoist monk, Abbot Wang Yuanlu, who had taken on the task of caretaker of the caves. He had proceeded to remove sand from many of the caves and started the many repairs needed at the site. In what is now called Cave 17, he discovered a small, walled-up chamber located to one side of a corridor leading to the main cave. The small chamber was packed from floor to ceiling with some 40,000 ancient objects, including manuscripts, scrolls, drawings, ephemera, and works of art — all dating from the fifth to eleventh century CE.

The cave had originally been dedicated to Hong Bian, a monk who died in 862 CE. His statue had been moved in what appears to have been an attempt to save the precious objects from being destroyed in imminent attacks by quickly sealing them in the cave chamber. The cave appears to have been sealed in the 11th century, since the latest manuscript discovered in the cave has been dated to 1002 CE.

Today, the cave stands totally empty except for the statue of Hong Bian, which has been replaced inside the cave. A stone stele nearby gives the details of the monk's life.

While most of the manuscripts found were in Chinese, manuscripts were found written in Tibetan, Uighur, Sanskrit, Sogdian, Hebrew, and the little-known Khotanese. Most of the manuscripts were Buddhist, but included were apocryphal works and prayer books, as well as Confucian, Taoist, and Nestorian Christian works. Examples included the Nestorian Jesus Sutras, the Dunhuang Go Manual, and ancient musical scores. Textiles found in the cave included silk banners, altar hangings, manuscript wrappings, monks' apparel, and fine silk embroideries.

Among the most important finds in the cave were various block-printed books, including the famous *Diamond Sutra*, regarded as the earliest completely printed book, dating to 868 CE. Printed on separate pieces of paper, some of the printed books had the sheets pasted together as scrolls.

The Treasure Hunters

The Abbot Wang Yuanlu took several of the manuscripts he had discovered to show to local officials, but he was ordered to reseal the cave in 1904. When the Hungarian archaeologist, Aurel Stein, heard of Yuanlu's discovery while on an archaeological expedition in 1907, he negotiated with Wang Yuanlu to purchase some of the documents discovered in the cave. Stein purchased approximately 7,000 complete manuscripts and 6,000 fragments for £130. In 1908 the caves were visited by Paul Pelliot, a 30-year-old monk and professor at the French University of Hanoi. Working for three weeks at the caves, Pelliot, who read Chinese, was able to ascertain which manuscripts were the finest and most important. He was also interested in the more unusual and exotic manuscripts. He was able to acquire nearly 10,000 documents in exchange for £90. In 1911, a Japanese expedition under Otani Kozui and a Russian expedition led by Sergei F. Oldenburg arrived and acquired hundreds of additional objects from the cave. What Yuanlu initially regarded as an act of piety in acquiring money to conserve and repair the caves ended in the Library Cave being ransacked of its treasures.

In 1909 a book, *Manuscripts of the Dunhuang Caves,* edited by the well-known scholar, Lue Zhenyu, was published. Lue Zhenyu proceeded to persuade the Ministry of Culture to send the remaining objects to Beijing in 1910, but not all the remaining objects were sent, and others were stolen. In 1924, the American explorer, Langdon Warner, arrived and removed murals and a statue from several caves.

In 1941, the painter Zhang Daqian repaired and copied some of the mural paintings. In 1944 the Research Institute of Dunhuang Art, later called the Dunhuang Academy, was set up. In 1961 the Mogao Caves were declared a protected historical monument, and more renovation work followed. Fortunately, the site escaped the devastation of the Cultural Revolution.

Today the Library Cave remains totally empty, with what were its original contents scattered around the world in various public and private collections.

International Dunhuang Project (IDP)

The IDP is an international project, founded in 1994 after a conference was held in 1993 to discuss the problems associated with the accessibility and conservation of the 40,000 manuscripts, paintings, and printed documents on silk and paper originally discovered at the Mogao Caves. Based at the British Library in London, the project was originally focused on cataloging and conservation, but that has since been extended to include digitizing, research, and education. IDP has local centers in Beijing, Dunhuang, St. Petersburg, Kyoto, Berlin, and Paris. Member institutions cooperating with the project are located in Taipei; New Delhi; Paris; Stockholm; Seoul; Washington, DC; Princeton, NJ; and Los Angeles, CA. IDP has also hosted regular international conservation conferences Digitizing of manuscripts was started in 1997, and they have been accessible online since 1998. Plans were to have ninety percent of the material digitized, cataloged, and online by 2015.

Preservation

When the age of the caves is taken into consideration, they are remarkably well preserved, largely due to the dry climate and their remote location. In 1961 the Mogao Caves were listed as one of the State Priority Protected Sites by the State Council, and in 1987 they acquired UNESCO World Heritage status. They have also been placed under the protection of China's law on the Protection of Cultural Relics. Boundaries of the protected area have been set by the Regulations for the Conservation of the Mogao Caves in Dunhuang of 2002 and the Master Plan for the Conservation of the Mogao Caves in Dunhuang. The caves are also administered by the Dunhuang Cultural Relics Research Institute.

Tourism

The Mogao Caves were visited by approximately 25,000 visitors in 1979. In recent years it is estimated that over a million tourists visit them every year, with ninety percent being local Chinese. The number of visitors has had to be limited to 6,000 per day, and tours now last approximately seventy-five minutes. In 2014, a $50 million visitors' center opened, built out beyond the buffer zone of the UNESCO heritage designated area. Visitors to the site now must first see two twenty-minute films at the new visitors' center, one an IMAX film and the other projected on a domed ceiling in a separate theater. Visitors are then transported via modern shuttle buses to the caves along a new, four-lane highway.

An English-speaking guide led our tour group into approximately a half dozen caves. Despite the limited time we were allowed at the caves themselves, it was obvious that we were shown many of the most important and unique caves, along with several of the smaller caves following similar ground plans and layouts. Unfortunately, no photography was allowed inside any of the caves, but several good books with full-color illustrations were available in bookshops at nearby locations.

The Mogao Caves were one of the first major sites that our group visited while on the tour of Xinjiang, China's westernmost province. As a result, much of the remaining tour seemed somewhat anticlimactic after seeing such a magnificent and outstanding, ancient site.

Adapted from:

http://whc.unesco.org/en/list/440

http://blogs.getty.edu/iris/14-facts-cave-temples-dunhuang/

http://en.wikipedia.org/wiki/Mogao_Caves

http://idp.bl.uk/pages/about.a4d

https://www.theguardian.com/artanddesign/2016/may/13/dunhuang-caves-artifacts-ancient-history-chinese-civilization-getty-institute-silk-road-los-angeles

CROATIA

Country name: Republic of Croatia (Croatian: Republika Hrvatska)

Site name: Split (formerly Spalato)

Location: Eastern shore of the Adriatic Sea, region of Dalmatia

UNESCO World Heritage Site: Inscribed 1979; no. 97

Date of Visit: 12 September 2012

DIOCLETIAN'S PALACE AT SPLIT

Split is Croatia's second largest city, while Zagreb, the capital, is the country's largest. Located on the eastern shore of the Adriatic Sea, it is the largest city in the region of Dalmatia. Sitting on a peninsula, it has become a transportation hub and one of Croatia's most popular tourist destinations.

The city's name, Split, is said to derive from a common, spiny shrub found in the area. Originally a Greek colony, the city was named Aspálathos or Spálathos. During the Roman period, the city's name in Latin became known as Spalatum or Aspalatum. In Serbo-Croatian it became known as Split or Spljet, while in Italian it became known as Spalato. The Croatian name eventually replaced the Italian version, and the city officially became known as Split in the country of Yugoslavia after World War I. That the city's name was derived from the Latin, "palatium," for "palace," is now thought to be erroneous.

In the third to second centuries BCE, the city was a Greek colony and known as Spálathos. After the Illyrian Wars, the nearby city of Salona became the capital of the Roman province of Dalmatia. With Salona thought to be the home city of the emperor Diocletian, it was the nearby city of Spalathos that the emperor chose as the site of his immense, imperial palace.

As the largest city on the Dalmatian coast, Split has had a tumultuous history and has been under Roman, Venetian, French, Italian, and Yugoslavian rule. Since the year 2000, it has developed into a major tourist destination for Croatia. New

Private homes have been built inside the ancient,
Roman palace of Diocletian at Split, Croatia.

infrastructure has been built to service new hotels and new office and apartment buildings.

What has made Split historically important and has qualified it as a UNESCO World Heritage Site are the remains of Diocletian's palace, regarded as one of the largest, most magnificent and best-preserved palaces of imperial Rome. The ancient Roman palace still functions as the core of today's Split.

Diocletian became a Roman emperor in 284 CE. In 305 CE, after reigning for twenty years, he retired from public life and commissioned for himself a vast, opulent palace on the bay of Split to be built by the architects Zotikos and Filotas. Constructed very much like a Roman military encampment, the huge structure measured 215m (705 feet) in length and 180m (590 feet) in width. Its thick walls measured 28m (92 feet) in height and possessed fortified towers and gateways piercing its four sides. Built like a Roman fortress and fronting the sea, the palace soon became surrounded by a city with a population estimated at 8,000 to 10,000 inhabitants.

Dating back to 295 CE, the ancient palace of Diocletian has become a small city in its own right inside the larger city of Split. In addition to the remains of the Roman palace and mausoleum, the ancient site now contains an estimated two hundred individual buildings and some three thousand inhabitants. Today the ancient palace contains twelfth and thirteenth centuries Romanesque churches, Gothic, Renaissance, and Baroque palaces, as well as a sixteenth century synagogue, various private residences, courtyards, and trendy shops. Especially notable are the ancient Temple of Jupiter, rededicated as a Christian church to the Virgin, and the Cathedral and Bell Tower of Saint Domnios, the patron saint of the city.

Unfortunately, our tour group had only a brief stay at Split. After a very short and perfunctory tour of Diocletian's palace, we were left on our own to tour the city. As a result, it was not possible to visit the Gallery of Fine Arts housed in a building dating from 1792 and many of the other historic sites of the city.

Since I did not even know of its existence, I was not able to visit the gallery devoted to the work of the famous Croatian sculptor, Ivan Mestrovic. At least I was able to photograph the 8.5 foot statue located at Split by Mestrovic of Gregory Nin, also known as Grgur Ninski, although I didn't get to rub one of his toes for good luck.

Adapted from:

https://en.wikipedia.org/wiki/Split,_Croatia

https://www.tripadvisor.com/Tourism-g295370-Split_Split_Dalmatia_County_Dalmatia-Vacations.html

https://www.nytimes.com/2015/06/28/travel/what-to-do-in-36-hours-in-split-croatia.html

http://whc.unesco.org/en/list/97

https://en.wikipedia.org/wiki/List_of_World_Heritage_Sites_in_Croatia

EGYPT

Country name: Arab Republic of Egypt (Arabic: Misr)
Site name: Abu Simbel
Location: On the western bank of Lake Nasser at the second
    cataract, near the village of Abu Simbel, near the Nubian
    border in southern Egypt, ca. 300 km southwest of Aswan
UNESCO World Heritage Site: Inscribed 1979, no. 88
Tour Dates: 18-30 September 2003

THE COLOSSAL TEMPLES OF RAMESSES II: ABU SIMBEL

Abu Simbel is one of Egypt's most impressive and iconic sites. It is reputed to be the country's most visited site after the pyramids of Giza. The temple complex is regarded as one of the greatest achievements of the pharaoh Ramesses the Great, who reigned from 1279 to 1213 BCE.

Abu Simbel is only one of six temples constructed by Ramesses II in the region of Nubia during his long reign. Located on the border with Nubia, the gigantic temples were intended to impress those to the south and to assert the rule of the pharaoh and the worship of the Egyptian religion in the region.

Abu Simbel's construction is reputed to have taken approximately twenty years. Some archaeologists believe it was constructed from approximately 1279-1213 or from 1264-1226 BCE. Its construction is thought to have probably been intended to celebrate the victory Ramesses claimed to have won over the Hittites in 1274 BCE in the battle of Kadesh. Some Egyptologists believe it could have been built starting in 1244 BCE. Others believe it was built to assert the power of Egypt on its southern border after the Nubian campaign.

Abu Simbel's larger temple was built in honor of the Egyptian deities, Ra-Harakhti, Amun-Ra, and Ptah, as well as the deified Ramesses. The smaller temple was dedicated to the goddess Hathor and to the pharaoh's favorite wife, Nefertari.

The site is thought to have been known in antiquity as the "Temple of Ramesses, beloved by Amun." The origin of the site's present name comes from a legend, often told by local guides. Abu Simbel is said to be named after a small boy who had led early explorers to the site. It is said that, in 1813 CE, the boy had led an early explorer, Johann Ludwig Burckhardt, to the site. Another version of the story states that the young boy actually led the explorer Giovanni Belzoni to the site in 1817. Burckhardt is thought not to have conducted excavations at the site where he found the Great Temple. Since Belzoni is credited as being the first to attempt the excavation of the temples buried by sands up to the necks of the façade's images., it is thought that the small boy had led Belzoni, rather than Burckhart, to the site. The legend of the small boy is therefore believed to have eventually caused his name to be applied to the site itself.

Of the two rock-cut temples at Abu Simbel, it is the larger of the two that has become the most famous. Its façade is decorated by four immense seated images of Ramesses II wearing the double Atef crown of Upper and Lower Egypt, with each figure measuring 20 meters in height. Atop the façade, measuring 35 meters in width, is a frieze of twenty-two baboons, depicted as sun worshippers. As a result of earthquake damage, the image of Ramesses II, located to the left of the temple's central entrance, retains only its lower half. The face of the image is missing, and only the torso and head of the pharaoh remain at the feet of the image.

Next to the legs of the four colossal images is a series of additional figures, each no taller than the legs of the colossal images of the pharaoh. Included are representations of the pharaoh's wife, Nefertari; the queen mother, Mut-Tuy; and the pharaoh's sons, Amun-her-khepeshet, and Ramesses. Also included are depictions of his six daughters, Isetnofret, Nebettawy, Meritamen, Nefertari, Baketmut, and Bintanath.

Decorating the temple's entrance are two images of the pharaoh worshiping an image of the falcon-headed deity, Ra Harakhti, which stands in a carved niche. The deity holds the

Façade of the temple of Ramesses II at Abu Simbel, Egypt

hieroglyph "user," as well as a feather, while the god of justice and truth, Ma'at, stands at his left side.

Inside the Great Temple are a series of chambers, decreasing in size as one goes further into the mountain. The hypostyle hall is notable for its immense pillars representing the deified Ramesses as identified with Osiris. Much of the interior decoration is given over to representations of the battle of Kadesh. Other scenes depict the pharaoh's victories in Nubia and Libya.

The end chamber, the sanctuary, is especially important for its representations of the four figures on its back wall. Depicted are the seated figures of Ra Harakhti, a representation of the deified Ramesses, Amun-Ra, and Ptah.

Much has been said about the orientation of the Great Temple. Only on two days during the year, February 22 and October 22, do the early morning rays of the sun penetrate the full length of the temple's interior and illuminate three of the images on the sanctuary's back wall. Ptah, god of the underworld, remains in darkness. The phenomena has caused some Egyptologists to surmise that the two dates mark the birthday and the date of the coronation of the pharaoh. Crowds of visitors throng to the site on those two days of the year to witness the sun's illumination of the temple's interior.

The temple of Hathor and Nefertari, also called the Small Temple, measures 12m (40 feet) in height and 28m (92 feet) in width. It stands approximately 100m to the northeast of the Great Temple. Its façade is decorated by colossal figures, with three located on each side of its central entrance.

The façade's figures represent Ramesses and his queen, with four images being that of the king and two being that of the queen. Each image measures 10m (32 feet) in height.

Especially notable is the fact that the queen is depicted at the same height as the pharaoh, since queens were usually represented as being smaller in size, The only other instance of the queen depicted as being equal in importance appears to be that of Nefertiti, who was often represented as being the equal of the pharaoh Akhenaton.

Inside the Small Temple are representations of Ramesses and Nefertari bringing offerings to the gods and depictions of the goddess Hathor. It is thought that the site was sacred to Hathor long before the construction of the Smaller Temple and that Ramesses selected the site for the temple dedicated to his wife and to Hathor for that reason.

Since Abu Simbel was threatened with being totally inundated by the waters of the Nile once the Aswan High Dam was completed, an international group of archaeologists and engineers, under the aegis of UNESCO, initiated a huge project of moving the massive temples to higher ground in 1964.

In 1962, based a scheme by William Macquitty, architects Jane Drew and Maxwell Fry and the civil engineer Ove Arup, proposed that a fresh water dam be built surrounding the temples. Water inside the dam would be kept at the same level as Lake Nasser. Underwater viewing chambers would allow the viewing of the temples by visitors to the site. It was argued that such a scheme would prevent the ancient monuments from suffering further damage from the effects of weathering and of erosion caused by the desert winds and sandstorms. Although it was acknowledged as being a very creative solution, it was rejected.

Instead, an international project costing an estimated USD $40 million and supported by funds from fifty different nations was undertaken from 1963 to 1968. After digging away the top of the cliffs, the temples were cut apart into approximately 16,000 individual stone blocks. Special care was taken to cut the temples apart at the least conspicuous locations. Then, when reassembled, joints between the ancient stores were sealed with a mortar composed of cement and desert sand. The temples, in their entirety, were then reassembled at a location 65m (213 feet) up the cliffs and 210m (690 feet) northwest of their original site. Built behind the reassembled temple façades was a man-made mountain to give the impression of the temples having been cut into the face of the mountain cliffs. Inside the artificial mountain, two huge domes were constructed of reinforced concrete and covered over by rocky rubble. Inside the two domes, the original interior walls and ceilings of the two temples were suspended from reinforced concrete frameworks.

All the smaller monuments and stelae at Abu Simbel were also moved to the new location. Included were the stele representing the marriage of Ramesses to the Hittite princess Naptera and the stele of Asha-hebsed, the foreman responsible for managing the workforce constructing the temples.

Today hundreds of tourists visit Abu Simbel each day. Cars and tour buses leave nearby Aswan daily, headed for the site. Other visitors arrive by air at a specially constructed airport near the site.

When I arrived at the site as part of my tour of Egypt, I was at first somewhat disappointed to be met by a large, nondescript, rocky hill. It was only after trudging around to the opposite side of the hill that the magnificent temples came into view. I was not only impressed by the scale of the conception of the pharaoh when constructing the temples. I was also overwhelmed by the magnitude of the project that had saved the enormous temples, rescued them from inundation by the Nile, and saved them for posterity.

Adapted from:

https://en.wikipedia.org/wiki/Abu_Simbel_temples
https://www.britannica.com/place/Abu-Simbel
whc.unesco.org › Culture › World Heritage Centre
http://whc.unesco.org/en/list/88
https://www.ancient.eu/Abu_Simbel

EGYPT

Country name: Arab Republic of Egypt (Arabic: Misr)

Site name: Sanctuary of Isis at Philae

Location: The island of Agilika, located in the Aswan Low Dam reservoir, 12 km south of Aswan

UNESCO World Heritage Site: Inscribed 1979; no. 88

Tour Dates: 18-30 September 2003

EGYPT'S RESCUED ISLAND TEMPLES AT PHILAE

Along with Abu Simbel, the ancient Greco-Roman temples of Philae, dedicated to Isis, have been relocated and rescued from the rising waters created by the Aswan High Dam. As a result of the international campaign initiated by UNESCO, the temple complex has been dismantled and transported to the nearby island of Agilika.

In ancient times the site was known as Pilak, meaning the "end," since the site marked the southernmost boundary of Egypt. The name "Philae" became the Greek and Latin name. The plural form of the name indicated that it referred to two small islands located above the first cataract of the Nile above Aswan. Early mentions of the site have included those of Strabo, Ptolemy, Seneca, and Pliny the Elder. During the Islamic period, Philae became known as El-Qsar, meaning "castle," and was also known as Gazinet Anas el-Wogud, after the hero of one of the *Arabian Nights.*

Although the earliest temple at Philae was built by Nectanebo I from 380-362 BCE, almost all of what is seen today was constructed by the Ptolemies during the two last centuries BCE and the first three centuries CE. Greeks and Romans, emperors and pilgrims, thronged to the island temples seeking to pay homage to Isis, the goddess of healing. Most of the construction is thought to have taken place during the reigns of Ptolemy II Philadelphus, Ptolemy V Epiphanes, and Ptolemy VI Philometor.

The crowded forecourt of the Temple of
Isis located on the island of Philae, Egypt

Reputed to be the site of the burial of Osiris, Philae was held in especially high regard by both the Egyptians to the north and the Nubians to the south. It was regarded as being so sacred that only priests were allowed to live on the island. Records indicate that Ptolemy VIII Physcon (170-117 BCE) was petitioned by priests to ban the island from secular settlement. Records of the priests' petition were recorded on an obelisk taken to London by William John Bankes in the nineteenth century, where the obelisk's hieroglyphics were used, along with the Rosetta Stone, to gain information on certain consonants of the Egyptian alphabet.

The principle deity venerated at Philae was Isis, although there were dedications to other deities such as Hathor. Philae may have been the last of the temples where the ancient Egyptian religion survived, as evidenced by an inscription as late as the fourth century CE. Finally, in the sixth century, the temple complex was shut down by the Byzantine emperor Justinian. It then became a Christian community, with ruins of a church having been discovered on the site, as well as traces of a chapel appearing to have been dedicated to both Jesus and Osiris. Until the Islamic period, it was the site of an active Coptic settlement.

Attracting the attention of explorers in the nineteenth century, Philae was visited by the British Egyptologist Joseph Bonomi the Younger in the 1820s. Later, the British novelist Amelia Edwards visited the site in 1973-1974.

The temples have been considered among Egypt's most beautiful and the island as one of its most scenic areas. The island temple complex began to attract large numbers of visitors each year, but then, with the construction of the first Aswan Dam in 1902, the temples began to be flooded by the waters of the Nile. The height of the dam had been raised twice, first in 1907-1912 and then again from 1929-1934. In spite of remaining largely intact from antiquity, the temples began to be inundated most of the year. Eventually a third of the temples were flooded year-round and could often be visited only from August to December. Then the construction of the Aswan High Dam threatened to totally engulf them. Fortunately, UNESCO's rescue program, carried out jointly with the Egyptian government between 1960 and 1980, was able to save Philae for posterity.

The massive engineering project to save the temples first entailed building a coffer dam around the entire island and pumping the water out from the enclosed area. The temples were then measured and cleaned. Using photogrammetry, the original building blocks of the temples were used in the temples' reconstruction, which took ten years. Each stone of the temple complex was numbered so that they might be reassembled, much like a giant puzzle. Disassembled into some 40,000 pieces for transportation to higher ground, the temples were reconstructed on the nearby island of Agilika, which is located approximately 500m (1,600 feet) from their original location.

Today, Philae bears many scars of having its images defaced after it no longer functioned as an Egyptian temple. Not only did it suffer from the zeal of early Christians to destroy pagan images. It also endured the iconoclasm of the Byzantine period when both Christian and pagan images were destroyed.

The trip to Egypt was my first after having retired in 2003. It also provided an opportunity to learn how to use a recently purchased digital camera. Although my trip in a small boat to the island seemed treacherous, being privileged to see the island's magnificent temples proved to be a trip highlight.

Today, the temple complex, as positioned on its new site, retains much of its original beauty. Viewed from the small boats that must be used to visit the island, the stately palms and the massive pylons of the temple rise almost magically like mirages out of the glistening waters of Lake Nasser. One can easily imagine how such majestic and monumental temples must have awed ancient Egyptian worshippers.

Adapted from:

https://en.wikipedia.org/wiki/Philae

http://www.planetware.com/egypt/philae-egy-asw-phil.htm

https://discoveringegypt.com/pyramids-temples-of-egypt/philae-temple/

http://whc.unesco.org/en/list/88

http://whc.unesco.org/en/activities/173

ETHIOPIA

Country name: Federal Democratic Republic of Ethiopia

Site name: Aksum (also spelled Axum)

Location: Mehakelegnaw Zone, Tigray region, Northern Ethiopia

UNESCO World Heritage Site: Inscribed 1980; no. 15

Tour Dates: 13-26 January 2011

ETHIOPIA'S SACRED CITY: AKSUM

Aksum is regarded as being Africa's oldest continuously inhabited city. It is also reputed to be Ethiopia's most sacred city and is an important pilgrimage destination. Two of the most important religious festivals of the Ethiopian Christians are centered at Aksum: the festival of Timkat, celebrated on 19 or 20 January, and the festival of Maryam Zion, celebrated on 24 November. It is also believed to be the location of the ancient Biblical Ark of the Covenant which resides in a small chapel in Aksum, the Church of Our Lady of Zion. Legends also suggest that Makeda, the Biblical Queen of Sheba, traveled from her home in Aksum to Jerusalem on her visit to see King Solomon.

Aksum was the center of the Aksumite Kingdom and was a great naval and trading center from 400 BCE until the tenth century. Although the city began to decline as early as the seventh century, kings continued to be crowned at Aksum as late as the 10th century.

When the kingdom was at its height in the fourth century, it was King Ezana, baptized as Abreha, who was converted to Christianity by Fromentius in 356 CE. Then during the reign of King Kaleb, Aksum joined with the Byzantine empire as an ally in opposing the Zoroastrian Persian Empire.

At its zenith in the third to sixth centuries, Aksum became the greatest center of trade in northeast Africa. It dominated the coast of the Red Sea, and its influence extended from the Gulf of Aden to the northern coast of modern Djibouti and Somalia. At its height, the Aksumite Kingdom was the most powerful state

Church of our Lady of Zion, reputed to be the location of the ancient Ark of the Covenant, Aksum, Ethiopia

between Persia and the eastern Roman Empire. In the early 6th century Aksum succeeded in reducing Yemen to that of a vassal, but later in the century invasions from South Arabia brought its power and influence to an end. Its trade within the area of the Mediterranean was effectively ended in the seventh and eighth centuries by the Arabs.

Once covering a large area of the Tigray Plateau, the Aksumite Kingdom left numerous impressive, monumental remains such as massive obelisks, ruins of palaces, and royal tombs dating primarily from the sixth and seventh centuries. Also found at Aksum was a series of stone inscriptions, with the Ezana Stone's trilingual inscriptions written in Sabaean, Greek, and the classical Ethiopian language, Ge'ez.

The stelae, called *hawilt* or *hawilti* in local languages, located in the Northern Stelae Park dating from the third and fourth centuries, are among its most impressive monuments. Thought to be grave markers, the stelae may have had metal disks engraved with designs attached to their sides. The largest stele still standing measures 24.6m high, 2.3m wide, 1.36m deep, and weighs 170 tons. One obelisk, probably having fallen while being erected, measures 33m high, 3.84m wide, 2.35m deep, and weighs 520 tons. It is believed to be the largest monolithic stele ever to have been created by humans. Located to the west of the city is the Gudit Stelae, interspersed with tombs, unlike those in the northern city area.

Another of Aksum's obelisks measures 24.6m high, 2.32m wide and 4.36m deep, and weighs 170 tons. Already broken into five sections, it was shipped off to Rome by Italian soldiers in 1937. Although a United Nations agreement was reached in 1947, disputes ensued, and the obelisk was not returned to Ethiopia until April of 2005. The obelisk's return, costing $4 million, was greeted with much fanfare, especially since it was seen as a symbol of Ethiopian pride and identity. Finally, in July of 2008, it was re-erected and dedicated on 4 September, 2008.

The Old and New Cathedrals of Saint Mary of Zion are Aksum's most sacred sites. The Old Cathedral, built in 1665 by Ezana, is believed to have been the first building at Aksum to house the ancient Ark of the Covenant. A massive structure with twelve naves, it was burned to the ground, then rebuilt, and destroyed again in the 1500s. Emperors Gelawdewos and Fasilides are credited with building the present structure. According to the beliefs of Ethiopian Christians, the ancient Ark of the Covenant housed in the temple in Jerusalem was stolen and replaced with a replica by Menelik, son of King Solomon and the Queen of Sheba. Kept hidden within the small chapel of Saint Mary of Zion, the ancient Ark is guarded by a single priest who is prohibited from leaving the precincts of the chapel and who is the only person allowed to see the ancient Ark. To this day, every Ethiopian Christian church, if it is to be regarded as a valid place of worship, is required to house a tabot, a small replica of the Ark.

The New Cathedral, standing near the old one, was built starting in 1955. Built as a result of a pledge by Emperor Haile Selassie to honor the liberation of Ethiopia from the Fascists, it is a strikingly modern structure. Selassie is said to have interrupted the visit of Queen Elizabeth II to Ethiopia to attend its dedication, while the Queen visited the new church several days later.

Other ancient monuments at Aksum include King Bazen's tomb, the reservoir called the bath of the Queen of Sheba, the Dungur palaces, the Abba Pentalewon and Abba Liqanos monasteries, the Lioness of Gobedra rock art, and the Ta'akha Maryam.

Although Aksum has been inscribed as a UNESCO World Heritage Site, there is a general lack of efforts at conservation. It remains under the protection and jurisdiction of the National Antiquities Authority of 1958 and the Authority for Research and Conservation of Cultural Heritage (ARCCH). The new museum built in 2011 near the Northern Stelae Park is somewhat of an intrusive structure next to such an important archaeological site, and flooding has adversely affected some of the ancient tombs.

Although some parts of the Festival of Timkat were observed at the nearby town of Adwa, it was at Aksum that our tour group was privileged to view the climatic moments of the yearly festival. Being permitted to see the many priests in their colorful religious regalia and carrying their large, lavishly decorated ceremonial umbrellas was one of the many highlights of the trip to Ethiopia in 2011.

Adapted from:

http://whc.unesco.org/en/list/15
http://whc.unesco.org/en/list/15
http://whc.unesco.org/en/news/456/

An Ethiopian priest exiting one of
Lalibela's rock-cut churches, Ethiopia

ETHIOPIA

Country name: Federal Democratic Republic of Ethiopia

Site name: Rock-Hewn Churches, Lalibela

Location: Semien Wollo Zone of the Amhara Region, 645 km from Addis Ababa

UNESCO World Heritage Site: Inscribed 1978; no. 18

Tour Dates: 13-26 January 2011

ETHIOPIA'S ROCK-CUT CHURCHES AT LALIBELA

Lalibela is regarded as Ethiopia's second holiest city, with Axum being honored by the Ethiopian Orthodox Christians as its holiest Christian city and place of pilgrimage. Ethiopia is known as being among the earliest countries to adopt Christianity, having done so in the early fourth century during the reign of the Zagwe dynasty king Gebre Mesqel Lalibela, who reigned from approximately 1181 to 1221 CE. Ethiopia's Christian roots go back further to the conversion of the Ethiopian eunuch by Philip the Evangelist, as recorded in the Bible's *Acts of the Apostles*, chapter 8. To this day, Lalibela's inhabitants are almost totally Ethiopian Orthodox Christians, and the city hosts a large number of resident priests and monks.

The exact dates of Lalibela's churches are a subject of much controversy. It is generally agreed that they date from the seventh to the thirteenth centuries, although the late twelfth to early thirteenth centuries are the dates most often given.

The carving of the churches has been attributed to King Gebe Mesqel Lalibela, whose full name means "he whom the bees recognize as king." Regarded as a saint, Lalibela is said to have envisioned the building of a "new Jerusalem" in his capital city which, at the time, was known as Roha. With the local river given the name, "River Jordan," Lalibela was built as a new holy city. It was thought that a new symbolic Jerusalem needed to be built, since the Holy Land had been captured in 1187 by Muslims led by Saladin.

It is generally thought that the carving of the churches must have taken much more time than the actual years of King Lalibela's reign. Some archaeologists have suggested that the carving of the churches was begun up to five hundred years earlier as palaces and fortifications and during a period when the kingdom of Axum was in decline. It is thought that the churches only later may have become associated with King Lalibela.

UNESCO has inscribed as heritage sites the following eleven rock-cut churches which have been divided into the following groups:

The Northern Group (north of the River Jordan):

Biete Medhane Alem (House of the Saviour of the World) - Lalibela's largest church measuring 10m (33 feet) in height, 33m (108 feet) in length and 22m (72 feet) wide

Biete Maryam (House of Miriam/House of Mary) - regarded as Lalibela's oldest church

Biete Golgotha Mikael (House of Golgotha Mikael) - reputed to contain the tomb of King Lalibela

Biete Meskel (House of the Cross)

Biete Denagel (House of Virgins)

The Eastern Group (south of the River Jordan):

Biete Amanuel (House of Emmanuel) - possibly once a royal chapel or royal residence

Biete Qeddus Mercoreus (House of Saint Mercoreos/House of Saint Mark)

Biete Abba Libanos (House of Abbot Libanos)

Biete Gabriel-Rufael (House of the angels Gabriel, and Raphael) - perhaps a former palace

Biete Lehem (House of the Holy Bread)

The eleventh church, the Biete Giyorgis (Church of Saint George), regarded as Lalibela's best-preserved church is separate from the two groups, but is connected to them via trenches. It is also probably Lalibela's most famous and photographed church because of its massive underground cruciform shape and the cross carved on its roof.

Removed at some distance from the other monolithic churches are the monastery of Ashetan Maryam and the Yimrehane Kristos Church. The church was built inside a cave and is thought to date from the eleventh century.

By being carved out of the local, living rock rather than constructed from cut and dressed stone, all interior spaces, doorways, windows, floors, roofs, and columns had to be carved from the stone. Many churches are connected by means of underground passages up to 11m (36 feet) deep. The interconnecting tunnels and ceremonial passageways also often lead to catacombs and caves of hermits.

The Portuguese explorer Péro da Covilha and the priest Francisco Álvages are thought to have been the first Europeans to have seen Lalibela's monolithic churches in the early 16th century. Plans of several of Lalibela's churches were published in a book by Álvages in 1550. A soldier, Miguel de Castanhoso, visited the churches sometime before 1544. But three hundred years passed before they were visited again sometime between 1865 and 1870 by Gerhard Rohlfs.

According to a local legend, King Lalibela was asked by an angel to build the churches. Men are said to have worked on the churches during the day, while angels worked on them at night. The carving of the Biete Giyorgis, dedicated to Saint George, is said to have been directed by the saint himself. It has also been suggested that the Ethiopians were assisted in the carving of the churches by the Knights Templar, but all evidence points to their having been produced by a Medieval Ethiopian culture, with Coptic influences evident in some of the churches' details. Regardless of whether or not the churches were actually carved during Lalibela's reign, the removal of massive amounts of rock and earth was involved. Mysteriously, no remains of any of the removed material have been found.

Also noteworthy is Lalibela's vernacular architecture. One group of round houses built of stone and having two stories has been called the "tukus" buildings. The second group, called the "chika" buildings, have been built of earth and wattle and are only one story in height.

Unfortunately, many of Lalebela's ancient buildings remain endangered. Drainage ditches have not been cleared of debris; buildings have suffered water damage; and some are in danger of collapse. Paintings and reliefs inside the churches have seriously deteriorated. Temporary structures have been built, but they visually impact the integrity of the sites. A draft of a plan to protect the sites from development has been prepared but has not been ratified. A conservation plan, drafted in 2006, has not been implemented. The sites are administered by the local Lasta district tourism and culture office, but plans for controls of the designated areas need to be strengthened.

I found Lalibela's monumental, monolithic churches to be among the most impressive sights seen on the tour of Ethiopia. In many respects, they are unique and deserve to be classified among Ethiopia's most important monuments representing its ancient Christian legacy.

Adapted from:

https://en.wikipedia.org/wiki/Lalibela
http://whc.unesco.org/en/list/18
http://www.ancient-origins.net/ancient-places-africa/rock-hewn-churches-lalibela-ethiopia-00154

ETHIOPIA

Country name: Federal Democratic Republic of Ethiopia
Site name: Tiya
Location: Located in the Gurage Zone of the Soddo region, 70 km south of Addis Ababa
UNESCO World Heritage Site: Inscribed 1980; no. 12
Date of Visit : 25 January 2011

ETHIOPIA'S MYSTERIOUS STELAE AT TIYA

Of all the awe-inspiring sites visited on the trip to Ethiopia, the field of stelae located outside the village of Tiya was the most mysterious. Tiya is regarded as the most important of the 160 archaeological sites located in the Gurage Zone of the Soddo region south of Addis Ababa. A lesser known area in the region with similar stelae is located between Lovada and Djibouti City.

The names of "Yegran Dingay" or "Gran's Stones," often given to the stelae by the local people, refer to the Adal Sultanate ruler, Imam Ahmad Ibn Ibrahim al-Ghazi. The largest such stela at Tiya rises to an impressive height of 3.7m (over 12 feet).

Thirty-six of the original forty-six huge ancient stone monoliths, bearing strange carvings of swords and various other signs and symbols, sit clustered in the tall grasses of a large field. Thirty-two of the stelae are decorated with various images and symbols that have yet to be deciphered.

Located less than 1 km (.6 miles) outside the small town of Tiya to the south of Addis Ababa, the archaeological site was designated one of Ethiopia's nine UNESCO World Heritage Sites in 1980. Other UNESCO sites in Ethiopia include: Axum, Lalibela, the Semien Mountains National Park, Fasiledes Castle, the lower valleys of the Awash River and the Omo, the Muslim Holy City Harar, and the Konso landscape.

General view of the field of stelea at Tiya, Ethiopia

The large stone stelae lie scattered about the site, which is estimated at 200 square meters and which is enclosed in a barbed wire fence. The site can be entered through a large metal gateway.

Joint venture excavations by French and Ethiopian archaeologists have unearthed stone artifacts and skeletons of humans varying from 18 to 30 years in age. The alignment of many of the stones along a common axis has led some to believe that the stelae mark mass graves and may be those of warriors killed in battle. Carbon testing has dated the human remains to the twelfth to fourteenth centuries.

Who created the stelae and what their purpose might have been, aside from the marking of graves, still appears uncertain. Despite early discoveries of the stelae by Neuville and Père Azslïs, work by German archaeologists in April, 1935, and in the years since then, the stones have received very little scholarly study.

The stelae have been separated by scholars into three types: anthropomorphic, phallic, and non-anthropomorphic/non-phallic. Examples of all three types have been found within the Gurage Zone.

The most common carvings on the stelae are the swords. It has been surmised that the number of swords carved on a stela may be indicative of the number of persons buried at the site or may symbolize the number of persons killed by a particular, buried warrior. Some of the swords on the stelae have been compared to the so-called "Gallo" sword types of the Oromo, while other swords have been compared to traditional Somali daggers.

Some of the carvings appear to be representations of schematic humanoids. Some circles on the stelae are thought to represent female breasts and to indicate that a nearby burial is that of a woman. Other carvings are thought to represent human body parts or tools.

Other carvings appear only as mysterious signs and symbols. There are what appear to be plant forms, with a very common motif being the so-called "false banana tree" or "fountain-like" shape recalling to some extent the semi-circular forms found topping the stelae at Axum.

What I believe to be the masterpieces of the ancient Ethiopian stone carvers are the two stelae located outside on the museum grounds in Addis Abbaba. Both are ornately carved with a plethora of swords and mysterious signs and symbols. The more remarkable of the two stelae is vaguely anthropomorphic in form. It is recommended that visitors to the museum should not miss seeing the two outdoor stelae.

Unfortunately, the studies of archaeological remains in Ethiopia have been few. Little research has actually been done at Tiya. There are some claims of finds of Middle Stone Age tools at Tiya and also evidence of tranchet blows on the stones that may date from the same time period. The most prevalent theory is that Tiya dates later, from the eleventh to thirteenth centuries CE.

The half-day trip from Addis Ababa to Tiya is best done with a local guide. The road to Tiya is one of Ethiopia's better blacktop highways, and the entrance to the site, which is only 400m from the main road, is easily identifiable by signs. An English-speaking, professional guide is usually at the site during daytime hours to admit visitors and to give tours.

There appear to be some plans to upgrade the site and to make it more developed and tourist-friendly. There have also been plans to set up training for guides and to provide visits to other such sites in the area. At the time of our visit, it remained a very serene, bucolic and undeveloped location.

The visit to the peaceful and serene site of Tiya, with its enigmatic stelae, was a welcome and worthwhile excursion outside the often crowded and chaotic capital of Addis Ababa.

Adapted from:

https://en.wikipedia.org/wiki/Tiya_(archaeological_site)
http://whc.unesco.org/en/list/12
http://www.worldheritagesite.org/sites/tiya.html

FRANCE

Country name: French Republic (French: République française)

Site name: Arles

Location: Bouches-du-Rhône department, southern France

UNESCO World Heritage Site: Inscribed 1981; no. 164

Date of Visit: 10 August 2016

THE ROMAN AND ROMANESQUE MONUMENTS OF ARLES

In 1981 a section of the central city of Arles measuring 65 hectares (160.6 acres), was inscribed as a UNESCO World Heritage site. Established by the Greeks in the 6th century BCE, it was named Theline. Captured by Saluvii in 535 BCE, it was renamed Arelate. In 123 BCE it came under the control of the Romans and reached its apogee in the fourth and fifth centuries CE. Today, the city still retains many of its ancient monuments, such as its medieval walls and a well preserved ancient amphitheater that is said to still host bull fights.

While Arles has numerous important antique and medieval monuments, it has become inextricably linked with the nineteenth century Dutch, Post-Impressionist painter, Vincent van Gogh (1853–1890). While living in Arles from February, 1888, to May, 1889, van Gogh is reputed to have created more than two hundred paintings, in addition to drawings, in only fifteen months. He was joined by Paul Gauguin late in 1888, but the two soon parted due to the quarreling between them. In December of that year, van Gogh cut off of his left ear. While at Arles, van Gogh painted many of his best known works, such as "Sunflowers," "Night Café," "Yellow Room," and "Starry Night." Due to his deteriorating mental condition, van Gogh left Arles in May of 1889 for the Saint-Paul asylum at Saint-Rémy-de-Provence.

The two sites associated with van Gogh which were seen on the trip in 2016 included the yellow café located near the city's

The cloister and bell tower of
Saint Trophime, Arles, France

ancient forum and the site of a reconstructed drawbridge. Not seen was the old Arles hospital which has been renamed Espace van Gogh, and has been devoted to the artist and his works. Among other museums of Arles that there was no time to visit were the Musée de l'Arles de la Provence Antique with its fine collection of Roman sarcophagi, the Museon Arlaten and the Musée Réattu.

The church of St. Trophime, formerly a cathedral, drew most of my attention during the brief stop in Arles. Its apse and transept date from the eleventh century, while the nave and bell tower date from the twelfth century. The long nave, measuring twenty feet in height, has side aisles and a transept that supports a central, square bell tower. In characteristic Romanesque fashion, it has a gloomy interior lit only by small high windows. Inside are several late Roman sarcophagi, various reliquaries, several Baroque paintings, and remains from other religious buildings.

It is the church's façade and cloister that are regarded as major examples of Romanesque art. Above the façade's central portal, Christ sits majestically in the tympanum while symbols of the four Evangelists are grouped around Him: the lion symbolizing St. Mark; the bull, St. Luke; the eagle, St. John, and the angel, St. Matthew. At the portal's right, the damned are led by grotesque demons into Hell, while on the left, the blessed are ushered into Heaven. At the right of the portal is also one of the façade's most engaging representations, a scene showing the soul of a Christian emanating from the person's mouth as an infant which is being welcomed into Heaven by angels. Also on the façade are such Biblical scenes as the baptism of Christ, the adoration of the Magi, and the massacre of the innocents. On a lower level are statues of various saints. Beside the portal are column bases with representations of Samson and Delilah, as well as Samson and the lion.

The church's adjacent cloister also ranks as an exceptional example of Romanesque art. Work was undertaken on the cloister's north gallery, followed by the eastern gallery. After the two galleries had been completed in 1210-1220, construction stopped until the western and southern galleries were constructed in the 1380s and 1390s.

The northern gallery retains the Romanesque style and has capitals decorated with Biblical scenes comparing Old Testament events with those of the New Testament. The eastern gallery displays Gothic elements and contains symbols of the four Evangelists and scenes of the life and passion of Christ. The southern gallery, given over to representations of the life of Saint Trophemus, dates from the 1380s and 1390s and is Gothic in style with pointed arches and columns with foliated capitals. The western gallery, dating from around 1375, contains scenes of the Annunciation, Pentecost, the coronation of the Virgin, the stoning of St. Stephan, and Samson slaying the lion.

The other two ancient monuments of Arles seen on the trip were the amphitheater, dated to 90 CE and holding 20,000 spectators, and the ancient Roman theater, dated to the first century BCE.

Not seen were the ancient forum, the fourth century Roman baths called the Baths of Constantine, and the Cryptoportius, a series of underground galleries.

While it was fascinating to visit several sites inspiring van Gogh in his paintings, seeing the church of St. Trophime was the highlight of the brief time spent at Arles. I especially enjoyed seeing the scene of the personified soul being ushered into heaven on the church's façade after having first seen only photographs of it decades ago when an undergraduate student majoring in art.

Adapted from:
https://en.wikipedia.org/wiki/Arles
https://en.wikipedia.org/wiki/
Church_of_St._Trophime,_Arles
http://us.france.fr/en/discover/arles-camargue-2

FRANCE

Country name: French Republic (French: République française)

Site name: Pont du Gard

UNESCO World Heritage Site: Inscribed 1985; no. 344

Location: Crosses the Gardon River near Vers-Pont-du-Gard, southern France

Date of Visit: 9 August 2016

A MASTERPIECE OF ROMAN ENGINEERING: PONT DU GARD

The Romans did not invent the Roman arch, but they employed the principles of the arch to engineer the building of massive structures on an unprecedented scale. By using the arch, they could span areas with stone as had never before been possible. The arch, with its voussoirs springing from the base of a hemispherical opening and capped with the keystone, could span distances not feasible with post and lintel construction or with the corbel arch.

France's Pont du Gard is a prime examples of Roman engineering genius. It is essentially a series of stone arches stacked one above another on three levels. Six huge arches make up its lowest level. A series of eleven smaller arches make up its second level, while the top level, supporting the the conduit channeling the water, is composed of a series of thirty-five arches. One of the aqueduct's lower arches is reputed to span a near record of 25m.

Rising 49m (161 feet) above the Gardon River, its width varies from 9m (30 feet) at the bottom to 3m (9.8 feet) at the top. The arches on the upper levels are recessed but built in line with each other. A slight curvature of the arches in an upstream direction on the upper levels was originally thought to have been deliberately built to strengthen the aqueduct against the

A side view of the Pont du Gard, a section of the
Roman aqueduct built over the Gardon River, France

flow of the river. It is now thought that it is merely a natural deformation created by the expansion and contraction of the aqueduct's stones reacting to the sun's heat.

Along with the aqueduct of Segovia in Spain, the Pont du Gard is one of ancient Rome's tallest and best preserved. The three-tiered stone bridge is only part of a 50 km long aqueduct that carried water to the ancient Roman city of Nemausus, present-day Nîmes. Using water emanating from a spring at Uzès, the aqueduct carried water across the gorge of the Gardon River.

It is estimated that the aqueduct supplied the city with some 40,000 cubic meters of water per day, taking some twenty-seven hours in its journey from the spring near Uzès to ancient Nemausus, where it ended in the *castellum divisorum*, a shallow open circular basin 5.5m in diameter by about one meter in depth. The huge basin is thought to have been covered by a small pavilion and surrounded by balustrades. Excavations have revealed roof tiles, remains of Corinthian columns and fragments of a fresco depicting dolphins and other fish. A pipe measuring 1.2m (3 feet, 11 inches) in circumference first disgorged the water into the basin and was then channeled into pipes measuring 40 centimeters (16 inches) in circumference. From there it was directed into water pipes feeding other parts of the ancient city.

Providing ancient Nemausus with water created very special problems for the designers of the ancient aqueduct. To the east and south there were only low plains, while to the west were hills making transportation of water from that direction toward the city much too difficult. Those in charge of planning the aqueduct therefore looked to the north and to the Uzès area where natural springs could be found. As a result, it was the Fontaine d'Eure near Uzès that was chosen as the source of the aqueduct's water supply.

The distance from the water source to ancient Nîmes is only 20 km, but it was necessary for the aqueduct to take a winding path, eventually measuring some 50 km in length. Among the various obstacles to be circumvented were the Massif Central's southern foothills, known as the "Garrigues de Nîmes."

Using only gravity for the flow of water, the giant bridge measures 48.8m (160 feet) high and is sloped downward only 2.5 centimeters (1 inch) for a gradient of only 1 in 18,241. The entire length of the aqueduct slopes in height by only 12.6m or 41 feet. At only 76m (249 feet) above sea level, the Fontaine d'Eure is only 17m (56 feet) higher than its outlet in ancient Nîmes. While the gradient of the aqueduct varies considerably, it is uniformly more shallow than is usual for Roman aqueducts. Its gradient is only about a tenth that of the aqueducts ending in Rome.

The construction of the aqueduct has been credited to the son-in-law of Marcus Vipsanius Agrippa in about 19 BCE, by linking the aqueduct's construction to its having been visited by Agrippa during that year. Recent archaeological research places the aqueduct's construction later, from 40 to 60 CE. Estimates are that the great aqueduct took 800 to 1,000 workmen approximately fifteen years to complete.

The ancient aqueduct is reputed to contain 21,000 cubic meters of stone, weighing over 50,000 tons. For its construction, a soft, yellow limestone was quarried from the Estel quarry located on the Gardon River's left bank and approximately 600m from the site of the aqueduct. The coarse stone, often referred to as *pierre de Vers,* could easily be carried by boat to the construction site on the right bank of the river.

The Pont du Gard was constructed largely without metal clamps or mortar. Most of the ancient stones were cut to fit together with no need of mortar. Inscriptions found on many of the stones gave instructions as to where stones were to be placed. There is also evidence of the use of scaffolding and of various forms of hoists. Templates may also have been used to create standardized sizes and shapes of stones used in the massive bridge.

The precision of the aqueduct's construction evidences that a team of highly skilled contractors and workers were involved in its design and construction. Cranes, as well as block and tackle pulleys run by human-powered treadmills, were probably used to lift many of the stones into their places. Large blocks still protruding from the aqueduct indicate that they served as supports for complex systems of scaffolding and framing.

Such a massive construction also came with huge costs. It is estimated that the aqueduct cost over 30 million *sesterces*, equal to fifty years of pay for five hundred members of a Roman legion.

Many problems have plagued the Pont du Gard during its long history. Although the water it carried was quite pure, it contained high concentrations of dissolved calcium carbonate leached out of the area's limestone. Maintenance of the aqueduct became complicated by increasing deposits of calcareous sinter, reducing the flow of water. Vegetation also penetrated the water channels' stone lids, clogging them with invasive roots that caused algae and bacteria to decompose in a process called biolithogensis.

Parts of the aqueduct are thought to have remained in use up until the sixth century, although sections could have become clogged as early as the fourth century. With the fall of the Roman Empire, the great aqueduct fell into disuse but still remained important as a toll bridge across the Gardon River. Repairs to the aqueduct in 1703 included filling cracks in the masonry and replacing lost stones. From 1743 to 1747, a new bridge was built by the engineer Henri Pitot next to the aqueduct's lower level. By 1835 it was reported that the aqueduct was in danger of collapse due to loss of stonework and erosion. In 1850 Napoleon III visited the Pont du Gard and, taking an interest in it, commissioned Charles Laisné to carry out repairs from 1855-1858. Stairs were built at one end of the aqueduct so tourists could safely walk along the structure's repaired conduit.

The great aqueduct has survived numerous natural disasters, including three floods in the last century. A flood in 1958 submerged the entire lower level, while a flood as recently as 2002 damaged some nearby structures.

Although the Pont du Gard is, by far, one of the best-preserved sections of the ancient aqueduct, other sections remain, including the Pont de Bornègre, the Pont de Sartanett, and sections of tunnels near Sernhac.

By the 1990's, the Pont du Gard had become such a huge tourist attraction that the bridge built next to it in 1743 was often clogged with traffic. Touristy shops and other illegal structures lined the banks of the Gardon River. In 1996, a major, four-year project was initiated, supported by the French state and local governments as well as by the European Union and UNESCO. Vehicular traffic has been banned, and the entire area has since been open only to pedestrians. A new visitors center has also been built on the river's northern bank.

Today, the Pont du Gard ranks among France's top five tourist destinations and attracts millions of visitors each year.

Adapted from:

http://www.pontdugard.fr/en/ancient-work-art

https://en.wikipedia.org/wiki/Pont_du_Gard

http://whc.unesco.org/en/list/344

http://www.avignon-et-provence.com/en/monuments/pont-gard-aqueduct

GERMANY

Country name: Federal Republic of Germany (German: Bundesrepublik Deutschland)

Site name: Museuminsel

Location: An island in the Spree River, Mitte district, Berlin

UNESCO World Heritage Site: Inscribed 1999; no. 896

Trip Dates: 1-15 August 2006

A MONUMENTAL MUSEUM COMPLEX: BERLIN'S MUSEUMINSEL

Berlin's Museuminsel is a small island located in the midst of the city's Spree River. Spreeinsel (Spree Island), along with neighboring Cölin, are cited as being the sites of the first settlements in the thirteenth century that were later to become known as Berlin.

As one of the world's most important and impressive ensembles of museum buildings, Museuminsel has its origins in the eighteenth century, the Age of Enlightenment. It is particularly notable for the five large public museums built on the island between 1824 and 1930.

Pergamonmuseum

Designed by the architect, Alfred Messel, it is Berlin's best-known and most popular museum. In its three wings are the remains of such outstanding ancient monuments as the immense Hellenistic Pergamon Altar, the Ishtar Gate and the Roman Market Gate of Miletus. The Museum of Islamic Art houses one of the masterworks of the Umayyad period, the reliefs from the façade of the Jordanian desert palace of Mshatta. A fourth wing will house the Tell Halaf façade, the Pharaoh Sahure columned hall, and the Kalabscha Gate. The massive gallery containing the Pergamon Altar has been closed for major renovations and is scheduled to reopen late in 2019.

Façade of the Altes Museum (Old Museum), Berlin, Germany

Bode Museum

Originally Kaiser Friedrich's Museum for European Renaissance Art, this museum, located on the northern tip of Museuminsel, has been named after Wilhelm von Bode, the museum's first director. The renovation of the museum was finally completed in 2006 after a five-and-a-half year project. It houses a large collection of sculpture dating from the medieval period to the late eighteenth century. It also contains the Museum of Byzantine Art and the Numismatic Collection.

Neues Museum (New Museum)

Construction on the museum, commissioned by Friedrich Wilhelm IV and designed by the Prussian court architect Friedrich August Stüler, was started in 1841. Extensively damaged in WWII, it remained in ruins until 1999. After ten years of reconstruction, budgeted at 20 million euros and conducted under the direction of the British architect David Chipperfield, it was reopened in 2009. It contains the Egyptian

Museum, the papyrus collection, the Museum of Prehistory and Early History, and a collection of Classical art.

When I visited Berlin in 2006, banners hung around the city advertised that the world-famous bust of the Egyptian queen, Nefertiti, had just been reinstalled in the Neues Museum. As a result, I found the area around the museum showcase displaying the famous bust mobbed by museum visitors.

Alte Nationalgalerie (Old National Gallery)

This museum was designed by Johann Heinrich Strack, the successor to Friedrich August Stüler. It was completed in 1876 after ten years of construction. After a major renovation, it reopened in 2001. It houses primarily German and other European paintings of the nineteenth century. I was especially pleased to see many outstanding works by the German artist Caspar David Friedrich in the museum's collection.

Altes Museum (Old Museum)

The initial ideas for a museum on Museuminsel were those of Alois Hirt, a German art historian and archaeologist in the field of ancient Greek and Roman architecture. Many of his ideas were used in the planning of the Altes Museum, the first major museum constructed on Museuminsel. Designed by the famous architect Karl Friedrich Schinkel, the museum opened in 1830. It is an especially impressive building with a neoclassical façade of Ionic columns, a rotunda, and large foyer. Its displays include works of art from ancient Greece and Rome.

Since German reunification, a massive effort was made to reunify the various Prussian collections that had become separated during the Cold War. Through 2010, Germany's federal government spent 20 million euros per year to modernize and restore existing buildings.

A master plan, initiated in 1999, includes a major renovation of the island in order to transform it into a state-of-the-art cultural complex. A building, designed by the architect James Simon as an entrance to the island's museums, is scheduled to open in 2018. Plans for the building include shops, cafés, and exhibition spaces.

The Humbolt Forum, located in the Berlin Palace and sitting opposite the Lustgarten, is scheduled to open in 2019. It is planned as the future site of the Ethnological Museum and the Museum of Asian Art.

A so-called "Archaeological Promenade" which will connect four of the five museums on the island, the Neues, Altes, Bode and Pergamon museums, is also being planned. Its subterranean galleries will feature exhibition spaces for interdisciplinary displays.

Other major features of Museuminsel are the large park, the Lustgarten, sitting in front of the Altes Museum, and the massive Berliner Dom (Berlin cathedral) bordering one side of the park.

Management of Museuminsel's buildings and their collections is the joint responsibility of the Stiftung Preussisher Kulturbesitz (Prussian Cultural Heritage Foundation) and the Staatliche Museen zu Berlin (State Museums of Berlin). The Landesdenkmalamt Berlin (Berlin Monuments Office) is responsible for the district's preservation and conservation. The Senatsverwaltung für Stadtentwicklung und Umwelt (Senate Department of Urban Development and Environment) is charged with the planning and development for the island.

Cited as a UNESCO World Heritage Site in 1999, Museuminsel has often been called Berlin's "Acropolis" of the arts. With its museums' collections spanning six thousand years of world art, it has also been called the "Louvre on the River Spree." It is also cited as an outstanding example of the evolution of modern museum design.,

Museuminsel is regarded as a unique ensemble of outstanding museum architecture and of museum collections. It is one of Berlin's prime tourist attractions, with the Pergamon Museum alone attracting over one million visitors every year.

Adapted from:

http://whc.unesco.org/en/list/896
https://en.wikipedia.org/wiki/Museum_Island
https://www.visitberlin.de/en/museum-island-in-berlin

GREECE

Country name: Greece (officially the Hellenic Republic)
Site name: Delos
Location: Prefecture of Cyclades, south Aegean region
UNESCO World Heritage Site: Inscribed 1990; no. 530
Date of Visit: 20 October 2016

THE AEGEAN ARCHAEOLOGICAL SITE OF DELOS

The uninhabited Aegean island of Delos, meaning "appearance" or "apparent" in ancient Greek, is regarded as one of Greece's most important historical and archaeological sites. It is also said to be an exceptionally extensive and rich site and is one of Greece's most extensively excavated archaeological areas. Today, it is preserved as a vast, ruined city that reached its height during Greece's archaic and classical periods.

Located in the Cyclades archipelago, Delos is a small island, measuring only 1.2 km wide and covering only 5 square km. Its position is approximately equidistant from mainland Greece and Asia, making it an ideal location for a cosmopolitan center of commerce and culture. It is a hilly, barren island with almost no natural resources, so it was not self-supporting and had to rely almost totally on imports. Its supply of water was also limited, and it was necessary to build a system of cisterns, aqueducts, and drains.

According to ancient legends, Delos was where the titaness Leto gave birth to the twin gods Apollo and Artemis, who were also children of Zeus. The jealous wife of Zeus, Hera, supposedly banished Leto from the earth, but Poseidon, taking pity on her, provided Leto with Delos as a safe place for the birth of her twins.

Colonized by the Ionians in the third millennium BCE, Delos was originally known as Ortygia, meaning "quail island." By

The ferry docked at the archaeological island of Delos, Greece

1000 BCE, Delos had become a religious capital and was regarded as being so sacred that no one was allowed to be born or die there. A number of "purifications" took place at Delos so that the island would be a fitting place for the worship of the deities. The first purge is recorded as taking place in the sixth century BCE, while another took place in the fifth century CE in order to rid the island of all its dead. It was after the second purification of the island that the first Panegyris, a festival honoring Apollo, took place. Held every five years, the festival included athletic, musical, and dance contests and drew visitors from the entire Aegean region.

Starting in 478 BCE, Delos is where the meetings of the Delian League took place. It was also the location of the treasury of the League until it was moved to Athens in 454 BCE.

By 166 BCE the Romans had made Delos a free port. It also became one of the largest centers of the slave trade. In 88 BCE, Delos was attacked by Mithridates VI of Pontus, who killed up to 20,000 of its inhabitants, and in 69 BCE it was attacked by pirates. Delos went into decline as a trading and religious center when it was replaced by Puteoli as the center of trade with the east. Invaded by Venetians, Saracens, Ottomans. and the Knights of St. John, Delos quickly fell into ruins, was used as a quarry, and had many of its remains burned for lime.

The four main areas on Delos are the maritime quarter, the theater district, the Sanctuary of Apollo, and the Lion District.

The maritime district was the primary residential area of Delos and contains the remains of many mansions and villas of the island's elite, such as the House of the Masks with its representation of a panther being ridden by Dionysus.

The Theater of Delos, said to be capable of accommodating 5,500 spectators, is located in the theater district. East of the theater is the House of the Dolphins, notable for its mosaic depicting the sea creatures.

A path from the theater district leads up to the cone-shaped hill of Mount Kinthos, located in the center of the island. It provides good views over the remains of the entire ancient city.

When visiting Delos, one usually first encounters the Agora of the Competialists, dating from approximately 150 BCE. To the left of the agora, one encounters the sacred way, bordered by marble bases and leading to the Temple of Apollo.

The great temple of Apollo, built in the Doric style, was begun in 477 BCE and completed in the 200s BCE. It became neglected after its treasury was transferred to Athens, and little of the temple remains today. Nearby stood a colossal statue of Apollo, the few remains of which are in the museum in Delos and in the British Museum.

The famous marble lions, dedicated by the people of Naxos and dating from the seventh century, once guarded the Sacred Lake, which today has been intentionally left dry. Copies have replaced the lions because of weathering from the north wind on Delos. The originals are now housed in the island's archaeological museum. Only five of the original nine lions remain.

Among the many other archaeological remains on Delos is a synagogue, which is said to be the world's oldest. In addition, there is a Temple of Isis, a Temple of Hera, and the platform of the Stoivadeion dedicated to Dionysus.

Since 1872 Delos has been excavated by the École française d'Athènes, which continues work there today. Monitoring of the island is the responsibility of the Hellenic Ministry of Culture, Education and Religious Affairs. In addition to its designation as a UNESCO heritage site, it is protected by a law, "On the Protection of Antiquities and Cultural Heritage" of 2002, and supervision of the site is carried out by the Committee for the Conservation of the Monument of Delos. Many of the artifacts found on Delos are now housed in the Archaeological Museum of Delos and the National Archaeological Museum in Athens.

Delos is visited by over 100,000 tourists every year. Daily ferry service from Mykonos is usually available, and during the summer months, boat service is said to be available from the islands of Naxos and Tinos. In addition to the archaeological museum, Delos has a visitors center, restaurant, and bar, but no overnight accommodations. Delos remains administered as a part of the municipality of Mykonos.

Unlike the island of Mykonos which can often be chaotic and crowded with hordes of other tourists, there were many areas on Delos that I could enjoy visiting all by myself.

Adapted from:
https://whc.unesco.org/en/list/530
https://www.ancient.eu/delos/
http://www.sacred-destinations.com/greece/delos

GREECE

Country name: Greece (officially, the Hellenic Republic)

Site name: Metéora

Location: Prefecture of Trikala, Region of Thessaly, near the town of Kalambaka

UNESCO World Heritage Site: Inscribed 1988; no. 455

Date of Visit: 12 May 2011

THE SUSPENDED MONASTERIES AND CHURCHES OF METÉORA

Metéora, meaning "suspended rocks" or "suspended in the air" in Greek, is said to have first been used in 985 CE as a place where a hermit named Barnabas could find solitude. In the eleventh century more hermit monks sought refuge in the lofty height of Metéora's pinnacles. In the fourteenth century, with the arrival of the Ottoman Turks and the decline of the Byzantine Empire, more monks arrived, and in 1382 the Great Meteoran Monastery was built. Eventually, there were twenty-four monasteries, but they were abandoned and allowed to fall into ruin during the nineteenth century. Today only six monasteries, dating primarily from the fourteenth to sixteenth centuries, survive as inscribed UNESCO World Heritage Sites.

The date of the establishment of the monasteries at Metéora is unknown, but a monastic community known as the Skete of Stagoi had formed around the church of Theotokos by the late eleventh to early twelfth century. Athanasios Koinovitis is known to have brought a group from Mount Athos to Metéora in 1344 and to have founded the Great Meteoron Monastery.

The monasteries stand up to 400m (1,200 feet) above the small town of Kalambaka in today's Greece. Seeking solitude and inner peace, the monks succeeded, over the centuries, in building monastic complexes on the tops of some of nature's most inaccessible sites.

Rising from the plain of Thessaly and standing above the Peneas valley, Metéora's rocky pinnacles are said to be composed of a mixture of sandstone and conglomerate rather than hard igneous rock. Metéora's stone has been dated to some 60 million years ago during the Tertiary period. It has been chemically analyzed as deltaic in origin and later formed by fluvial erosion and earthquakes.

The Theopetra cave, which is open to the public and is located 4 km (2.5 miles) from Kalambaka, has been found to have contained many Paleolithic and Neolithic artifacts. Radio carbon dating has yielded evidence of human habitation in the cave up to 50,000 years ago.

There is much controversy over how Metéora's monasteries were constructed on such lofty sites. It is thought that the monks, having no water or electrical supplies, might have constructed their monasteries by laboriously hauling building materials up to the great heights by means of baskets, nets, rope ladders, winches, and windlasses. Somehow the rocky pinnacles must have been initially scaled. Perhaps kites might have been flown to establish footholds on the building sites. When questioned about the safety of their ropes and ladders, monks are said to have replied that they needed to be replaced only "when the Lord allows them to break." When under threat, monks only needed to draw up the long rope ladders, nets, and baskets.

Today, Metéora's monasteries stand as monuments of the Orthodox Christian faith, as well as preserving prime examples of post-Byzantine painting in their sixteenth century frescoes. Metéora's six monasteries inscribed as UNESCO World Heritage Sites are as follows:

Great Meteoron Monastery

This is the largest and oldest of the monasteries and was erected in the mid-fourteenth century and restored and embellished in 1483 and 1552. The Katholikon or main church, dated to the mid-fourteenth century, is dedicated the Transfigur-

Monastery of St. Stephen, built atop one of
the rock pinnacles at Metéora, Greece

ation of Christ. It has a small museum and is said to have only three monks in residence.

Varlaam Monastery

The second largest monastery, it was built in 1541 and embellished in 1548. Its church is dedicated to All Saints and is reputed to contain the shoulder blade of St. Andrew and the finger of St. John. It is said to house seven monks.

Monastery of Rousanou/St. Barbara

Possibly named after the first hermit to live on the site, its cathedral was founded in the mid sixteenth century and decorated in 1560. It remains a flourishing nunnery with thirteen nuns in residence.

Holy Trinity Monastery

Reputed to be Metéora's most inaccessible monastery, it was built in 1476 and renovated in 1684, 1689, 1692, and 1741.

St. Nikolaos Anapafsas Monastery

Built in the sixteenth century, its small church was decorated by the Cretan painter Theophanis Strelitzas in 1527. In 2015 it had only one monk in residence.

St. Stephen's Monastery

Reputed to be the most accessible monastery, its small church, dated to the sixteenth century, was decorated in 1545. It was shelled during World War II and is now a nunnery. As of 2015, it housed twenty-eight nuns.

Today, rock-cut stairways built in the 1920s and buses using back roads allow thousands of tourists to visit the monasteries every year and have allowed them to become thriving businesses catering to tourists. Metéora's almost surreal landscape continues to awe those who visit what is regarded as one of Greece's most inspiring, scenic, and photogenic areas. It has an almost magical and mystical quality and is such a spectacular setting that one can easily imagine why ancient monks would have sought Metéora out as a place of retreat for solitude, meditation, and prayer.

Adapted from:

https://www.visitmeteora.travel/en/what-to-see/the-meteora-monasteries

http://whc.unesco.org/en/list/455

https://en.wikipedia.org/wiki/Meteora

http://whc.unesco.org/en/list/455

HONDURAS

Country name: Republic of Honduras (Spanish: República de Honduras)

Site name: Maya Site of Copán

Location: Located on the west bank of the Copán River, Copán Department, western Honduras, near the border with Guatemala, 1.6 km (one mile) from the modern village of Copán Ruinas

UNESCO World Heritage Site: Inscribed 1980; no. 129

Date of Visit: 13 November 2008

RECORDS OF A MAYAN DYNASTY: COPÁN

Copán's Hieroglyphic Stairway was excavated by John C. Owens and George Byron Gordon in 1892-1893. It is the longest known Mayan inscription and is regarded as one of the foremost remains of Mayan culture. Measuring 10m (33 feet) wide and 21m (69 feet) long, the stone stairway contains approximately 2,200 Mayan glyphs. When discovered, it was in a ruinous state but is reputed to list the names of a dynasty of sixteen rulers from 426 to 822 CE. Construction on the stairway is stated to have been initiated in 710 CE by Copán's thirteenth ruler, Uaxaclajuun Ub'aah K'awiil. Another ruler, Yipyaj Chan K'awiil, is thought to have moved the stairway from an earlier building and installed it in his own version of the list. He is said to have set up Stela M with his own image and to have doubled the length of the text, as well as adding five life-size statues dressed as warriors, each seated on his own step on the stairway. The statues are thought to represent the most important rulers of the dynasty. The stairway's list ends with a ruler named "Smoke Shell" and with an enigmatic, bilingual inscription.

The Mayan ruler, Tax Kuk Mo, who became the first recorded king, is thought to have been a foreigner and may

Stele "P," depicting the Mayan king,
K'ak' Chan Yopaat, at Copán, Honduras

have come from Tikal, arriving in the Valley of Copán in 427 CE. His tomb has been preserved beneath the pyramid-shaped Temple 16. His reign was followed by various short-lived rulers. Records also tell of warfare with the Mayan city of Quirigua and the capture and sacrifice of the thirteenth ruler of Copán.

The history of Copán has also been preserved in various stelae and altars. Altar Q, built by the last of the kings, Yax Pasaj Chan Yopaat in 776 CE, tells of fifteen kings coming before him and gives the names of the rulers of the dynasty founded in 426-427 CE.

The ancient name of Copán is thought to be *Oxwitik* meaning "three *witiks*," but the exact meaning of the name remains obscure. In 1530 a local chieftain, Copán Calel, staged an uprising against the Spanish, and it is said that it was his name that became associated with the site.

The site of Copán was discovered by Diego García in 1570, and a mention of it has also been found in a letter dated March 1576. No excavations took place at Copán until the early 19th century when it was visited by Jean-Frédéric Waldeck. In 1834 it was visited by an expedition led by Colonel Juan Galindo. In 1839 the explorers Frederick Catherwood and John Lloyd Stephens arrived, with Catherwood making detailed drawings of the site. Later it was also visited by Alfred Maudslay.

In the 1930s and 1940s restoration work took place sponsored jointly by the Carnegie Institution in Washington, D.C. and the Honduras government. Several expeditions sponsored by the Peabody Museum of Harvard University took place in the late nineteenth and early twentieth centuries.

Copán is thought to have been founded as a small farming settlement as early as 1,000 BCE. The present archaeological site covers 250 acres (100 hectares) including the city's residential areas, while its core area measures 37 acres (150,000 square meters). Copán is thought to have been one of the most densely populated cities of its time. At its height, it may have had 20,000 residents and an area of 250 square km (100 square miles). Thought to have been completely abandoned by 1200 CE,

Copán's last recorded date has been found to be 822 CE. The reason for its being abandoned has been the subject of much debate. Drought is thought to be the most probable cause.

Copán has been divided into many various groups of archaeological remains by archaeologists, including an acropolis and several main plazas. The site has also been divided into various groups such as the Main, Cemetery, and Sepulturas Groups.

Of special note is the site's ball court, remodeled several times and decorated with mosaic sculptures of macaw heads. Thought to have been dedicated to a bird deity, hieroglyphs have dated it to 738 CE. Built by Copán's ill-fated thirteenth ruler, what has been called Structure 22 is thought to have been a throne room, while Building 101-2 is regarded as having been a royal residence complex.

In 1997, with the construction of Copán's Sculpture Museum, several original sculptures were moved to the museum, and replicas were placed at their original locations.

Especially notable is the copy of the Rosalila building excavated by Ricardo Aguncia and reconstructed inside the museum. It is regarded as one of the best-preserved phases of Temple 16 and as having been built over the remains of five earlier temples. A dedicatory inscription on one of the steps of the temple dates it to 571 CE. In the early eighth century, Uaxaclajuun Ub'aah K'awiil encased the Rosalila temple in a new temple building and as a result preserved the brightly painted sixth century version of the temple which is now represented by the copy in the site's museum.

Copán was designated a UNESCO site in 1980, and between 1982 and 1999, UNESCO approved funding of USD $95,825 for conservation work at the site. Today, the site is managed by the Honduras Institute of Anthropology and History (IHAH) and is protected by the "Constitution of the Republic of Honduras" of 1982 and the "Law for the Protection of the Culture Heritage of the Nation" of 1997. It is also covered by a presidential decree of

1982 which created the National Monument of Copán, covering a 30 km area.

Unfortunately, Copán continues to be endangered by erosion from the Copán River and the sprawl of neighboring towns. It is also in a seismic zone and has sustained damage from at least two earthquakes. An extension of the boundaries of the Copán Archaeological Park is being negotiated in order to expand the protected area beyond the present boundaries of the World Heritage property and to create an enlarged buffer zone. In addition, looting at the site remains a problem, with one tomb being looted in 1998 while it was being excavated.

When I booked a trip to Guatemala, I was fortunate to have a travel agent at the time who agreed to organize an extension of the trip to include an excursion across the border into Honduras so I might visit Copán. I remember very well feeling somewhat ill at ease while crossing the border, especially when the local English-speaking guide asked for what was the equivalent of a few extra dollars to bribe the border guards in order to get us both over the border.

The trip extension to Copán became one of the highlights of the trip. I could easily see why Copán is regarded as one of the most important sites of the Mayan civilization and as one of the greatest Mayan cities of the Classic Mayan period from 300 to 900 CE.

Adapted from:

https://en.wikipedia.org/wiki/Copán
https://whc.unesco.org/en/list/129
https://www.britannica.com/place/Copan
https://www.livescience.com › History

The Neo-Classical façade of Saint
Stephan's Basilica, Budapest, Hungary

HUNGARY

Country name: Hungary (Hungarian: Magyarország)

Site name: Budapest, including the Banks of the Danube, the Buda Castle Quarter and Andrássy Avenue

Location: bisected by the Danube River, central Carpathian Basin, central Hungary

UNESCO World Heritage Site: Inscribed 1987; extension, 2002; no. 400

Dates of Visits: 13-15 May 2007; 8-10 September 2012

A TALE OF TWO CITIES: BUDAPEST

In 1849 the WT Clark suspension bridge connected two cities on opposite sides of the Danube River, Buda on the right bank and Pest on the left. Although the area located on the Danube had been inhabited since Paleolithic times, it was during the Roman period that a settlement named Aquincum was established and centered on Óbuda, capital of a region known as Pannonia. Today, only the ruins of a Mithraeum and two amphitheaters survive. Later, during the Middle Ages, a settlement was established on the Pest side of the river, only to be destroyed in 1241-1242.

In 1265, King Bela IV built Buda Castle to house the Hungarian kings. Gothic art and culture spread throughout the Magyar region during the fourteenth century, as well as during the reign of Matthias Corvinus. In 1872-1873, the unification of Pest, Buda and Óbouda took place. Beginning in 1862, the Hungarian Academy was housed in a Neo-Renaissance building. Then from 1884 to 1904, the massive Neo-Gothic Parliament building was constructed on the Pest side of the Danube River.

Since the construction of the first bridge in 1849, additional bridges have been built to unite the two cities into what is known as Budapest today, including the Chain Bridge, the Liberty Bridge and the Elizabeth Bridge.

In 1987, Budapest became Hungary's eighth UNESCO World Heritage Site and was cited as being one of the most culturally diverse urban landscapes in Europe. Included in the protected Buda Castle Quarter were the Castle, built in 1265; the Sándor Palace; the Matthias Church; the Holy Trinity Square; Fisherman's Bastion, and the Royal Palace which today contains the Hungarian National Gallery and the National Széchényu Library. Also included were such landmarks located along the banks of the Danube as the Rudas Baths, the Chain Bridge, Gresham Palace, the Hungarian Academy of Sciences, the Vigadó concert hall and the Neo-Gothic Parliament building.

In 2002 UNESCO extended the protected area to include Margaret Island and an area up to the Grand Boulevard (Nagykörút). Included was Andrássy Avenue (dated 1872-1885), named after Count Gyula Andrássy who was Prime Minister between 1867 and 1871. The broad avenue was originally lined with grand buildings with exclusive apartments. In addition, the Millennium Underground Railway (dated 1893-1896), the first underground railway in Europe, was built under the grand avenue and connected Deák Ferenc Square to the City Park area. Both the avenue and the underground railway helped to radically change many of the urban areas of Pest.

Along the avenue are such landmarks as the Hungarian State Opera, designed by Miklós Ybl; the Academy of Music, founded by the famous Hungarian composer Ferenc Liszt; the Drechsler Palace, and the villas of the Kodály Circus. Today many of the apartment buildings, originally built along the avenue for Budapest's elite, have been converted for commercial uses and have become cafés, restaurants, and upscale boutiques.

Located at the far end of Andrássy Avenue are Heroes' Square, the Museum of Fine Arts and the Kunsthalle. Heroes' Square is especially notable for being decorated with fourteen statues of historical figures arranged in a semicircle around a column topped with an image of the archangel Gabriel. Located behind Heroes' Square are the City Park, Vajdahunyad Castle and the Széchanyi Baths.

Parts of Budapest's UNESCO heritage site were protected since 1965, but the area was enlarged in 2005 by the extension of the UNESCO heritage site in 2002 and under the Act on the Protection of Cultural Heritage. The Gyula Forster National Centre for Cultural Heritage Management has been made the management organization under the national world heritage act of 2011.

I was especially privileged to have visited Budapest on two separate occasions, in 2007 and 2012. Although I realize that there is still much of Budapest that I failed to see, I especially regret that it was not possible to tour Budapest's massive, Neo-Gothic Parliament built on the banks of the Danube. It has become such an iconic landmark, used over and over again by tour companies running riverboat tours. Their advertising often shows their clients leisurely lounging in their elegant staterooms as they slowly glide past the massive building on the Danube.

Adapted from:

https://en.wikipedia.org/wiki/History_of_Budapest

http://whc.unesco.org/en/list/400

https://everything-everywhere.com/unesco-world-heritage-site-136-historic-budapest/

http://visitbudapest.travel/guide/world-heritage-sites/

INDONESIA

Country name: Republic of Indonesia (Indonesian: Republik Indonesia)

Site name: Borobudur Temple Compounds

Location: Kedu Valley, Regency of Magelang, Province of Central Java; 40 km northwest of Yogyakarta

UNESCO World Heritage Site: Inscribed 1991; no. 592

Tour Dates: 3-15 April 2005

EARTH'S LARGEST BUDDHIST MONUMENT: BOROBUDUR

Borobudur has become an iconic symbol of Indonesia and is Indonesia's major tourist attraction. Along with Prambanan, it is largely responsible for the tourism industry in Central Java centered in its major city, Yogyakarta. In 1974, 260,000 visitors, 36,000 of whom were foreigners, visited Borobudur. By the middle of the 1990s, 2.5 million are said to have visited Borobudur, with eighty percent of them being foreign visitors.

Borobudur, also known as Candi Borobudur and Candhi Barabudhur, is regarded as having been built in the ninth century CE during the golden age of the Sailendra dynasty and finished during the reign of king Samaratungga in 825 CE. It drew pilgrims for hundreds of years until it was abandoned sometime between the tenth and fifteenth centuries,.

The name Borobudur was first used by Thomas Stamford Raffles in a book on Java's history. No earlier written sources are thought to exist except for an old Javanese manuscript written by a Buddhist scholar in 1365 CE mentioning a Buddhist monument called Budur.

No written records exist giving the dates or the purpose of Borobudur's construction. It is estimated that it took approximately seventy-five years to build and that it was built at about the same time as Java's great Hindu temple, Prambanon.

An image of the Buddha sits inside the remains of one of the stupas on Borobudur's upper levels, Indonesia

When Borobudur was abandoned is also unknown. Although it was undoubtedly never completely forgotten, it sat hidden for centuries under volcanic ash and jungle vegetation.

The discovery of Borobudur is credited to the brief period of British rule in Java from 1811 to 1816. Having an interest in Java's ancient history, the Lieutenant Governor-General Thomas Stamford Raffles sent a Dutch engineer, H. C. Cornelius, on a tour to Semarang in 1814. Although Raffles is generally credited with Borobudur's discovery, it was Cornelius and two hundred of his men who cut down jungle vegetation, removed volcanic ash, and revealed the great monument that had been hidden for centuries.

Commissioned by the government of the Dutch East Indies, F. C. Wilsen, and later, J. F. G. Brumund, succeeded in studying Borobudur and in making hundreds of drawings. Also appointed by the government, C. Leemans published the drawings of Wilsen and Brumund in a monograph. In 1872 the first photographs of Borobudur were taken by Isidore van Kinsbergen, a Dutch-Flemish engraver.

Sadly, Borobudur soon became the target of looters and souvenir hunters, many of whom had the support of the government. In 1896, the king of Thailand was permitted to carry off eight cartloads of Borobudur's sculptures. Today, the sculptures remain on exhibition in the Java Room of Thailand's National Museum in Bangkok. Other sculptures from Borobudur are located in the Indonesian National Museum in Jakarta, the British Museum in London, and the Tropenmuseum in Amsterdam.

It is estimated that 55,000 cubic meters (72,000 cubic yards) of stone were taken from nearby rivers and streams for the construction of Borobudur. It is thought that it was built without mortar and that its reliefs were carved after its stones were in place. They are also thought to have been carved starting at the top, with work proceeding to the ground.

As a low pyramid measuring 15m (49 feet) above the surrounding plain, Borobudur is often regarded more as a shrine or stupa than a temple, but it is generally agreed that it has always been an important place of pilgrimage. By climbing its various levels, and by circumambulating the monument clockwise, called *pradakshina*, the pilgrim was ascending into higher and higher levels of enlightenment.

Built atop a low bedrock hill, Borobudur was built in three basic levels. Aside from the hidden level or "foot," the first level was composed of five square, concentric terraces. Next were its three concentric, circular levels containing a total of seventy-two, bell-shaped, openwork stupas. At the top is a single massive stupa. As a model or *mandala* of the Buddhist universe, the various levels are thought to represent the various levels of human desire. Represented by the base is the *kamadahtu* (the world of desires). *Rupadhatu* (the world of forms) is represented by the monument's five square levels, and *arupadhatu* (the world of formlessness) is represented by its top three circular levels.

Borobudur possesses 2,672 individual reliefs, with 1,460 being narrative in nature and 1,212 being decorative. The total area of bas-reliefs on the monument is estimated to be 2,500 square meters. They are said to represent the largest collection of such Buddhist scenes in the world.

Borobudur's hidden lowest level, also called the "foot," contains 120 reliefs and has been identified as representing karmic law. Reliefs on the upper levels tell of the life of the Buddha and legends about his earlier lives. Other reliefs tell of his teaching of the Buddhist law and illustrate his search for enlightenment.

Borobudur has 504 representations of the Buddha, many of which are in the lotus, meditative, or cross-legged position and are located in niches on the five lower, square levels. Although appearing similar, there are subtle differences among them. Variations in the *mudras* or hand positions of the images can be seen in the images facing the different cardinal directions.

The hidden "foot" of Borobudur was discovered in 1885. While some of its panels contain only short inscriptions, 160 illustrate the lowest level of the world of desires, the *kamadahtu*. The hidden level of Borobudur remains very much a mystery, with some archaeologists claiming that it was buried in order to stabilize the vast monument and others believing that it was hidden for its being improperly designed. On the other hand, many of its panels are regarded as being among Borobudur's most expertly carved.

Archaeologists discovered traces of colored pigments, including black. green, red and blue, as well as gold leaf, when excavating Borobudur, so it may not have originally been the dark gray monument we see today. It may also have been covered in *vajralepa* plaster prior to being painted, as seen at such nearby temples as Candi Kalasan and Candi Sewu.

Borobudur has been identified as being part of a complex of three Buddhist monuments, all lying in a line leading to the main shrine of Borobudur. To the east stand two other smaller temples, Candi Mendut and Candi Pawaon. Together all three temples were to be seen as representing different levels in attaining enlightenment. While Candi Mendut contains an image of the Buddha flanked by Bodhisattvas, Candi Pawon no longer contains its image.

A comprehensive plan was drawn up for Borobudur in 1973, and a major restoration of the monument was undertaken from 1975 to 1982. As a result of the "Save Borobudur" campaign launched in 1968, the Indonesian government united with UNESCO in a massive conservation effort. Borobudur's five lower platforms were dismantled, and 1,460 relief panels were cleaned. A new drainage system was also added. Six hundred workmen were involved in the project at a cost of USD $6,901,243. It is estimated that more than a million stones were disassembled and then reassembled over an eight-year period.

On 21 January, 1985, Borobudur was attacked by terrorists and severely damaged by nine bombs. As a result, a blind Muslim imam, Husein Ali al-Habsyie, was sentenced to life imprisonment, and two of his followers were sentenced to twenty years. In 2014, security was tightened after a threat was made by what was said to be a branch of ISIS. Terrorists also threatened to destroy Borobudur and other sites in Indonesia which contained images.

Despite all preservation measures, Borobudur remains endangered, with earthquakes being one of its major threats. On 27 May, 2006, an earthquake caused severe damage in Central Java, but Borobudur was largely unaffected. In October and November of 2010, the eruption of nearby Mount Merapi caused a layer of volcanic ash up to 2.5 cm (1 inch) to cover the monument. Since the acidic ash could seriously affect Borobudur, it was closed for cleaning from November 5th to the

9th. On 14 February, 2014, Borobudur was again closed after being inundated with volcanic ash from the eruption of the Kelud volcano located 200 km from Yogyakarta in eastern Java.

Measures need to be taken at Borobudur to prevent tourist vandalism. There is also soil erosion, especially on the monument's southeastern side, and missing parts of the monument still need replacement. Numerous missing heads and relief panels were restored by Theodor van Erp between 1907 to 1911. He also restored the three-tiered parasols, the *chhatra*, atop Borobudur's main stupa at the monument's summit. Later he dismantled the stupa's top, claiming that not enough original stones remained to restore it properly, so today, the remains of the monument's original top resides in the nearby Karmawibhangga Museum.

Today, few guards are stationed at Borobudur, and visitors remain unsupervised. Despite warning signs, visitors often climb on top of the monument and proceed to vandalize it. There is also the custom, thought to bring good luck and often encouraged by local guides, of tourists reaching in and touching the images of the Buddha hidden inside the seventy-two stupas on the monument's upper levels.

There is also no limit on the number of visitors allowed on the site. Deterioration of the stone stairways is also a problem resulting from the large volume of visitors, so wooden stairs have been built over several stairways.

I felt privileged to have had two half-day visits at Borobudur, one on my own and another with a local guide, but I still felt I had seen only a very small portion of what Borobudur has to offer to those who visit it.

Adapted from:

http://whc.unesco.org/en/list/592
https://en.wikipedia.org/wiki/Borobudur
https://www.nationalgeographic.com/travel/world-heritage/borobudur-temple/

INDONESIA

Country name: Republic of Indonesia (Indonesian: Republik Indonesia)

Site name: Prambanan Temple Compounds

Location: Near the Opak River, Province of Central Java

UNESCO World Heritage Site: Inscribed 1991; no. 642

Tour Dates: 3-15 April 2005

INDONESIA'S LARGEST HINDU TEMPLE: PRAMBANAN

Constructed in the ninth to tenth centuries CE, Prambanan is Indonesia's largest Hindu temple complex and is one of the largest Hindu temples in all of Southeast Asia.

The first temple at Prambanan is thought to have been built by Rakai Pikatan of the Hindu Sanjaya dynasty of the Mataram kingdom in approximately 850 CE and then expanded by kings Lokapala and Balitung Maha Sambu. It was then expanded by other Mataram kings such as Daksa and Tulodong who built the smaller *perwara* temples around the main temple complex. The original name of Prambanan, also called Rara Jonggrng, was probably Shiva-grha, meaning "house of Shiva."

The Prambanan complex originally included two hundred and forty temples. Also known as Loro Jonggrang, Prambanan was built in three major sections: the outer zone measuring approximately three hundred meters per side, an inner zone containing hundreds of smaller temples, and the inner, holiest sector containing the site's eight major temples and eight smaller shrines.

The temple dedicated to Shiva is the tallest and largest in the Prambanan complex, measuring 47 m (154 feet) in height and 34 m in width. Its main gate on the eastern side is flanked by two guardian deities, Mahakala and Nandhisvara. The temple's central shrine has five chambers, four of which are located in the four cardinal directions. The fifth chamber, in the temple's center, contains a 3 m high statue of Shiva Mahadeva. Some archaeologists believe the image may be a personification of King Balitung, thought to be a reincarnation of Shiva. Three of the other smaller chambers contain images of Agastya; the elephant-headed deity, Ganesha; and Durga as the slayer of the bull demon.

The balustrades of the three main temples are decorated with scenes from the Ramayana and the Bhagavata Purana. The scenes are arranged to be read from left to right while circumambulating the temple clockwise in what is called *pradakshina*. Other walls of the temples' galleries are decorated with such images as devatas, apsaras, and Brahman sages.

To the north sits the temple dedicated to Vishnu, while to the south sits the temple dedicated to Brahma. Each temple faces east and measures 20m in width and 33m in height.

The three shrines in front of each of the larger temples are dedicated to the vehicles or *vahanas* of the three primary deities. In front of the temple dedicated to Shiva sits the shrine dedicated to the bull, Nandi. Nearby stand images of Chandra, god of the moon, and Surya, god of the sun. In front of the temple dedicated to Vishnu stands a temple dedicated to Garuda, while in front of the Brahma temple sits a shrine, probably dedicated to Hamsa or Angsta. Today, both shrines remain empty.

Sitting in the innermost zone of the complex are two *apit* or flanking temples, possibly dedicated to Sarasvati and Lakshmi, consorts or *shaktis* of the main temple deities.

The second, walled area around the inner zone contains the *pervara* temples. Measuring approximately 225m on each side, the area contains four rows of small temples containing 44, 52, 60, and 68 temples in various rows. Of the 224 temples, only two have been restored.

Four *partok* temples sit in the corners of the temple's inner area. Sitting outside the four gateways, located in the four cardinal directions, are four small *kelir* temples.

A common motif decorating the lower, exterior walls of Prambanan's temples is so characteristic of Prambanan that it

General view of the temples of Indonesia's
largest Hindu temple complex at Prambanan

has become known as a "Prambanan panel." Standing in small niches are *sihas* or lions flanked by scenes representing the *kalpataru* or *kalpavriksha* tree. The trees are often flanked, in turn, by *kinnaras*, animals in pairs such as monkeys, horses, elephants, and deer.

Prambanan was constructed to symbolize the Hindu cosmos and the sacred mountain of Meru. Much like Borobudur was built to symbolize the Buddhist universe, Prambanan was built to symbolize the three levels of the Hindu cosmos. At the lowest level was *bhurloka*, the region of humans and animals. On the *bhuvarloka* level were the lesser gods and such holy men as rishis and ascetics. The highest level, *svarloka* or *surgaloka*, was the realm of the gods.

Located in the vicinity of the main temple complex of Prambanan are the temples of Candi Sewu, Candi Lumbung, Candi Bubrah and Candi Asa. Together the four temples are one of the largest complexes of Buddhist temples in Indonesia, second only to Borobudur. Except for Candi Sewu, the temples are in a very ruined condition. Candi Bubrah, with "bubrah" meaning "ruined," exists primarily only as foundation stones. My local guide expressed amazement when I asked to tour the temples, saying that they were seldom visited and almost never visited by foreign visitors.

Prambanan was very seriously impacted by the earthquake of 27 March, 2006, resulting in closure of much of the site. Prambanan was opened again to the public later in the year, but the interiors of some of Prambanan's temples were still closed in 2009 due to concerns about their safety. With the eruption of Mount Kelud on 14 February, 2014, both Prambanan and Borobudur were closed to be cleared of volcanic ash. While the eruption of Mt. Merapi in 2010 left Borobudur covered in ash, Prambanan remained almost totally unaffected.

As with Borobudur, Prambanan began to receive international attention beginning in 1911 during the brief period of British rule in Indonesia. The site was discovered by chance by Colin Mackenzie, a surveyor employed by Sir Thomas Stamford Raffles. Although Raffles had commissioned a full investigation of the site, it remained largely neglected during subsequent Dutch East Indies rule. Some excavations took place in the 1880s, but they succeed primarily in encouraging looting of the site. The Dutch carried off parts of the temples as garden ornaments, and local residents looted the temples for building materials. Only in 1930 was restoration work begun, and by 1953 the restoration of the main temple of Shiva had been completed. Most of the smaller temples still exist only as foundation stones and will probably never be fully restored.

Prambanan was designated a UNESCO World Heritage Site in 1991 and as a National Cultural Property in 1998. It is also protected by the Management of Prambanan Temple Compounds and by a presidential decree of 1992. A marketplace was removed from the area in the 1990s, and today an archaeological park has been created, including Prambanan, Lumbung, Bubrah, and Sewu temples.

Today Prambanan is one of Indonesia's most popular tourist attractions. In 2008, over 856,029 local visitors and 114,951 foreign visitors were recorded as having visited Prambanan.

On my trip to Central Java, I was privileged to tour Prambanan with two different local guides. It was also possible to attend an evening performance of a traditional Javanese ballet based on the story of the Ramayana and enacted by lavishly costumed dancers at the open-air theater located to the west of the temple complex and across the Opak River. On the evening of the ballet performance, it was possible to dine at a nearby restaurant with the magnificent, lighted temples of Prambanan visible in the distance.

Adapted from:

http://whc.unesco.org/en/list/642
http://whc.unesco.org/en/news/1212
http://www.worldheritagesite.org/list/Prambanan
https://en.wikipedia.org/wiki/Prambanan

IRAN

Country name: Islamic Republic of Iran (formerly known as Persia)

Site name: Gonbad-e Qabus

Location: City of Gonbad-e Kavus, province of Golestan, northeastern Iran

UNESCO World Heritage Site: Inscribed 2012; no. 1398

Date of Visit: 16 May 2014

IRAN'S ENIGMATIC TOWER: THE GONBAD-E QABUS

The Gonbad-e Qabus had been on my wish list of travel destinations for over four decades. It was in 1966, while an art history graduate student at the State University of Iowa, Iowa City, that I had selected the Iranian tower as the subject of my master's degree thesis. As a naive, young student, little did I realize what a formidable task I had taken on when writing about the tower and in evaluating the legend which had grown up around it. While much is known about the tower as to who commissioned it and when it was built, I questioned the reason for its construction and why it appeared to have no historical precedents.

I felt elated when I found that it would be possible to extend my tour of Iran in 2014 to visit the tower located in the northeastern section of Iran and close to the border with Turkmenistan.

Starting from Tehran, it had taken nine hours to reach the modern city of Gonbad-e Kavus, in Golestan Province in northern Iran east of the Caspian Sea. While riding through the typical Iranian city, we suddenly stopped. Only then, looking up out of the car window, did I realize we had arrived at our destination.

The Gonbad-e Qabus was once located 3 km north of the ancient Zayid capital of Gurgan, also known as Jorjan, and possibly on a trade route from Merv to Gurgan which was

General view of the Gonbad-e Qabus, northeastern Iran
Note the circle that visitors can stand in to hear an echo.

destroyed by Mongol invasions in the fourteenth and fifteenth centuries. The tower is a monument which would have been a landmark visible from all directions.

Standing alone on a low artificial hill in the city's central park, the Gonbad-e Qabus, meaning "Dome of Qabus," is a massive tower, reputed to be the world's tallest structure built exclusively of unglazed, fired brick. Rising 72m (236 feet), including its platform measuring 15m in height, the tower is a cylinder with a diameter tapering from 17 to 15.5m and 3m thick walls. Ten equally-spaced, right-angled flanges around the central cylinder create a ground plan in the form of a decagon. The only openings in the tower are an entrance at the tower's base, topped by a window grille, and a small window facing east, penetrating the tower's conical, brick roof. Otherwise, the tower is a solid mass of unglazed brick.

The tower's only decorations are two bands of inscriptions, located between the tower's flanges at two separate levels. The lower inscription is located 8m (26 feet) above ground level, while the upper inscription sits directly under the corbels supporting the conical roof. It has been noted that the brickwork of the inscriptions does not match the quality of the remainder of the tower and that a coating of plaster slip, which has since disappeared, may have once covered the Kufic characters.

The inscription, which is duplicated on both levels, has been translated as follows:

"In the name of Allah the Beneficent, the Merciful, this tall castle for the prince Shams ul-Ma'ali Amir ibn-e Amir Qabus ibn-e Woshmgir ordered to build during his life, in the year 397 lunar Hajira and the year 375 solar."

Giving both the lunar and the solar dates is quite unusual, since using only the lunar date was the norm. It has therefore been surmised that Qabus was extraordinarily concerned with its being known exactly who built the tower and when, as also evidenced by the duplication of the inscriptions on the tower at two levels.

The bricks of the roof have been specially formed to create one, uninterrupted smooth surface. The mortar on the tower has been identified as being of a type called *saruj*, which is composed of lime, sand, and ashes.

The Arabic inscriptions in the Kufic style are made of fired brick and were made as part of the fabric of the tower. They state that the tower was commissioned by the Ziyarid amir, Shams al-Ma'ali Qabus ibn Wushmgir (reigned 978-1012 CE) who has been noted as being a "literati" and as being a sophisticated and learned ruler. Since the dates in the inscription correspond to September, 1006, to March, 1007 CE, the Gonbad-e Qabus is regarded as Iran's earliest building bearing its own date of construction. It is recorded that Qabus was assassinated at the fortress of Jinaskh in 1013 CE (403 AH), so he actually had little time to appreciate the completion of his tower.

The inscriptions mention the tower as being a "kasr," also often transliterated as "qasr." The term is usually translated as "castle," "palace," or "dwelling." As a result, many scholars have interpreted the inscription as meaning that the tower was intended as the final resting place or "castle" of Qabus.

No evidence of any burial has been found, however, during any of the investigations undertaken inside or outside the tower. Excavations by Russians in 1899 to a depth of 10.75m (35 feet) revealed that the tower's walls extend below the excavated depth. They also uncovered no signs of a burial site.

On the day that I visited the tower, an elderly man at the site stated that he remembered a deep pit in the center of the floor inside the tower which has since been covered over with cobblestones. He also stated that there is a local belief that the burial of Qabus may have been at one side of the tower's interior.

Even with the lights installed inside the tower, it would be a dark and inhospitable space if it were to be lived in. The interior has been built with solid brickwork and with no stairway or any form of access to its top, making it unsuitable as a lookout tower or an astronomical observatory. In addition, since the tower sits off-center on its hill, it appears unlikely that it could have functioned as a form of sundial.

No significant amount of light enters the tower through the roof's very small window, and one can see only a dark void when looking up inside the tower. It is thought that, rather than having symbolic significance, the roof window may have been created merely for the ventilation of the tower's interior.

The legend associated with the Gonbad-e Qabus has been ascribed to an Iranian historian named al-Jannabi. A reference to him was eventually found stating that he had visited both Mecca and Medina in 1556 CE. His full name was found to be Abu Mahammed Mustapha Ebnol Saiyed Hasan al Jannabi. He is said to have been born at Jannaba, a city in ancient Persia not far from Shiraz. He is credited in descriptions of the Gonbad-e Qabus with initiating the legend that Qabus was encased inside a glass coffin and hung by chains at the top of the tower's interior. It seems especially noteworthy that the legend materializes some five and a half centuries after the date of the tower. Similar descriptions of such burials in glass coffins have been associated with both Alexander the Great and the Biblical prophet Daniel. No concrete evidence has been found to substantiate any of the legends about the burial of Qabus, Alexander the Great, or the prophet Daniel.

No evidence has also been found of any remains at the top of the Gonbad-e Qabus's interior other than solid brickwork. It has also not been determined if the tower has any form of double dome or if there is a void between its inner ceiling and outer conical roof. It has been thought that the tower's interior may merely follow the outlines of its brick exterior.

Without any evidence of the tower having been used as a place to commemorate a burial, the best explanation for the construction of the tower appears to be that suggested by the authorities at the Gonbad-e Qabus World Heritage base in the nearby town of Gorgan in Golestan Province. They believe that Qabus built the tower primarily to glorify and immortalize himself. It could also have been built to establish his control of the region, as well as a symbol of Islam having control of a region where Zoroastrianism had previously been the major religion. If so, it has been over a millennium that the tower has been a prominent landmark on a major overland trade route. It is largely because of the tower that one hears about Qabus and the Zayarid dynasty.

One of the early Westerners to visit the tower was the British travel writer, Robert Byron, who claimed that after seeing a photograph of the Gonbad-e Qabus, he became motivated to visit Iran. In his book, *The Road to Oxiana*, he stated that "the Gumbad-i-Kaus ranks with the great buildings of the world."

If Qabus built the tower as part of his legacy and to survive the vicissitudes of time, he did very well. Especially since there appears to be no historical precedent for such a tower, it is thought to be a highly original structure within the development of ancient Persian architecture. There have been numerous suggestions that the tower displays influences from the local domestic tents or yurts in that they also are circular structures with conical roofs. It can be argued, however, that the differences between the tall, monumental Gonbad-e Qabus and the low, modest, Central Asian yurts are very significant.

On the other hand, the Gonbad-e Qabus is seen as being the prototype for many of the later tomb towers and commemorative monuments throughout Iran and Central Asia.

The Gonbad-e Qabus became a protected site in 1930 with the enactment of Iran's National Heritage Protection Act. In 1975 it was cited by the Iran Cultural Heritage, Handcrafts & Tourism Organization (ICHHTO, no. 1087). In 2012, it was designated a UNESCO World Cultural Heritage Site. The Plan for Gonbad-e Qabus Town was drafted in 1989, and a more detailed plan was created in 2009.

When I visited the site in 2014, a ramp had been cut into the artificial hill to give visitors access to the tower, and a circle had been built in front of the tower. It is said that an echo can be heard bouncing off the tower when one stands in the circle. The hill appears somewhat unkempt, but irrigation of the hill had been stopped, since it was softening the soil and affecting the stability of the tower. I was also told that a drainage ditch around the base of the tower needed repairs and updating.

After standing on its artificial hill for over 1,000 years, the tower has finally been recognized as a major masterpiece of world architecture. The influence of the Gonbad-e Qabus has also extended into the 20th century, as can be seen in the open-work tower built in 1954 atop the mausoleum of the Persian philosopher Avicenna, located in Hamadan, Iran.

Adapted from:

https://en.wikipedia.org/wiki/Gonbad-e_Qabus_(tower)

http://whc.unesco.org/en/list/1398

https://www.tripadvisor.com/ShowUserReviews-g672704-d6993882-r360758093-Gonbad_e_Qabus_Tower-Gonbad_e_Kavus_Golestan_Province.html#

http://wikimapia.org/8550728/Gonbad-e-Kavus-Tower

http://islamic-arts.org/wp-content/images/0276a9725761_FA8D/Gunbad-i-Kabus-in-Jurjan.png

http://hotelmagazine.ir/news_clipping_1706_3214.jpg

ISRAEL

Country name: State of Israel
Site name: Tel Aviv's White City
UNESCO World Heritage Site: Inscribed 2003; no. 1096
Date of Visit: November 2008

TEL AVIV'S WHITE CITY

If you think Israel is important only for its ancient sites, think again. The architecture of one of Israel's nine UNESCO World Heritage Sites dates from the early 20th century.

Having just arrived at the Ben Gurion airport outside Tel Aviv, I found that I had an afternoon at leisure before rushing off to see such ancient sites as Capernum, Qumran and Masada. Fortunately, I had an Eyewitness Travel guide to *Jerusalem and the Holy Land* that mentioned Tel Aviv's so-called White City, designated a UNESCO World Heritage site in 2003.

Founded in 1909, Tel Aviv was built north of the walled port city of Jaffa under the British Mandate of Palestine from 1917 to 1948. Since then, it has become a vibrant urban metropolis and the major economic center of Israel. Commissioned by Tel Aviv's first mayor, Meir Dizengoff, the architect and city planner Sir Patrick Geddes was given the job of laying out the new city, which essentially provided him with a blank slate for trying out new ideas in architecture and urban design.

Designed and built by immigrant architects from Europe from the early 1930s until the 1950s, Tel Aviv is reputed to have over 4,000 buildings in the new Bauhaus or International Style. The Bauhaus, for which the style was initially named, was an architecture, art, and design school in Germany from 1919 to 1933, led by such notable founders of the modernist movement as the architect Walter Gropius.

The architectural style's emphasis on simplicity and functionality was considered appropriate for the socialist ideals of the Zionist movement, giving rise to the founding of the new city of Tel Aviv. Simple, functional design was seen as allowing quick and inexpensive construction. Much of the new architecture was built with reinforced concrete, and characteristics of the new style included plain, unadorned, and asymmetrical façades of white stucco with ribbons of horizontal, strip windows. Vertical stacks of windows, often called "thermometer" windows, lighted the stairwells.

Transferring an architectural style from Europe to the desert and Mediterranean climate required a number of adaptations. White was found to reflect light and heat. Large glass areas were replaced by smaller, recessed windows and were shaded by overhangs. Pitched roofs were replaced with flat ones, and narrow balconies allowed residents to sit outside and catch breezes from the Mediterranean. Buildings raised on pillars, or *pilotis*, allowed winds to blow under buildings and created ground-level play areas for children.

The three major zones of Bauhaus style buildings are the central White City area, the Lev Hair and Rothschild Boulevard area and the Bialik area. The area is also defined by Allenby Street to the south, Begin Road and Ibn Gvirol Street to the east, the Yarkon River to the north, and the Mediterranean to the west.

Wandering from my high-rise hotel located on the waterfront of the Mediterranean, I found the largest concentration of Bauhaus buildings on Tel Aviv's Rothschild Boulevard and the neighboring Ha'am Street. Rothschild Boulevard was found to have central garden areas, kiosks, and benches, while Sheinkin Street was more commercial with boutiques and cafés.

I never did find the Bauhaus Center at 99 Dizengoff Street where I would have found books, souvenirs, and information relating to Bauhaus architecture. I learned later that the center runs weekly guided tours. Plans for a White City Heritage Center to promote architectural preservation is planned to open in the Max-Leibling House on Idelson Street in 2018.

Fortunately, I found a book in the bookstore of the Yad Vashem **Museum** while in Jerusalem: *Bauhaus Tel Aviv; an*

An International style apartment building with projecting balconies in Tel Aviv's White City, Israel

architectural guide, by Nahoum Cohen with photographs by Jachin Hirsch (London: Batsford, 2003. 276p).

It is recommended that you wear comfortable shoes for a lot of walking and to be prepared to see many buildings in a sad state of repair, although there are efforts currently underway to renovate many of the deteriorating buildings. You'll not see such a large concentration of Bauhaus/International Style architecture anywhere else in the world.

Adapted from:

https://en.wikipedia.org/wiki/White_City_(Tel_Aviv)

http://whc.unesco.org/en/list/1096

www.bauhaus-center.com/

https://www.touristisrael.com/the-white-city-tel-aviv/344/

http://www.visit-tel-aviv.com/white-city-tel-avivyafo#.WW54FkvpUnE

https://www.amazon.com/s/ref=nb_sb_noss?url=search-alias%3Dstripbooks&field-keywords=Cohen%2C+Nahoum.+Bauhaus+Tel+Aviv

ITALY

Country name: Italian Republic (Italian: Repubblica italiana)
Sicily (Italian: Sicilia; officially: Regione Siciliana)
Site name: Cathedral-Basilica of Cejalú (Italian: Duomo di
Cefalú)
Location: Cefalú, Province of Palermo; located on the
Tyrrhenian Sea, northern coast of Sicily, approximately
70 km east of Palermo and 185 km west of Messina
UNESCO World Heritage Site: Inscribed 2015; no. 1487
Date of Visit: 12 April 2008

CEFALÚ'S CATHEDRAL: A MASTERWORK OF NORMAN ART AND ARCHITECTURE

In 2008, UNESCO inscribed, as a single heritage site, a group of Norman monuments under the title of "Arab-Norman Palermo and the Cathedrals of Cefalú and Monreale." Built during the Norman period in Sicily (1130-1194 CE), they were cited as prime examples of a socio-cultural syncretism combining Islamic, Byzantine, and Western European cultural and stylistic elements. In addition to the citation of UNESCO, the sites have been given the protection of the 2004 Italian code of the Cultural and Landscape Heritage. Today, the sites reflect relatively few effects of neglect or of being compromised by later developments.

Construction of Cefalú's Cathedral began in 1131 CE shortly after the Normans had conquered Sicily in 1091 CE. It is said to have been commissioned by Roger II, king of Sicily, as a result of making a vow when landing on the city's beach after surviving a storm. Today the fortress-like building dominates the city's skyline and survives as a powerful symbol of the presence of the Normans in northern Sicily at the time of its construction.

The cathedral's mosaic decoration was begun in 1145. That same year, the sarcophagi Roger II had made for himself and his wife were placed in the cathedral. In 1215, the sarcophagi were transferred to Palermo by Frederick II of Hohenstaufen. After a period of decline, work on the cathedral resumed in 1215. Its façade was completed in 1240, and it was finally consecrated by the Bishop of Albano, Rodolphe de Chevriéres, in 1267. The portico between the two towers on the cathedral's façade by Ambrogio da Como was added in 1472.

According to legend, the large terrace located in front of the cathedral was originally a cemetery, and it is said that earth from Jerusalem brought to the site caused the mummification of all those who had been buried there.

The immense cathedral, as it stands today, has a Latin cross ground plan and has two huge Norman-style towers on its façade, one being square in plan and the other, octagonal. Inside, the cathedral has a central nave flanked by two side aisles, separated by arcades supported by antique columns. Twelve of the nave's columns are thought to date from the 2nd century CE, while the two large capitals of the triumphal arch probably date from the middle of the twelfth century.

Parts of the cathedral have been constructed lower than the transepts. Also notable is the fact that, although the construction is essentially Romanesque in style, the cathedral contains a number of pointed arches, appearing to predict the arrival of the Gothic style. An example is the façade's portico which has a central, rounded arch and two flanking, pointed arches.

The two side apses of the cathedral, decorated on the exterior with crossed arches and blind arcades, are lower than the central apse, which is thought to have originally contained windows which were later closed to allow for interior mosaic decoration. Notable on the exterior are the corbels supporting the blind arcades, with their sculptures of masks, animal heads, and contorted, human figures.

While mosaics may have been planned for the entire cathedral, they are today located only in the apse and on parts

Interior view of the Byzantine style mosaic
decoration of the Duomo (Cathedral) of Cefalú, Sicily

of side walls. As a result of Roger II bringing experts in mosaic work from Constantinople, Cefalú contains some of the finest examples of Byzantine art superimposed on what is essentially a Northern European, Romanesque style building.

Dating from around 1170, mosaics in the apse depict the Virgin flanked by angels and figures of apostles, prophets, and various saints. On the cross vaults of the ceiling are representations of cherubim and seraphim. On the wall of the presbytery at the right are depictions of royalty located near the royal throne. To the left, near the bishop's chair, are representations of priests.

It is the mosaic located in the semi-dome of the cathedral's central apse that is usually regarded as a masterpiece of the Byzantine mosaicists' art. The immense image of Christ Pantokrator dominates the entire apsidal end of the cathedral. Christ is portrayed with one hand in benediction and the other holding a copy of the Gospel of Saint John. In the Gospel He holds, verse 12 of the 8th chapter of the gospel is cited in both Greek and Latin: "I am the light of the world. Who follows Me will not wander in the darkness but will have the light of life."

In the image of Christ Pantokrator, the blue of Christ's robe contrasts with the glitter of the gold background, giving the entire composition a vibrancy and luminosity. The mosaic is often cited as one of Italy's finest works and as being on an aesthetic level comparable to the finest Byzantine work in Constantinople.

Other notable features of the cathedral are a twelfth century baptismal font, a large, two-manual organ, and various funerary monuments. Especially controversial are the seventy-two, very modern, abstract compositions in the stained glass windows by Michele Canzoneri, a Palermo artist, which were installed in the cathedral starting in 1985.

I found the cloister located adjacent to the cathedral of special interest. Surrounding a central area was an arcade composed of pointed arches resting on slender, double columns. It was the lively figures on the capitals of the double columns that captured most of my attention. What I found to be especially fascinating were the Byzantine-style capitals portraying animals such as lions and eagles, with many of the capitals featuring mirror images.

Unfortunately, only a very short stop was made at Cefalú before returning to Palermo. Time did not allow a visit to the small museum just down the street from the Cathedral, but I found it interesting to note that Cefalú's Museo Mandralisca owned an outstanding painting by Antonello da Messina, "Portrait of an Unknown Man," displayed on a poster on the museum's façade.

Adapted from:

http://whc.unesco.org/en/list/1487
https://en.wikipedia.org/wiki/Cefalù_Cathedral

ITALY

Country name: Italian Republic (Italian: Repubblica italiana)
Sicily (Italian: Sicilia; officially: Regione Siciliana)

Site name: Cathedral (Italian: Duomo)

Location: Monreale (Sicilian: Murriali); Province of Palermo;
15 km (9 miles) inland from Palermo

UNESCO World Heritage Site: Inscribed as "Arab-Norman
Palermo and the Cathedral Churches of Cefalú and
Monreale," 2015; no. 1487

Date of Visit: 7 April 2008

BYZANTINE MOSAIC MASTERPIECES: SICILY'S CATHEDRAL AT MONREALE

The Cathedral of Monreale is regarded as Sicily's most important Norman monument. It is important not only for being one of Sicily's most beautiful buildings, but also for its outstanding fusion of architectural styles.

Even more remarkable and impressive is what one finds inside Monreale's cathedral. Superb mosaics cover almost every wall surface of the cathedral's interior. Covering 6,340 square meters, the mosaics make up the largest cycle of Byzantine-style mosaics in all of Italy.

In 1174, King William II ordered the building of the church dedicated to the nativity of the Virgin, a commission which is memorialized in one of the cathedral's mosaics in which William presents a model of the church to the Virgin. Upon the completion of the church in 1182 CE, its status was elevated to that of a metropolitan cathedral by Pope Lucius III.

Measuring 102m (334 feet) in length and 40m (131 feet) in width, the cathedral is regarded as one of the primary national monuments of Italy. Its ground plan has been described as a fusion of Western and Eastern elements. While the nave is very much like a typical Western basilica, the eastern end, with its large choir and its triple apses, is cited as being more typical of Eastern examples.

The cathedral's wide nave has narrow side aisles defined by monolithic granite columns topped primarily with Corinthian capitals. The high clerestory's windows provide light and show off the mosaics to advantage. The eastern end has been built higher than the nave and has a central section and two side aisles, each ending with an apse. A painted, openwork, wooden roof covers most of the building's interior.

On the cathedral's west end are two towers with a central entryway between them. What was once a large atrium has been replaced by a Renaissance-era portico dating from the sixteenth century.

The cathedral's most impressive feature is the mosaic decoration on its interior. Almost all the interior wall surfaces, including soffits and the jambs of arches, have been decorated with glittering mosaics. Arranged in tiers, the mosaics are divided by both horizontal and vertical bands. The choir is especially notable for its five tiers of various scenes and figures, one sitting atop another.

At the eastern end, the half dome of the central apse contains a monumental image of Christ Pantocrator. Below Christ is a representation of the seated Virgin and Christ. In the side apses are depictions of Saints Peter and Paul. Inscriptions in Latin and Greek label the various figures and scenes. In the nave are scenes from the Bible's Old Testament beginning with the book of Genesis. In the choir are scenes from the New Testament depicting Christ's miracles and His Passion, as well as representations of evangelists, apostles, and various saints. Not only are the mosaics very Byzantine in style, but their high quality is evidence that they were the work of skilled, local artisans as well as master craftsmen from Constantinople. A source for many of the cathedral's scenes depicted in the mosaics has been suggested as being the *Menologion* of Basil II, compiled by the emperor in the 10th century.

Worthy of mention are the tombs of William I of Sicily and William II in the cathedral's choir. On the north side are the tombs of Margaret of Navarre and of her two sons and an urn

Cloister of the Duomo (Cathedral) of Monreale, Sicily,
with its double columns decorated with mosaics

said to contain remains of Saint Louis of France. As a result of the fire of 1811, much of the choir has been reconstructed.

The cathedral's magnificent organ with six manuals and 120 stops dates from 1967. Two Baroque style chapels, usually closed off from the remainder of the cathedral, date from the seventeenth and eighteenth centuries.

The cloister, adjoining the cathedral and part of the cathedral abbey, should also not be missed while at Monreale. It is regarded as one of Italy's finest cloisters for its size, beauty, and attention to detail. Completed in 1200 CE, the cloister possesses 108 pairs of white marble columns topped by capitals carved with foliage and allegorical and Biblical subjects. A feature unique to the cloister is the ornamentation of every other column with patterns of mosaics. Decorating the columns are bands of glass tesserae in patterns of gold and other colors. Located at one corner of the cloister is a small pillared pavilion containing a marble fountain, thought to have been intended as a *lavatorium* for the abbey's monks.

The cathedral is protected under the 2004 Italian Code of the Cultural and Landscape Heritage. It has also been designated a national monument, in addition to its inscription as a UNESCO World Heritage Site.

The name, Monreale, is a contraction of "monte-reale," meaning "royal mountain." The city is situated on a promontory, Monte Caputo, which overlooks Sicily's capital of Palermo. The hilltop location of the cathedral provides spectacular panoramic views of Palermo and the Conca d'Oro, the crescent shaped harbor of the Mediterranean upon which Palermo is located.

On my first trip to Sicily in the 1980s, our local guide recommended that an English-speaking, Spanish gentleman on the tour and I should view the harbor from the cathedral's rooftop walkways. After climbing up a stone, spiral stairway in one of the towers on the cathedral's façade, we finally emerged at the walkways atop the roof covering the cathedral's nave.

Knowing of the many conquests of Palermo by numerous invading armies, the elderly gentleman remarked, as he viewed the impressive, panoramic scene, "Palermo is indeed like a beautiful woman. Everyone has wanted to possess her."

Adapted from:

https://en.wikipedia.org/wiki/Monreale

http://whc.unesco.org/en/list/1487

http://www.wondersofsicily.com/palermo-monreale-cathedral.htm

http://www.planetware.com/monreale/monreale-cathedral-i-si-monct.htm

JAPAN

Country name: State of Japan (Japanese: Nippon or Nihon)

Site name: Horyuji;

Location: 7.5 miles outside of Nara

UNESCO World Heritage Site: Inscribed 1993; no. 660

Date of Visit: 21 July 2005

WORLD'S OLDEST WOODEN STRUCTURES: HORYUJI

There were three sites in Japan that were not on the itinerary of my tour in 2005 that I wanted very much to visit. One was the monumental bronze image of the seated Buddha at Kamakura. Since then I was privileged to see the image of the Unification Buddha in South Korea in 2015, which is the larger of the two iames. I had also wanted to see one of Japan's holiest Shinto shrines, the Ise Grand Shrine. But access to it is strictly limited, and it is largely obscured by the four-foot wall that surrounds it.

The third site I wanted to see was the Buddhist temple complex of Horyuji, located 12 km outside of central Nara. Since I had an extra day at leisure in Japan, I decided to attempt to see Horyuji on my own. Little did I realize what an adventure it would become.

Earlier I had managed to find my way to the National Museum in Tokyo, but although what I saw there was most worthwhile, I totally missed seeing the 300 objects donated to the imperial household by Horyuji in 1878 that are displayed in a separate building at the museum.

Since I was staying in a hotel in Kyoto, I found that I first had to take a train to Nara. Then I had to change to another train on the *Yamatoji* Line to the railway station at Horyuji. Getting off at the station, I found that there was no Buddhist temple in sight. Fortunately, a helpful Japanese fellow who understood my confusion motioned me to follow him. He

View of the Sai-in area and its
pagoda at Horyuji, Japan

pointed me in the right direction past a group of small shops, and I ultimately came upon a long, broad, tree-lined sidewalk.

In the distance I saw the Great South Gate, rebuilt in 1438, of the western section of Horyuji, the *Sai-in*. I had finally arrived at the site of the world's oldest wooden buildings and the area containing Japan's earliest Buddhist monuments. I had also arrived at Japan's first, inscribed UNESCO World Heritage Site. As early as 1993, Horyuji, along with Hokki-ji, had been declared a UNESCO site.

Founded by Crown Prince Shotoku in the seventh century CE, the temple was built in honor of the prince's father and dedicated to Yakushi Nyorai, the Buddha of healing. The name, Horyuji, is said to mean "Temple of the Flourishing Law" while another name, Horyu Gakumonji means "Learning Temple of the Flourishing Law." At the time of the temple's construction in 607 CE, the temple complex was called by yet another name, Ikaruga-dera.

Just as I was ready to leave the site, I happened to notice a building I'd not visited. It was the Gallery of Temple Treasures built in 1998 to display part of the ancient temple's vast collection of works of art. Needless to say, I was in awe of the excellence of the art on exhibit in the building's galleries.

Only later did I find that Horyuji had two main areas and that I'd only found it possible to visit one of them. Most of my time spent at Horyuji was devoted to the western or *Sai-in* area. The eastern section, the *To-in*, with its octagonal Hall of Dreams or *Yumedono* Hall, located 122m to the east was the area I totally missed. I also failed to realize that the full extent of the site contains quarters for monks, libraries, and lecture and dining halls. I also later discovered that the entire area designated a UNESCO site located in the Nara prefecture covers forty-eight ancient wooden buildings located at the two sites of the Horyuji and Hokki-ji temples. The temple of Horyuji covers 14.6 hectares while the smaller temple of Hokki-ji covers .7 hectares.

Not only are many of the structures at Horyuji the world's oldest wooden buildings. They are also considered masterpieces

179

of wood construction. Using a post-and-lintel system, intricate series of brackets transfer the weight of the heavy, tiled roofs to the huge supporting columns. The buildings at Horyuji are also notable for the entasis of their columns and for the cloud-like forms of the brackets supporting the roofs.

The western section of Horyuji contains the central gate or *Chumon*, the main hall or *Kondo*, and the pagoda of five stories. All have been dated to the Asuka period (538-710 CE). Although there is controversy over what exactly was destroyed in a fire of 670 CE, most of the buildings have survived intact. They have undergone numerous renovations over the many centuries, with repairs being made in the twelfth century CE and then again in 1374 and 1603 CE.

Entering the western area's main gate, I first encountered two of Japan's oldest *Kongo Rikishi*, a pair of huge, fearsome figures guarding the gate. The most prominent structure once inside the western precinct is the five-story pagoda, standing at 32.45m (122 feet) in height and measuring 20 by 20m in width. It is the pagoda that has been dated as one of the world's oldest wooden buildings. Dendrochronological research on its central pillar points to a date of 594 CE. At the base of the pillar extending three meters below ground level, a fragment of a bone of the Buddha is reputed to be enshrined. The pagoda contains four scenes depicting the life of the Buddha pointing out in the four cardinal directions.

Next to the pagoda stands the *Kondo*, also regarded as one of the world's oldest wooden buildings. The great hall measures 18.5m by 15.2m and has been built in two stories. In the later Nara period, the first story was provided with a double roof supported by added columns. Although damaged in a fire of 1949, fifteen to twenty percent of the original building is believed to have survived.

Also located in the western precinct is the great lecture hall or *Daikodo*, where images dating from the Heian Period (794-1185 CE) are exhibited.

Among the very important, early Buddhist images at Horyuji is the so-called Shaka Triad, dated to 623 CE in which Sakyamuni is flanked by images of Bhaisajyaguru and Amitabha. There is also the Yakushi Nyorai, dated from before the fire of 670 CE. The notable Yumedono Kannon measuring over six feet in height and made of gilded wood, is thought to have been intended as a representation of Prince Shotoku, the temple's founder.

I found that only a half day at Horyuji was inadequate. A full day at the site would have allowed much more time to appreciate its many ancient buildings and hundreds of temple treasures.

I was especially surprised that I found myself to be the only Westerner at the site on the day of my visit and that there was only one tour bus in the temple's parking area. It appeared that the visitors to the site that day were only Japanese or other Asians. Such a great national treasure as Horyuji seemed sadly neglected by many foreign travelers visiting Japan.

Adapted from:

https://en.wikipedia.org/wiki/Hōryū-ji

http://whc.unesco.org/en/list/660

http://www.horyuji.or.jp/horyuji_e.htm

http://www.japanvisitor.com/japan-temples-shrines/horyuji-temple

http://www.ancient.eu/Horyuji/

JORDAN

Country name: Jordan (The Hashemite Kingdom of Jordan)

Site name: Qasr Amra (also spelled Qusayr Amra and Quseir Amra)

Location: Located 85 km (53 miles) east of Amman and 21 km (13 miles) southwest of Al-Azraq on Highway 40

UNESCO Site Designation: Inscribed 1985; no. 327

Date of Visit: 16 April 2006

AN EARLY ISLAMIC PLEASURE PALACE: QASR AMRA

I knew of Qasr Amra's importance as a major, early Islamic site and wanted very much to visit it, along with much better-known sites in Jordan as Petra and Jerash. On a trip outside of Amman on one free afternoon, I found it located out in the midst of what has to be one of the most forlorn and desolate sites I've ever visited. For mile after mile in every direction, all I could see was a totally flat, arid, desert landscape.

I had found it possible to hire a local guide to take me on a half-day desert castle loop trip east of the city and close to the border with Saudi Arabia. The three castles visited on the trip were Qasr Amra, Qasr al-Kharana, and Qasr al-Azraq. Of the three castles visited, Qasr Amra, one of Jordan's five UNESCO sites, was the one I wanted the most to see.

Qasr Amra is located some 85 km (53 miles) east of Jordan's capital of Amman on Highway 40 and about 21 km (13 miles) southwest of Al Azraq. It is located next to Wadi Butum, a seasonal water source. With an area measuring 25 hectares (62 acres), the site includes what remains of a much larger complex which was an early-eighth-century garrison, fortress, and residence of the Umayyad caliphs. The site also includes a well, water tank, a water-lifting mechanism, remains of drainage pipes, and a cesspool.

Qasr Amra is thought to have been built between 723 and 743 CE. For many years it was the caliph Walid I who was regarded as the builder and primary user of the pleasure palace. It is now believed that one of two princes, who later became caliphs, Walid II or Yazid III, was more likely to have built Qasr Amra.

What still exists of the original Umayyad palace is a complex of low buildings of limestone and basalt. A northern section, standing two stories high, contains a triple-vaulted ceiling, while a western section is composed of a series of small domes.

It is Qasr Amra's frescoes that are its most notable features. Starting with the main entry vault are scenes of hunting, drinking of wine, fruits, and nude women, with some of the representations of the animals suggesting Persian influences. Also depicted is the construction of a building and an enthroned king. A section of the frescoes, now in Berlin's Pergamon Museum, depicts a boat along with an abundance of birds and fish.

Among the more interesting frescoes are those known as the "six kings." Four have been identified as Byzantine emperors, while others have been recognized as being representations of the Visigothic king, Roderic, the Ethiopian, Negus, and a Sassanian shah. The Greek inscription, "NHKN," meaning "victory," is thought to imply the Umayyad caliphs' domination over their enemies. Also, the kings' gestures of supplication are seen as being directed at the caliph who would have been seated in the hall.

One of the most interesting, extant sections of the desert palace is the hammam or bathhouse. In typically Roman fashion, it includes an apodyterium (changing room), a tepidarium (warm bath), and caldarium (hot bath).

The apodyterium contains scenes including animals playing music and what appears to be an angel looking down at two shrouded lovers. On the ceiling are blackened faces thought to represent the stages of life. Some believe that the central figure may be a representation of Jesus Christ.

The warm bath or tepidarium contains depictions of plants and animals interspersed with nude women. The frescoes,

Exterior view of the Umayyad pleasure palace
of Qasr Amra in eastern Jordan

depicting scenes of hunting, lovers, and gardens with palm trees, are thought to represent what contemporary physicians regarded as the three vital principles of the human body, the natural, the spiritual, and the animal.

The frescos of the caldarium, or hot bath, are regarded as among Qasr Amra's most important. Represented on its hemispherical half-dome is what is believed to be the very first such representation of the heavens on other than a flat surface. Identifiable are thirty-five different constellations, arranged from the north celestial pole rather than from the North Pole. The angle of the zodiac appears to be represented remarkably well, while the counterclockwise arrangement of the various stars suggests that the scene was probably copied from a flat representation.

Qasr Amra was discovered in 1898 by the Czech explorer Alois Musil, but it was the drawings of Alphons Leopold Mielich, an Austrian artist, made for Musil's book, that made the site famous.

Today, in addition to its UNESCO designation in 1998, the site is managed from an office at Zara by Jordan's Ministry of Tourism and Antiquities. The site is said to now be fenced and secured by four permanent guards, although I did not see any such security being given to the site at the time of my visit in 2006. It is also said that there is now a visitors' center where a fee is collected to visit the site.

Qasr Amra continues to be threatened by sandstorms and by seasonal flooding. As protection against flooding, a diversion dike and a modern reservoir have been built. Threats to preservation continue to be created by seasonal increases in humidity and the increasing numbers of tourists. Walls continue to be threatened by plaster becoming detached from them. On the other hand, accumulations of graffiti, dirt, and the deposits of insects and birds were removed during the restoration projects of the 1970s and 1990s.

Although much of Qasr Amra still remains in poor condition, conservation work continues as supported by the World Monument Fund, the Instituto Superiore per la Conservazione ed il Restauro, and Jordan's Department of Antiquities.

Strongly influenced by earlier classical and Byzantine precedents, Qasr Amra reflects what must have been a very sybaritic lifestyle of the Umayyad caliphs. Not only was it a garrison and a fortress, but it was a residence, desert retreat and pleasure palace of the caliphs.

Today it is regarded by many as one of the prime examples of early Islamic art. As an early Islamic monument, Qasr Amra remains a unique site displaying some of the highest artistic achievements of the Umayyad period.

Adapted from:

https://en.wikipedia.org/wiki/Qasr_Amra

https://www.nationalgeographic.com/travel/world-heritage/quseir-amra-jordan/

https://www.metmuseum.org/exhibitions/listings/2012/byzantium-and-islam/blog/where-in-the-world/posts/qusayr-amra

JORDAN

Country name: Jordan (The Hashemite Kingdom of Jordan)

Site name: Wadi Rum, aka as Valley of the Moon, Roman Valley, and Valley of the Rum

Location: southern Jordan, 60 km (37 miles) east of Aqaba

UNESCO World Heritage Site: Inscribed 2011, no. 1377

Date of Visit: 22 April 2006

JORDAN'S SCENIC WADI RUM

Wadi Rum, Jordan's largest wadi, became its fourth UNESCO World Heritage Site on 25 June, 2011, by a unanimous decision of members of the World Heritage Convention. It is inscribed as a heritage site along with Jordan's Petra, Qasr Amra and Um er Rassas.

Located in southern Jordan near the Saudi border, the site is a large area of desert landscapes, sandstone mountains, narrow gorges, natural rock arches, caverns, ruined temples, and massive, towering cliffs. It is also the site of some 25,000 petroglyphs and 20,000 ancient Nabatean, Thamudic, and Arabic inscriptions.

The Wadi Rum Protected Area (WRPA) covers a site of 74,2000 hectares. Identified as a possible nature preserve in 1978, the area is today covered by the Law of the Department of Antiquities and is managed by the Administration of the Aqaba Special Economic Zone.

As a very isolated area and one inhospitable to permanent residents, Wadi Rum is populated by only several thousand nomads, Bedouins, and villagers. So far, it appears to be a largely unspoiled landscape. One sees only the goat hair tents of the Bedouins, a few nondescript concrete buildings, a few shops in a small village, and the headquarters of the Desert Patrol Corps.

Located only a short distance on a side road from the Desert Highway between Amman and Aqaba is the Wadi Rum Visitors

A view of Jordan's scenic Wadi Rum

Center. At the time of my visit to Jordan in 2006, the very new and modern visitors center had just opened. Once inside, we were treated to state-of-the-art displays and by a professionally made video presentation on the site and its ecology.

Only a short distance from the visitors' center, we were treated to a view of one of the area's most spectacular sights, the so-called "Seven Pillars of Wisdom." A series of rocky cliffs, the desert rock formation was so named in the 1980s after the book written by the British officer T. E. Lawrence, also known as Lawrence of Arabia. Lawrence had penned his book after time spent in the area in 1917-1918 during the Arab Revolt against the Ottomans.

Climbing into the back of a four-wheel drive vehicle, we were driven across the desolate desert landscape to a Bedouin tent set up for tourists such as ourselves. After being served a fragrant cup of tea, we were treated to a tour of several of the more spectacular sights in the area. Especially impressive was the Khaz'al Canyon, a very narrow defile between towering cliffs in which we discovered a small spring, as well as numerous examples of rock drawings and ancient inscriptions. Fortunately, the petroglyphs and inscriptions appeared relatively well preserved, except for naturally occurring erosion and weathering. On the other hand, there were also numerous, distracting examples of modern graffiti.

As an added bonus, while at a rest stop at the very small village of Wadi Rum, our local guide recommended a visit to the recently discovered ruins of an ancient Nabatean temple just up a hill from the village. I found it especially enlightening to see the ruins of such a temple, constructed from quarried pieces of the local rock and not of the rock-cut variety seen earlier at Petra.

Recently, Wadi Rum has become increasingly popular as a site for eco-adventure tourism. It has become somewhat of a mecca for foreign visitors who are trekkers, climbers, and day trippers from Petra and Aqaba. The area is becoming known for its luxury tourist camps, horseback riding, hiking, and mountain climbing, and more and more all-terrain vehicles (ATVs) and Jeeps are to be seen carrying tourists around to see the various sights. More and more car tracks are being left on the desert landscape. The village of Wadi Rum also has the potential to encroach upon the landscape, and exploitation of the area's groundwater and the collection of firewood by the local people are also becoming concerns of preservationists.

The stark, barren landscape of Wadi Rum has not escaped the notice of film-making crews who have often substituted Wadi Rum as the background for science fiction epics taking place on the planet Mars. The 1962 film by David Lean, "Lawrence of Arabia," is undoubtedly the best-known movie filmed in large part at Wadi Rum.

Wadi Rum was very much one of the highlights of the trip to Jordan. Not only did its desolate sand dunes have a certain beauty, but it had soaring, rocky cliffs, granite and sandstone mountains, narrow canyons, and the remains of millennia of history, as evidenced by its many petroglyphs, inscriptions, and ancient ruins.

Adapted from:

http://whc.unesco.org/en/list/1377

https://wikitravel.org/en/Wadi_Rum

http://www.unesco.org/new/en/amman/about-this office/single-view/news/wadi_rum_a_new_unesco_world_heritage_site/

KAZAKHSTAN

Country name: Republic of Kazakhstan (with change to the Latin alphabet: Qazaqstan)

Site name: Tamgaly Archaeological Park

Location: In the Chu-Ili mountains, Almaty Oblast, ca. 170 km northwest of Almaty

UNESCO World Heritage Site: Inscribed 2004; no. 145

Date Visited: 7 October 2005

PETROGLYPHS OF KAZAKHSTAN'S TAMGALY GORGE

There are estimated to be not just hundreds of petroglyphs at the Tamgaly Gorge, but thousands -- some 5,000 in fact. It is said to be the most important site of rock art in Central Asia. It is reputed to be Central Asia's largest concentration of petroglyphs and to be important for the quality and quantity of its images.

Tamgaly means "painted or marked place" in Kazakh and other Turkic languages. It is located in the arid Chu-Ili mountains and is best visited as a day trip by car from Kazakhstan's capital of Almaty. The site is quite remote and can be difficult to locate, so it is best to see the site with a knowledgeable guide and driver. The time of day should also be considered, since many of the rock engravings are best viewed in a raking light.

The petroglyphs are clustered in forty-eight areas and are estimated to date from the second millennium BCE to the early twentieth century. Tamgaly is only one of the areas in the region with petroglyphs. Other sites include Gobustan, Mong Altai, Hail Alta, Tanum and Valcamonica.

The Chu-Ili mountain spur at the western end of the Tienshan Mountains is the location of the gorge created by the Tamgaly River. It is an area with springs and vegetation, unlike the mountains on the border of Kazakhstan with Kyrgyzstan and the arid central Kazakhstan plains in the north. The

One of the many petroglyphs
at Tamgaly Gorge, Kazakhstan

somewhat circular site covers 900 hectares. The largest concentration of petroglyphs is located in the central canyon which, in addition to the petroglyphs, contains many graves and altars used for sacrificial offerings.

The site includes Mount Tamgaly, 982m in height. Running through the center of the area is the Tamgaly River flowing to the plains to the north. Located in the gorge are black rock faces that rise in stages. It is an area that has attracted pastoral communities since the Bronze Age.

Five sites contain the largest concentrations of petroglyphs, estimated at some 3,000. Located on the surfaces of the local rock, the most impressive and best-preserved petroglyphs have been created by a technique of incising the images on the rock with stone or metal implements. Most prevalent is the wide variety of animals, including images of horses, camels, deer, and goats, in addition to warriors and scenes of animal sacrifice. One erotic scene has been identified, while another depicts an unborn calf still inside its mother.

Of much interest to archaeologists are the images of zoomorphic creatures, abstracted forms of people, and what appear to be solar deities. It is thought that some of the petroglyphs may represent a pantheon of gods with representations of dancers, women giving birth, and groups of worshippers. Especially controversial are the so-called "sun-headed deities" with some scholars associating them with the ancient Indo-Iranian solar deity, Mithra.

The largest number of petroglyphs are thought to date from the Bronze Age, with a smaller group dating from the Iron Age. There are also glyphs dating from the Middle Ages, as well as some from more modern times. That the area was a place of burials is evidenced by its many box-like enclosures or cists and the mounds of earth or kurgans dating primarily from the Middle to Late Bronze Age.

Unfortunately, the site was being given little security. There was no entrance fee, and the site was accessible only by private transportation. A lone soldier might be found at the entrance.

Signs in Russian gave little information about the site. As a result, it was very difficult to understand much about the site without being accompanied by a knowledgeable guide. A visitors center is located at the nearby small village of Karabastay, but it was said to be usually closed. At Tamgaly's primary site there was only a parking area, a guard house, picnic shelters, and rest rooms.

In 2001 Tamgaly was inscribed as a Property of National Significance on the List of Monuments of History and Culture. In 2003, it was designated as the State Archaeological Reserve of Tamgaly under the auspices of the Ministry of Culture of the Republic of Kazakhstan. In 2004 it received UNESCO World Heritage status.

Most of the petroglyphs appear to be in a good state of preservation, but cracks in the rock caused by weathering and earthquakes can be seen. Foliating of the rock is also seen in some areas due to the action of freezing water. There is also evidence of modern graffiti and of damage caused by visitors to the site.

While I had seen many ancient petroglyphs elsewhere, I'd never seen such a profusion of petroglyphs nor such a variety of images. In spite of all the expert explanations of our local guide, I still could only wonder what symbolism and meaning many of the images must have had for the people who created them.

Adapted from:

http://en.wikipedia.org/wiki/Tamgaly
http://whc.unesco.org/en/list/1145
http://www.worldheritagesite.org/list/Tamgaly
http://culture360.asef.org/organisation/state-archaeological-reserve-museum-tamgaly/

KOREA

Country name: Republic of Korea (South Korea)
Site name: Gyeongju Historic Areas
Location: Gyeongju City, Gyeongsangbuk-do Province
UNESCO World Heritage Site: Inscribed 2000; no. 976
Date of Visit: 20-21 October 2015

GYEONGJU: CAPITAL OF KOREA'S SILLA DYNASTY

Gyeongju is often called "the world's largest museum without walls." As the capital of the Silla dynasty ruling Korea for nearly nine hundred years (57 CE - 935 CE), it is especially notable for its outstanding examples of Korean Buddhist art and architecture. While the capital of the Silla dynasty, the city was known as Seorabeol, meaning "capital." In 940 King Taejo changed the city's name to Gyeongju meaning "congratulatory district."

Gyeongju has 52 designated cultural properties registered as World Cultural Heritage sites and is home to 31 National Treasures. There are 35 royal tombs and 155 tumuli in central Gyeongju and 421 tumuli in the outskirts of the city. Many of Gyeongju's treasures date from the United Silla period which ended with the Joseon period (1392-1910), when Gyeongju no longer had national importance but still remained a regional center.

The Gyeongju Historic Areas are composed of five distinct sections:

The Mount Namsan Belt is situated north of the city and includes ruins of 122 temples, 64 pagodas, and 53 stone statues. Also included in the area are the ruins of the Namsen Mountain fortress, the site of the Poseokjeong Pavilion and the Seochulji pond.

Silla dynasty images of the Buddha at
Gyeongju, South Korea

The Wolseong Belt includes the site of the ruined Wolseong Palace, the Gyerim woodlands or "Chicken Forest," the Anapji pond, the ruined Imhaejeon Palace, and the Cheomseongdae Observatory, which is regarded as the oldest observatory in the Far East.

The Tumuli Belt contains three royal tomb groups. Included is the tumulus with the famous depiction of a winged, heavenly horse painted on birch bark

The Hwangnyongsa Belt contains two Buddhist temples, the Bunhwangsa stone pagoda and the ruins of Korea's largest temple, the Hwangynongsa Temple,

The Sanseong Fortress Belt is Gyeongju's least known and most infrequently visited section. It is composed primarily of fortresses and includes the 400 year old Myeonghwal Mountain Fortress and the Bu Mountain Fortress which is located in Geoncheaon-eup.

The Mount Namsen and Sanseong Belts are primarily rural and are regarded as not being threatened by development as are the other historic sites which are within urban areas. The Gyeongju Historic Areas are owned by the Korean government and are state-designated cultural heritage under the Cultural Heritage Protection Act. The area is also designated a national park under the National Park Law.

Before any construction is permitted within the historic areas, a Cultural Heritage Impact Assessment must be made. Protection of historic areas is enforced by the Cultural Heritage Administration (CHA). Land surrounding the protected areas has been purchased as buffer zones, and the East Sea Southern Railway has been removed as of 2014.

The Gyeongju National Museum, founded in 1945 and built in 1968, is devoted primarily to artifacts from the Silla dynasty. Located adjacent to the royal tomb complex, it houses 16,333 ancient objects such as the Emille Bell and several of the impressive, golden Silla crowns. Its collection has become so enormous that a large warehouse has been built on the site for objects that cannot be exhibited in the museum. Also located at the museum is an archaeological research department.

Ranked as one of Korea's top tourist attractions, Gyeongju's historic areas are said to draw six million visitors each year, including 750,000 foreign visitors.

This foreign visitor to South Korea missed by only one day being able to see the exhibition, "Silla: Korea's Golden Kingdom," at the Metropolitan Museum of Art, New York, from 4 November 2013 to 23 February 2014. Fortunately, I was able to purchase the large, scholarly catalog of the exhibition. By reading the catalog, I realized how little I knew about Korean art. Setting off on a trip to Korea in October of 2015, I found that it not only lived up to my already high expectations but exceeded them.

Adapted from:

http://whc.unesco.org/en/list/976

https://en.wikipedia.org/wiki/Tourism_in_Gyeongju

https://en.wikipedia.org/wiki/Gyeongju

http://english.visitkorea.or.kr/enu/ATR/SI_EN_3_1_1_1.jsp?cid=995361

http://asiasociety.org/korea/unesco-world-heritage-series-part-3-gyeongju-historic-areas t

LAOS

Country name: Lao People's Democratic Republic (colloquial name: Muang Lao)

Site name: Vat Phou (also known as Wat Phu)

Location: At the base of Mount Phu Kao (also spelled Phou Khao); 45 km south of Pakse, 6 km from the Mekong River, Champasak province, southern Laos

UNESCO World Heritage Site: Inscribed 2001; no 481

Date of Visit: 20 January 2007

A LOATIAN KHMER STYLE TEMPLE: VAT PHOU

Vat Phou, also known as Wat Phu, meaning "mountain temple," is one of the oldest and largest archaeological sites in Laos.

Vat Phou has been regarded as a sacred site by at least three cultures: the Chen La kingdom (sixth-eighth centuries CE), the pre-Angkor Khmer empire (ninth-thirteenth centuries) and the Lan Xang kingdom, which converted the complex from Hinduism to Theravada Buddhism.

The top of the mountain, Phu Kao (original name, Lingaparvata), upon which the temple complex was built, was thought to resemble the symbol of Shiva, the lingam. The permanent spring at the base of the mountain's cliffs also served to anoint the lingam in the temple sanctuary with water.

Although Vat Phou was the site of a temple as early as the fifth century CE, most of what survives today dates from the eleventh to fifteenth centuries. The site was originally associated with the city of Shrestapura, located on the banks of the Mekong River and to the east of the mountain of Phu Kao. Inscriptions have linked it to both the Chen La and Champa kingdoms.

In the early tenth century and as early as the reign of Yasovarman I, Vat Phou became part of the Khmer empire

A guardian figure (dvarapala), venerated as King
Kammatha, at the Khmer style temple of Vat Phou, Laos

centered at the capitol of Angkor located to the southwest in present day Cambodia. During the eleventh century Vat Phou was largely replaced by structures in the Koh Ker and Baphuon styles of Angkor. Few changes were made to the site in succeeding centuries until it was converted to Theravada Buddhism in the thirteenth century.

Beginning at the Mekong River, the temple complex rises in three basic levels. Unusual for being built upon the side of a mountain, Vat Phou is composed of seven terraces arranged on an axis with the river. Starting at the river and the ruined city of Shrestapura, of which little survives, one first encounters a series of reservoirs or *barays*. Only the middle reservoir measuring 600 by 200m retains its water. Other reservoirs existed to the north and south. A pair of *barays* remain near the long walkway bordered by boundary markers leading to the temple complex.

Midway up the walkway are two structures that have been called the north and south palaces, although what their actual purpose once was is unknown. Also called the men's and women's palaces and dated to the eleventh century, they are thought to have been used for ritual ceremonies. To the south is located the "Ho Thao" and to the north, the "Ho Nang." The two structures are notable for their intricate carvings on their pediments and lintels in the early Angkor style. Depicted are such deities as Shiva and his consort. Both structures possess courtyards with an entrance and corridor on their sides facing the central axis of the temple complex. To one side of the southern palace sits a shrine dedicated to Nandi, the sacred bull.

Proceeding up the mountain, one encounters several structures that once housed lingams, while on the fourth terrace stands an image of a guardian, a *dvarapala*. Venerated as King Kammatha, the mythological builder of the temple, the figure has been decked out in colorful robes by the local people.

On the highest terrace sits the temple sanctuary that once contained a lingam dedicated to Shiva. Measuring sixty by sixty meters, the terrace provides spectacular views of the flat plains, the central walkway, and the large reservoirs, ultimately leading back down to the Mekong. Since Theravada Buddhism replaced Hinduism in Laos, the temple's sanctuary now houses a large Buddha image, in front of which sit three smaller images clad in saffron-colored robes.

The sanctuary is notable for its sculptural decoration in the early Khmer style. Among the many figures depicted on the lintels and pediments are *apsaras, devatas,* guardian figures, and representations of such Hindu deities as Vishnu, Krishna, and Indra.

Also located at the top level are the remains of a small library and several rock sculptures including a stone carved with the footprint of the Buddha and depictions of an elephant and a crocodile. It is the carving of the crocodile that is thought to have been the location of human sacrifice according to a Chinese text. Another stone has been carved to represent the Hindu *trimurti,* with its representations of the three main deities of Hinduism, Shiva, Vishnu, and Brahma.

Scientific work conducted at Vat Phou includes several joint UNESCO and Laotian projects. Starting in 1991, excavations have been performed at Vat Phou by the Projet de Recherches en Archéologie Lao (PRAL) in order to produce an accurate map of the archaeological site. Then in 2001 the site was given UNESCO World Heritage status.

Today, the temple complex remains open for worshippers as well as for tourism. A small museum at the site contains a collection of both Hindu and Buddhist sculptures.

Vat Phou is the site of an annual, local festival called *Boun Wat Phou Champasak.* Held during the third lunar month (usually in February), it becomes the scene of ritual ceremonies, musical and dance performances, cock fighting, elephant racing, and a trade fair.

Vat Phou is one of the oldest and most important archaeological sites in Laos. It is also important as an example of an outpost of the Khmer Empire and as one from the early

Khmer period, predating Angkor Wat, which is located at the Khmer capital of Angkor across the border in Cambodia.

Adapted from:

https://en.wikipedia.org/wiki/Vat_Phou

http://whc.unesco.org/en/list/481

http://www.vatphou-champassak.com/en

https://www.renown-travel.com/laos/pakse/wat-phou.html

http://www.visit-laos.com/champasak/wat-phu.htm

http://thetraveluster.com/2013/01/unesco-world-heritage-site-vat-phou-champasak-laos/

MALTA/GOZO

Country name: Republic of Malta (Maltese: Repubblika ta' Malta)

Site name: Megalithic temples of Malta and Gozo

Location: the Mediterranean islands of Malta and Gozo

UNESCO World Heritage Site: Inscribed 1980; extension, 1992; no. 132

Date of Visit : 23-24 May 2009

PREHISTORIC TEMPLES OF MALTA AND GOZO: ĠGANTIJA AND TARXIEN

The prehistoric, megalithic temples of Malta and Gozo are reputed to be among Earth's earliest manmade, free-standing structures. They are considered to be older than Stonehenge and the pyramids of Egypt. So far only the site of Göbekli Tepe, located in southeastern Anatolia, present day Turkey, has been determined to be older.

In 1980, the temple of Ġgantija was inscribed as a UNESCO World Heritage Site. In 1992, the UNESCO committee extended the inscribed site to include five other prehistoric temples on Malta and Gozo: Ħaġar Qim, Mnajdra, Skorba, Ta' Ħaġrat, and Tarxien. All six temples have been dated from the fourth millennium to the third millennium BCE.

My trip to Malta and Gozo was an afterthought, since they were part of an extension to a trip to Tunisia located only a short distance to the south in North Africa. During the short trip to Malta and a half day excursion to Gozo, I found it possible to visit two of the temple sites, Ġgantija and Tarxien.

The prehistoric remains on Malta and Gozo have been divided into eleven phases based on recalibrated radiocarbon dating. The earliest is the Neolithic Ghar Dalam phase dated to approximately 5,000 BCE. The period dating approximately from 4,100 to 2,500 BCE has been divided into five phases with

Interior view of the temples at Tarxien on the island of Malta

the two earliest phases represented primarily by pottery shards. The period of temple construction has been divided into three major phases: the Ġgantija phase (3600-3200 BCE), the Saflieni phase (3300 - 3000 BCE), and the Tarxien phase (3150-2500 BCE).

The basic plan of the temples is that of a forecourt situated in front of a concave façade. The walls are usually composed of upright stones (called *orthostats*) capped with horizontal stone slabs. It is thought that the temples had corbeled ceilings topped by horizontal beams. The outer walls are usually composed of larger stones with the space between the inner and outer walls filled with rubble and earth.

The temple interiors were usually composed of semicircular, apse-like forms arranged symmetrically along a center axis, with the number of apses varying from two to six. The harder coralline limestone was usually used for exterior walls, while the softer globigerina limestone was used for the inner walls. Numerous stones have drilled holes, and reliefs of spirals and various plants and animals have been found on some of the temple walls.

The many remains of animal bones and fire residue indicate that animal sacrifice was conducted at the prehistoric temples. Remains of holes in the floors have also led to the belief that ritual libations may have been poured into them.

The temples are generally regarded as being in a relatively good state of preservation, especially when their great age is taken into consideration. Photographs of the various sites often date back to the early twentieth century. Preservation measures have included capping walls with cement and removing stones with decorations indoors to museums to prevent further weathering.

The temples are protected by the Environment and Development Planning Act of 2010 and by the Malta Environment and Planning Authority. Of special concern is that the sites be given adequate buffer zones.

Several statuettes and other prehistoric objects have been preserved in the Gozo Museum of Archaeology. Other prehistoric remains are located in the Museum of Archaeology in Valletta. Of special note are the representations of "fat ladies," thought to be fertility figures or mother goddesses. The representations of a prehistoric sleeping "fat lady" in small, plaster copies are especially popular as souvenirs.

Tarxien

(pronounced tar-sheen;
derived from "Tirix" meaning "large stone")

Tarxien was the first of the two prehistoric temple sites visited on the tour. Located on the island of Malta, this temple site is located in the midst of the modern village of Paolo. After passing through an entrance building, one is immediately transported back into prehistoric times.

Located approximately 400m east of the Hypogeum of Hal-Saflieni, the temples were excavated early in the twentieth century by Temi Zammit. The southern temple possesses a forecourt, a curving façade and an ancient cistern. The temple to the northeast is regarded as the earlier temple and is dated to 3600 to 3200 BCE. It possesses two semicircular apses separated by a central aisle. The east and south temples have been dated to 3150 and 2500 BCE.

Ġgantija

(pronounced j-gan-tee-yah)

Ġgantija, meaning "giants' grotto" and dated from 3600 to 3000 BCE, was visited on an optional half-day excursion to Malta's adjacent island of Gozo. In a local legend, the temples are said to have been built in one day and one night by Sunsuna, a giantess, while she was nursing her child. As a result, many archaeologists believe that the temples were dedicated to a fertility goddess or a great earth mother. The site is also thought to have been that of an oracle as well as a site for prayers for healing.

Sitting on the Xaghra plateau of Gozo and facing to the southeast, the two temples are enclosed by a boundary wall.

The temples are composed of five apses and have some traces of plaster covering their walls.

The temple at Ġgantija is regarded as being one of the most complete. Covering an area of 10,000 square feet, its walls reach an impressive seventeen feet in height.

Early records indicate that the plan of the temple was correctly mapped by Jean-Pierre Houël in the eighteenth century before excavations were conducted at the site. In 1827, debris was removed from the site, and several years later the temples were depicted in a painting by Brochtorff, a German artist.

Ħaġar Qim

Located on a ridge two kilometers from the village of Orendi, this temple site has a wide forecourt and a passage running down its middle. Its four interior spaces can be accessed through a separate entrance in the soft globigerina limestone. Especially on the site's south, exterior wall, weathering has caused extensive flaking of the soft limestone,.

Ta' Ħaġrat

Located on the eastern edge of the village of Mġarr and about one kilometer from the Ta' Skorba temple, this temple complex has two adjoining temples, both trefoil in shape. Excavated in 1925-1927 by Sir Temi Zammit, it is a less-organized and a smaller site than other temple complexes on Malta. The Mġarr phase pottery unearthed at the village site predates the site by centuries.

Mnajdra

(aka L-Imnajdra)

Regarded as a separate site, this temple complex sits only 500m from the site of Ta' Ħaġrat. The site is centered on a circular forecourt with three adjoining temples located at one side. The site's middle temple with four apses is regarded as being the most recent in date. It has been determined that the southern temple is oriented to the sun's equinoxes and solstices. The rays of the rising sun can be observed passing directly through the site's main doorway to shine on the temple's central niche.

Skorba

(aka Ta'Skorba)

A village is thought to have existed at this site, predating the temple by up to twelve centuries. With its three apses, one of the temple complexes has been largely leveled to the ground with only the stone paving at its entrance remaining. To the east is a Tarxien-period second temple with four apses and a central niche. The site's oldest structure is an 11-meter-long wall located to the west. Material gathered from the site has been dated to Malta's earliest period, the Ghar Dalam phase. Radiocarbon dating has dated fragments of charcoal found at the site to 4,850 BCE.

The extension of my trip to include Malta and Gozo resulted in my being privileged to visit sites that were among the trip's major highlights. I had never thought I would see such ancient, prehistoric sites on a trip which I had originally planned as only a tour of Tunisia.

Adapted from:

https://en.wikipedia.org/wiki/Ġgantija

http://heritagemalta.org/museums-sites/ggantija-temples/

http://www.sacred-destinations.com/malta/ggantija-temples

https://www.visitgozo.com/where-to-go-in-gozo/archaeological-sites/ggantija-temple

http://en.wikipedia.org/wiki/Megalithic_Temples_of_Malta

http://www.maltacultureguide.com/index.php?page=article&article_id=30

http://whc.unesco.org/en/list/132

http://en.wikipedia.org/wiki/Tarxien_Temples

MEXICO

Country name: United Mexican States (Spanish: Estados Unidos Mexicanos)

Site name: Pre-Hispanic City and National Park of Palenque

Location: State of Chiapas, Municipality of Palenque, Yucatán

UNESCO World Heritage Site: Inscribed 1987; no. 411

Date of Visit: 7 December 2004

A CLASSIC MAYAN SITE: PALENQUE

Located in the Mexican state of Chiapas, Palenque, known in ancient times as Lakamha. meaning "big water," reached its height during the Mayan Classic period. Established during the Late Pre-Classic period, it flourished from approximately 500 to 700 CE and is thought to have been abandoned in the ninth century. With an area of 1780 hectares and an estimated 1,400 known structures, less than ten percent of the site is thought to have been explored. Although Palenque is considered a medium-sized site and is smaller in area than Chichen Itzá, Tikal or Copán, it contains some of the finest Mayan architecture, relief carvings, and pierced, stone combs atop its temples.

As a ceremonial and civic center, Palenque is renowned for its refined and harmonious architectural style and for the relative lightness of its construction. It is also known for its corbel vaulted interior spaces, its T-shaped windows and its pierced temple crests.

Located in the center of the ancient city is what has been called the Palace, built on an artificial terrace as a complex composed of a series of buildings and courtyards. Constructed over four centuries, the complex is thought to have been used for civic functions, entertainments, and religious ceremonies. One of the Palace's most unusual features is its four-story tower called the Observation Tower, with what appears to be a Mansard roof. Its baths were supplied with fresh water from a

The Temple of Inscriptions at
the Mayan site of Palenque, Mexico

complex hydraulic system and by an aqueduct carrying water under the site's main plaza from the Otulum River.

Construction on the Temple of Inscriptions is thought to have been started in 675 CE. It was built to house the tomb of one of Palenque's most notable rulers, K'inich Janaab' Pakal, known as Pakal the Great (reigned 615-683). It contains one of the longest Mayan texts of glyphs known, second only to the hieroglyphic stairway at Copán, located in Honduras. It records nearly one-hundred and eighty years of the site's history. The massive pyramid measures 60m in width, 42.5m in depth and 27.2m in height. With its largest stones weighing up to 12 and 15 tons, its total volume has been estimated to be 32,500 cubic meters.

In 1952, the archaeologist Alberto Ruz Lhuillier discovered a lengthy passageway and stairway leading to the tomb of Pakal inside the Temple of Inscriptions. The elaborately carved lid of the sarcophagus of Pakal has been the subject of much study and debate among archaeologists, with one interpretation being that Pakal is depicted as the Mayan maize god coming up from the underworld. Ancient alien theorists have said the complex carving on the tomb's lid represents Pakal aboard an ancient spaceship.

Another subject of debate is the possibility of the alignment of passageways in the pyramid allowing the sun to shine on Pakal's tomb at the time of the winter solstice. The tomb has also yielded the richest jade collection ever found in a Mayan tomb. A mosaic of jade has been found covering the face of Pakal, while a covering of carved jade pieces held together with gold wires was found covering his body.

Also noteworthy is the separate group of three temples that includes the Temple of the Cross, the Temple of the Sun, and the Temple of the Foliated Cross. Sitting atop steep pyramids are temple interiors with elaborate carvings depicting figures flanking a central object or religion icon. The objects appearing as crosses to early explorers and used to name the temples are now thought more likely to represent the Mayan mythological tree of creation located at Earth's center.

Other structures at Palenque include the Temple of the Skull and the Temple of the Red Queen, also known as the Temple of the Beautiful Relief. Another temple, the Temple of the Count, was given its name as a result of its being lived in by the explorer Jean Frederic Waldeck, reputed to be a count. Other structures at Palenque include a ball court and a stone bridge over the Otulum River.

Palenque is reputed to be the most studied and written about of Mexico's Mayan sites. One of the earliest visitors to Palenque was Don Ramon de Ordoñez y Aguilar in 1773. The architect Antonio Bernasconi was the first to make maps and drawings of Palenque, while Luciano Casteñeda made additional drawings at the site. In 1831 Juan Galindo visited Palenque and was the first to report that the depictions of humans at the site looked like the local people and that the site should not be attributed to Polynesians, Egyptians, or to Israel's Lost Tribes as other early explorers suggested.

The first photographs of Palenque were taken by Désiré Charnay in 1858. In 1882 a book on Palenque was published in London. From 1890 to 1891, Alfred Maudslay resided at Palenque, and in 1923, Frans Blom from Tulane University mapped the site. From 1949 to 1952, Alberto Ruz Lhuillier undertook excavations at Palenque and succeeded in discovering Pakal's tomb after four years of work at the Temple of Inscriptions. The first Palenque Mesa Reconda (Round Table), led by Merle Greene Robertson, was held at the site in 1973. In the 1970s a small museum was built at the site.

In 1920, researchers from Pennsylvania State University discovered that the Peidras Bolas Aqueduct was a pressurized, spring-fed water channel, the first to be identified in the Americas. Recently, many additional investigations have taken place at Palenque, but it is still said that only approximately five to ten percent of the site has been excavated.

Protection of Palenque is the responsibility of the National Institute of Anthropology and History (INAH) and the National Commission for Protected Areas (CONANP). The site was inscribed as a heritage site by UNESCO in 1987, and in 1993 was made an Archaeological Monument by the Mexican government and came under the protection of the Federal Law on Archaeological, Artistic and Historic Monuments and Sites.

Today, the number of tourists visiting Palenque continues to grow, and there are estimates that it draws up to 600,000 visitors a year. For centuries, the site was abandoned and overtaken by the dense jungle, which did much to preserve it, but today many ongoing measures need to be taken to prevent deterioration of the site from weathering, the encroachment of the surrounding jungle, and the great influx of tourists. Although the Temple of Inscriptions was closed to tourists when I visited Palenque in 2004, the Palace and many of the other temples atop pyramids were open to the hundreds of visitors climbing over the ancient ruins.

Adapted from:

http://whc.unesco.org/en/list/411
https://en.wikipedia.org/wiki/Palenque

MEXICO

Country name: United Mexican States (Spanish: Estados Unidos Mexicanos)

Site name: Uxmal (aka Uchmal; Mayan: Óoxmáal)

Location: 80 km (50 miles) south of Mérida, Yucatán State, Mexico

UNESCO World Heritage Site: Inscribed 1966; no. 791

Date of Visit: 6 December 2004

MEXICO'S LATE CLASSIC MAYAN SITE OF UXMAL

Uxmal, meaning "thrice built" in the Mayan language, is regarded as representing one of the high points of Mayan culture. The name may also have been derived from "Oxmal" or from "Uchmal," the latter meaning "the future, what is to come." Located on Mexico's Yucatán peninsula, it sits 150 km (90 miles) from the Mayan site of Chichén Itzá. The ancient city center covers an area of 60 hectares (150 acres). Along with the related sites of Kabah, Labna, and Sayil, Uxmal is considered a high point in the development of Mayan art and architecture.

Founded in 700 CE, the city may have had, at its height, a population of 25,000 inhabitants. It reached its high point in the Late Classic Mayan period from about 850 to 950 CE. Around 1000 CE, construction at Uxmal declined when invading Toltecs set up their capital at Chichén Itzá, and it is thought to have ceased by 1100 CE. Uxmal remained an inhabited site, however, until the 1550s.

The architecture of Uxmal is regarded as representing many of the primary features of the Puuc style. The Puuc region, located in the southwestern section of the state of the Yucatán, was a major area of trade. "Puuc," meaning "hill or low mountain chain," was an area measuring approximately 2500 square km. Characteristics of the style included buildings with two stories, the lower being undecorated and usually only having doorways. The upper stories were heavily ornamented

Detail view of the architectural decoration of the
Quadrangle at the Mayan site of Uxmal, Mexico

with many decorative elements and especially with depictions of the rain deity, Chac. As a result, the upper stories often possess what appears to be a mosaic-like frieze.

The ancient city sits in a dry savanna region surrounded by forested areas. The city's water supply came primarily from nearby *cenotes*, or sinkhole-type wells in the area's limestone substrata. An adequate supply of water for the city was a major preoccupation of the city's residents as evidenced by the prominence of the images of the rain deity, Chac (aka Chaac), on so many of the city's buildings.

Located near the entrance to the archaeological site is Uxmal's tallest pyramid, the so-called Pyramid of the Magician (also called the Pyramid of the Soothsayer (Spanish: Pirámide del Adivino). It rises in five levels to a height of 27.6m (90.5 feet) and measures 69 by 49m (227 by 162 feet) at its base. Also called the House of the Dwarf (Spanish: Casa del Enano), the massive structure is said to have been constructed by a dwarf in only one night. At the pyramid's top sits a temple with a doorway decorated with a mask of the rain deity, Chac.

Located to the west of the pyramid sits the so-called Nunnery Quadrangle. Four rectangular buildings, with a total of seventy-four individual rooms, sit around a large courtyard measuring 79 by 65m (260 by 212 feet). The complex is thought to have been used either as a palace or as a residence. Masks of the deity, Chac, decorate each of the complex's four sides.

To the south and sitting on a wide platform measuring 8.8.m high (29 feet) is the so-called Governor's Palace. It is said to possess pre-Colombian America's longest continuous façade. It is also regarded as one of the finest examples of the Puuc style. Astronomers have determined that the large edifice was used for observing the rising and setting of the planet Venus. The central section of the palace measures 19.8m (65 feet) in height and is flanked by smaller structures on each side. Connecting the three structures are typical Mayan-style corbeled vaults. Sitting on a smaller platform in front of the palace is a throne decorated with two jaguar heads.

Also worthy of mention are the ball court (Mayan: pok-ta-pok) located near the Quadrangle, the Great Pyramid located to the west of the Governor's Palace, the House of the Tortoises with its sculptural frieze of tortoises, and the House of the Pigeons with its upper level pierced with what appear to be pigeon holes. There are also complexes of buildings called the North and South groups, the Cemetery Group, and the so-called House of the Old Woman (Spanish: Casa de la Vieja).

Uxmal, along with the sites of Sayil and Labná, remains well preserved due to being in remote and sparsely populated areas. Preservation and conservation efforts have been limited primarily to consolidation and cleaning. Conservation work is recorded as having taken place in 1913 and 1914, and work was undertaken by American archaeologists in the 1940s. Improvements to the site include new signage, an improved parking area, and the construction of a small museum in 1986.

The site is protected by the Federal Law on Monuments and Archaeological, Artistic, and Historical Zones of 1972. Management of the site is the responsibility of the Yucatán Regional Centre of the National Institute for Anthropology and History (INAH). The Cultural Institute of the State of Yucatán and the Ministry of Social Development are also responsible for site management.

Along with Palenque and Chichén Itzá, Uxmal is one of the major Mayan sites on Mexico's Yucatan peninsula, and it is strongly recommended for inclusion on an itinerary when visiting Mexico.

Adapted from:

http://whc.unesco.org/en/list/791
https://en.wikipedia.org/wiki/Uxmal
https://www.britannica.com/place/Uxmal

PALESTINE

Country name: State of Palestine (Arabic: Dawlat Filasṭīn)
Site name: Church of the Nativity (Latin: Basilica Nativitatis)
Location: Bethlehem, 10 km south of Jerusalem
UNESCO World Heritage Site: Inscribed in 2012; no. 1433
   Included on UNESCO's List of World Heritage in Danger
Tour Dates: 3-11 November 2008

CHRISTENDOM'S ENDANGERED SITE: CHURCH OF THE NATIVITY, BETHLEHEM

On 29 June, 2012, the Church of the Nativity was declared a UNESCO World Heritage Site by a 13 to 6 vote of the 21-member World Heritage Committee and became Palestine's first heritage site. An emergency candidacy procedure bypassed the usual process of eighteen months despite the opposition of Israel and the United States, since they both contended that Palestine should not be recognized as a UNESCO member. UNESCO also placed the site on its endangered list, and in 2008 the site was placed on the World Monuments Fund's list of the most endangered 100 sites. Today the Church not only has the distinction of being one of Christianity's most sacred sites. It is also considered to be the oldest Christian church in continuous daily use.

Controversy among scholars still wages over whether or not Jesus of Nazareth was born in Bethlehem. Only two of the four Gospels mention His birth. Luke tells of His being placed in a manger and of the visit of the shepherds. Matthew's account tells of the visitation of the Magi, the massacre of the innocents, and the flight into Egypt.

No archaeological evidence has been found to support Christ's birth in Bethlehem, nor is there any evidence that early Christians considered the present church site as sacred. The emperor Hadrian is reputed to have built a temple dedicated to the pagan deity, Adonis, on the site in 124 CE. Justin Martyr appears to be among the first to report, in his dialogue with Trypho, that it was in a cave outside Bethlehem where the Virgin and Joseph had found lodgings and where Christ was born. Then in the third century CE, Origin of Alexandria visited Palestine and also reported that Christ's birth took place in a cave in Bethlehem.

Early in the fourth century CE, the emperor Constantine sent an imperial delegation to Palestine to identify sites associated with the life of Christ. It was the council of Nicaea which decreed that sites associated with the life of Christ be memorialized by building Christian churches above them. As a result, the construction of a church over the site in Bethlehem was commissioned by the emperor Constantine and his mother, Helena, in 327 CE. Built under the supervision of Makarios, bishop of Jerusalem, the structure was completed by 339 CE. The church featured an octagonal rotunda built over the Grotto, an atrium and a forecourt with double aisles. Subsequently, in 529 or 556 CE, the original church was destroyed by a fire during the Samaritan Revolts.

In 565 CE, a new basilica was built on the site by the Byzantine emperor Justinian. It is his structure which basically survives to this day.

The Church of the Nativity is a typical Roman basilica separated into five sections by Corinthian columns and with a sanctuary at its eastern end. The once-golden mosaics on its side walls are today quite badly deteriorated, and the original Roman style marble floor has been largely covered over. A trap door in the existing floor can be opened to reveal a small section of the original mosaic pavement of Constantine's structure. At the eastern end stands a gilt iconostasis, while spiral stairways on either side lead down to the Grotto.

Entrance to the church is through a low doorway only approximately four feet in height and which is today called the "Door of Humility." Contrary to what some believe, it was not built to make pilgrims bow when entering the sacred site but

View of tourists entering the "Door of Humility" at
the Church of the Nativity in Bethlehem, Palestine

was constructed after the Crusades to help prevent looters from entering the Church on horseback and on camels.

When visited in 2008, I found the Church to be dark, gloomy, and in a very sad state of repair, as well as being overrun by hordes of tourists.

We had been forewarned by our tour leader to bring our passports with us, since we would be passing from Jerusalem in Israel over into the West Bank of Palestine. The passage into Palestine went smoothly. We first had lunch in what appeared to be a large banqueting hall before visiting Manger Square in front of the Church.

The Manger Square is a large, paved plaza in front of the Church. On Christmas Eve, it is where crowds gather, singing Christmas carols in anticipation of the traditional midnight mass.

Once inside the Church we encountered long lines of pilgrims waiting to enter the Grotto at the Church's eastern end. After a short wait, we were ushered toward the front of the line ahead of everyone else. After going down a narrow flight of stone steps, we entered the very small, claustrophobic area of the Grotto. Due to the crowd of other pilgrims, I could only find a place to stand at the back of the Grotto area and could only look down over many heads to take a quick photograph of the silver star marking the circular opening to a cavern below.

The fourteen-pointed silver star located in the Grotto is reputed to mark the place of Christ's birth. It is probably the most famous feature of the Church and the most popular subject of photographs. Set in a marble floor, it bears the inscription: "Hic De Virgine Maria Jesus Christus Natus Est-1717 (Here Jesus Christ was born to the Virgin Mary-1717)." Removed in 1847, the star was reinstalled in 1853 by the Turkish government.

Around the star in the floor are fifteen silver lamps representing the three branches of Christendom having authority over the Grotto area. The Greek Orthodox have six lamps; the Roman Catholics, four; and the Armenian Apostolic

Church, five. Catholics and those of the Armenian Apostolic Church have jurisdiction over the altar known as the Altar of the Nativity. Catholics maintain the area of the Grotto named the "Grotto of the Manger" where the Virgin is thought to have laid the Christ Child in a manger, while the Altar of the Magi sits opposite the site of the manger.

I found the Grotto so claustrophobic that I was glad to find an exit door. Hastily leaving the area, I soon found myself inside the nearby Roman Catholic, neo-Gothic church dedicated to Saint Catherine of Alexandria. Its light, airy and well-lit church interior was such a welcome relief after experiencing the gloomy, derelict, and claustrophobic confines of the ancient Church structure next door.

The venture over into Palestine was not over, however. Returning to the checkpoint where we had passed from Israel in Palestine, our tour bus suddenly stopped and sat to one side of the checkpoint on the Palestinian side. There we sat for well over half an hour as we saw vehicle after vehicle passing back into Israel with no apparent difficulty.

Finally, our tour leader returned to our tour bus with a tall Israeli soldier clad from head to toe in camouflage gear and armed with an impressive array of weapons. With a scowl, he proceeded down the aisle of our tour bus, carefully scrutinizing each of our passports. Then, after the tour leader said he had to make a phone call to an official to gain clearance for us, we were finally allowed back into Israel. It was the only time while on the entire trip that I felt in danger, not knowing why there was the delay in our entrance back into Israel. Although I would have been disappointed not to have seen the Church of the Nativity, I found the entire experience of visiting the Church to be one of the most underwhelming of the trip.

Considering all that the ancient Church of the Nativity has experienced, it seems miraculous that it has survived at all. It has endured fires, earthquakes, invasions, changes in regimes, and, most recently, a siege.

In April of 2002, fifty armed Palestinians sought by Israeli Defense Forces (IDF), along with approximately 200 monks and other Palestinians, locked themselves inside the Church. Only after the siege had lasted 39 days did it end after some of those inside had been shot by IDF snipers.

In 614 CE, the Church was threatened with destruction by the Persian army of Chosroes II. It is said that it escaped being destroyed due to a depiction inside of the three Magi in Persian clothing.

When the Crusaders conquered the Holy Land in 1099 CE, they established a force of 100 knights to protect the Church. During the Latin Kingdom of Jerusalem, the Crusaders made many additions and repairs to the building and, until 1131 CE, used it as the coronation church for the Crusader kings. They added mosaics to the building in addition to encaustic paintings of saints to its interior columns. Very faint vestiges of the columnar paintings can still be seen today.

Roof reconstruction and renovations took place in 1480 CE, only to have earthquakes and many aftershocks cause extensive damage to the Church between 1834 and 1836.

By 1846 the Church had been subjected to looting, and much of its marble floor was removed and used in other local buildings. In 1964 St. Jerome's Cave was connected to the Cave of the Nativity by a passage in order to give pilgrims better access to the subterranean sites.

Then in 2014, soon after the visit of Pope Francis to the Church, curtains in the Grotto caught fire, creating considerable damage.

Recently, the Church has been undergoing extensive repairs and renovations. After years of negotiations among the various Christian groups having authority over the Church, a massive restoration project was finally initiated in September of 2013. As a result, it is a Palestinian Presidential Committee that is overseeing the project with the restoration work being done by an Italian company, Piacenti S.p.A. The badly deteriorated roof has been repaired; new windows have been installed; and mosaics and other works of art have been restored.

It seems especially ironic that it is the predominantly Muslim Palestinians who found it possible to unite the various Christian communities in the restoration of the Church. They regard it as a major site attracting hordes of Christian pilgrims and also as one of their national treasures.

Not only has the Church of the Nativity felt the impact of centuries of neglect and the thousands of pilgrims visiting the site. In addition to the Church of the Nativity and the adjacent church dedicated to Saint Catherine, there are convents and churches of the Catholics, Greek Orthodox, Armenians, and Franciscans. There are also the bell towers, gardens, and the pilgrimage route.

The areas surrounding the sacred site are also lacking in any control over development and tourism. The volume of traffic, insufficient parking and the proliferation of many small businesses have created significant increases in air pollution affecting the façade of the Church as well as the exteriors of many buildings along the Pilgrimage Route.

Despite the 250-year-old agreement among the various Christian communities called the "Status Quo," the dissension among Christians continues. Four monastic communities occupy the area around the Church: the Greek Orthodox, Roman Catholic, Syriac Orthodox and Armenian Orthodox. Brawls among the monks of the various Christian groups occur with frequency over the areas where they have jurisdiction, and the Palestinian authorities have often had to be called to restore law and order.

As one example, during a recent holiday season, there was a well-publicized territorial dispute. When Greeks were dusting a chandelier, they happened to move their ladder into an Armenian controlled area, resulting in a major altercation.

Unfortunately, the words of the Christmas carol do not readily apply to today's Bethlehem.

If only the words of the song were true today:

"Oh little town of Bethlehem. How still we see thee lie…"

"Oh morning stars together, proclaim the Holy Birth. And praises sing to God the King, and peace to men on earth."

Adapted from:

https://en.wikipedia.org/wiki/Church_of_the_Nativity

http://whc.unesco.org/en/list/1433

https://www.smithsonianmag.com/travel/endangered-site-church-of-the-nativity-bethlehem-51647344/

"Finding Jesus," *National Geographic*, December 2017, p. 46

PERU

Country name: Republic of Peru (Spanish: República del Perú)

Site name: Nasca Lines; officially, the Nasca and Pampas de Jumana Lines and Geoglyphs

Location: Peru's arid coastal plain, 400 km south of Lima

UNESCO World Heritage Site: Inscribed 1994; no. 700

Date of Visit: 9-21 September 2007

WORLD'S LARGEST GEOGLYPHS: PERU'S ENIGMATIC NASCA LINES

Peru's Nasca Lines are the world's largest and most varied group of geoglyphs. They are unrivaled in size, quantity, and diversity and are the world's most studied. They also remain the most controversial. Why they were created, who created them, and what their intended meaning was, remain largely a mystery.

The geoglyph called the "Astronaut," with an arm
raised in greeting (seen in the inset)
at the site of the Nazca Lines, Peru

Covering 75,358 hectares and lying on one of Earth's driest deserts, the lines are located on a high, desolate, arid plateau stretching over 80 km (50 miles) between the towns of Palpa and Nasca on the Pampas de Jumana, 400 km (250 miles) south of Lima. The lines etched in the desert earth represent a wide variety of zoomorphic and anthropomorphic figures, geometric forms, and long, straight lines. While there are hundreds of geometric forms and straight lines, the most famous are the more than 70 zoomorphic designs, including depictions of birds, fish, jaguars, monkeys and llamas. In addition to a few anthropomorphic forms, there are also representations of flowers and trees.

New geoglyphs continue to be discovered, such as those found in August of 2014, July of 2015, and in the spring of 2016. In 2012, a Japanese team founded a research center to study the lines for the next 15 years and, as a result, some 100 new geoglyphs have been located.

Estimated to date from the eighth century BCE to the eighth century CE, the lines have survived for nearly two millennia. Covering almost 450 square km (170 square miles), some of the figures have been determined to measure almost 370m (1,200 feet) in size. Among the larger geoglyphs are: the hummingbird, measuring 93m (330 feet) in width; the condor, 134m (440 feet); the monkey, 93m (190 feet), and the spider, measuring 47m(150 feet).

Still in a remarkable state of preservation, the lines have been compared to contemporary, ancient artifacts. They have been divided into various periods such as the Middle and Late Formative (500 BCE - 200 CE) and the Regional Development Period (200 CE - 500 CE). They have also been divided into the Paracas phase (400 - 200 BCE) and the Nasca phase (2000 BCE - 500 CE).

How the lines were created by ancient people is easier to determine than their meaning. They are thought to have been laid out with little more than ropes, wooden stakes, and simple surveying equipment. They have been carved into the earth composed of reddish-brown iron oxide-covered pebbles of the desert to a depth of 10-15 centimeters (4-6 inches) to uncover the lime-rich, light-colored soil underneath. Because of the concentration of lime in the subsoil, it soon hardened, protecting the lines from weathering and wind erosion. As one of the driest places on Earth, the desert in which the lines are located has little rain and wind, helping to keep the lines visible.

The first mention of the lines was as early as 1553 by Pedro Cieze de León, who believed they were markings of trails. Visible from nearby hills, the lines were also mentioned by the local Peruvians and military personnel. Seeing the lines while hiking, the Peruvian archaeologist Toribio Mejíia Xesspe discussed them in a conference in 1939 in Lima.

The first archaeologist to subject the lines to serious study was Paul Kosok from Long Island University. Later, a German archaeologist and mathematician Maria Riche subjected the lines to further study and suggested that they had astronomical significance, such as marking the rise of the sun and certain constellations.

Archaeologists and other scholars continue to conjecture as to what the significance and meaning of the lines might be. Some believe that the ancient Nasca people drew the lines to be seen by deities residing in the heavens. Scholars such as Kosok and Riche have said they constitute a sort of astronomical observatory and that they facilitated tracing astronomical sightings as part of the religious cosmology of the ancient people. Riche also believed the figures represented constellations etched into the earth.

Others have asserted that the lines were created in the worship of various mountains and sources of water. They have suggested that the lines were used in the worship of deities associated with the availability of water. Some scholars believe that the geometric lines might have indicated lines of water sources and networks of irrigation systems. It has also been suggested that such figures as the plants, birds and the spider might represent fertility symbols. One scholar has proposed that the huge spider figure is a diagram of the constellation, Orion, and that three lines associated with the figure symbolize the three stars of Orion's belt.

Conjecture has also surrounded whether or not ancient people creating the lines might have developed some means of viewing them from the air. Although many of the lines are visible from surrounding hills and mountains, the use of hot air balloons by ancient peoples has been proposed.

The best that can be said is that controversy and conjecture over the meaning of the lines continues unabated.

The lines are presently protected under the National Constitution (article 36) and Law no. 28296 of the General Law for National Cultural Heritage. They have also been made the responsibility of the Peruvian government's Ministry of Culture. A management plan, the "System de Gestión para el Patrimonio Cultural y Natural del Territorio de Nasca y Palpa" has been formed and is being implemented. In addition, in 1994, the lines were designated a UNESCO site. The lines have also been included on the 2012 World Monuments Watch. In August of 2015, the U.S. Ambassadors Fund for Cultural Preservation set aside $150,000 for a campaign to protect the area from the effects of El Niño.

Despite all the preservation measures, threats to the lines continue. Little damage was done by mudslides in 2007, but in 2013, limestone quarry machinery obliterated a section of one line and damaged another. In 2012 and 2013, damage was reported as having been done outside the area of the lines by the Dakar Rally, an international, off-road race. The race was later banned in 2014.

In December of 2014 the most publicized damage to the lines was that done by Greenpeace activists They placed a banner reading "Time for Change! The Future is Renewable," inside the lines of one of the most notable of geoglyphs, the hummingbird. It is claimed that irrefutable damage was done around the area of the huge figure by rocks being ground into the soil and by those placing the banner not wearing the specialized shoes required to prevent damage to the lines. Although Greenpeace has since apologized, many have felt that the apology was insufficient. Only one activist was eventually fined and given a suspended sentence.

Even more recently, in February of 2018, the lines again came under attack. A truck driver named Jainer Jesús Flores Vigo intentionally drove his tractor/trailer off the Pan-American highway that runs through the protected site. Driving past signs that warned of the site's protected status, the driver left deep scars on an area measuring 100 by 300 feet and on three straight line geoglyphs. The driver was arrested and charged with attacking "cultural heritage," according to Peruvian sources.

Today, the Nasca Lines are among Peru's top tourist attractions. Although the South Pan-American Highway cuts directly across the area and there is a lookout tower nearby, most visitors to Peru choose to take one of the small, commercial, airline flights over the lines to view them to the best advantage. Fortunately, such a short flight over the lines was part of the tour I took to Peru in 2007. A small propeller-driven airplane seating only about 15 to 20 people was finally made available for us to take an all-too-short flight over the lines.

It was quite a wild ride, to say the least. The pilot obviously tried to impress us as being quite the daredevil and took us on a very low flight over one of the long, straight lines thought by some scholars to be ancient runways. On the other hand, he did an admirable job in allowing those of us on both sides of the plane to get good views of many of the most remarkable ancient lines.

With only seconds to see many of the gigantic figures, I was certain that the photographs I attempted to take out of the plane's small windows would be totally worthless. I was therefore amazed that I had managed to photograph recognizable views of many of the figures seen on the flight. Reworking the photos in PhotoShop revealed that I had captured much more detail in many of the geoglyphs than I had originally thought.

While the flight over the lines was of very short duration, it will always remain as one of my most memorable experiences and as one of the highlights of the trip to Peru.

Adapted from:

http://whc.unesco.org/en/list/700

http://www.iflscience.com/environment/greenpeace-irrevocably-damages-fragile-nazca-lines-peru-during-publicity-stunt/

https://www.wmf.org/project/lines-and-geoglyphs-nasca

https://en.wikipedia.org/wiki/Nazca_Lines

SPAIN

Country name: Kingdom of Spain (Spanish: Reino de España)

Site name: Works of Antioni Gaudí

Location: Barcelona and environs, Catalonia

UNESCO World Heritage Site: Inscribed 1984, extension, 2005; no. 320

Tour Dates: 1-9 January 2008

ANTONI GAUDÍ AND CATALAN MODERNISM

Antoni Gaudí i Cornet (25 June, 1852 – 10 June, 1926) created seven architectural masterworks in and around Barcelona inscribed in a group as a UNESCO World Heritage Site. But he is undoubtedly best known for his last work, the Sagrada Familia, which occupied his full attention from 1915 until his death in 1926.

Gaudí is rightfully called the grand master of the Catalan Modernism style. Often called "Modernista" and "Modernisme," the style had naturalistic and organic forms as its basic inspiration. Gaudí's early influences include the Gothic style as well as the Mudejar. Although unique in many ways, Gaudi's work is often viewed as being a synthesis of a number of other late nineteenth century and early twentieth century movements, including Arts and Crafts, Symbolism, Expressionism, and Rationalism. Gaudí is also seen by many architectural historians as changing the course of architecture and as creating a style that even today is regarded as highly innovative and unique, almost to the point of being surreal. Although often eclectic, his highly personal style is also seen in his designs of gardens, sculpture, and the decorative arts.

A graduate of the Escola Tècnica Superior d'Arquitectura in Barcelona, Gaudí proved to be only a mediocre student. When he was finally awarded the degree of architect in 1878, Elies Rogent is reputed to have said of him, "Who knows if we have given this diploma to a nut or to a genius. Time will tell."

Unfortunately, my very limited time spent in Barcelona allowed for my visiting only three of the works by Gaudí inscribed on the UNESCO list. While it was possible to visit the Sagrada Familia both as part of a guided tour as well as on my own, I could only view and photograph the exteriors of the Casa Batlló and the Casa Milà.

The seven works by Gaudí inscribed as UNESCO sites are the following:

Casa Vicens (construction started 1883)

This family home was commissioned in 1877 by Manuel Vicens i Montaner, an owner of a brick and tile factory in Barcelona. Often considered the first building constructed in the Art Nouveau style, it was Gaudí's first commission for a private home. Now a museum, it has received only basic restorations and conservation work.

Palau Güell (1886-1888)

Now a tourist and cultural monument, this work by Gaudí was also originally a family home. It was built very much in the tradition of a Catalonian city mansion and is notable for its main entrance in the form of a parabolic arch, its decoration in a Mudejar style, its spire in the form of a lantern tower, and its façade decorated with colorful tiles.

Parc Güell (construction started 1900)

As one of Gaudí's best known works, the Parc Güell is still used for its original purpose as an open space and public park. Today it is one of Barcelona's most popular tourist destinations. Gaudí's distinctive style is seen especially in the park's undulating benches covered in colorful tile mosaics.

Casa Batlló (1904-1906)

A pre-existing building, originally designed by Emili Sala Cortés, this building was extensively renovated by Gaudí in a commission by Josep Batlló i Casanovas. Keeping the original rectangular balconies, Gaudí redesigned them into curvilinear, mask-like forms and added the building's fifth floor. The façade was modified by the addition of warped surfaces in Montjuïc sandstone and with multicolored ceramic fragments.

Casa Milà (aka La Pedrera, meaning "The Quarry," 1906-1910)

Commissioned by Pere Milà I Camps, this massive structure is built around two curvilinear courtyards. Its famous, undulating façade was constructed of limestone from Vilafranca del Penedès. Consisting of five stories, it is especially notable for its highly sculptural chimneys covered in colorful tiles.

Colònia Güell, church crypt (construction started 1908)

Designed as a church for Colònia Gúell, an industrial village, this was the last project commissioned by Gaudí's patron, Eusebi Güell. Only the crypt of the church was built, as the project was abandoned after the death of Gaudí's patron. The church was designed as an oval with a central aisle and two aisles on each side. The structure displays the first use of parabolic vaults, while circular brick columns alternate with leaning basalt columns. Its stained glass windows are said to resemble butterfly wings and flower petals.

Sagrada Familia, Nativity façade and crypt (1915 - 1929)

This iconic Barcelona landmark is reputed to be Spain's most visited tourist site. Taking over the project from its original architect, Francisco de Paula, in 1883, Gaudí devoted himself exclusively to its construction starting in 1915. Considered Gaudí's *magnum opus*, it was only partially completed before his untimely death. He managed to oversee the construction of only the massive church's apse, crypt, and a portion of the Nativity façade.

The Sagrada Familia's crypt and apse had been completed in the Gothic style, but the remainder of Gaudí's work on the structure was in his much more organic style, in which the architect envisioned the building's interior as resembling a forest of branching tree-like forms.

The Modernista façade of the Casa Batlló
by Antoni Gaudí in Barcelona, Spain

Designed with a cruciform plan, the Sagrada Familia was planned as a structure with an apse having seven apses and a nave bordered by two side aisles on each side. When completed, it will have three façades dedicated to the Nativity, Passion and Glory of Christ. It will have eighteen towers. There will be four towers on each side, making twelve towers dedicated to the apostles. Four towers will be dedicated to the evangelists, while one on the apse will be dedicated to the Virgin. The central tower, planned to reach a height of 170m (560 feet), will be dedicated to Christ.

Construction on the grandiose structure continues to this day with completion predicted for 2026. When I visited the Sagrada Familia in 2008, the entire area was very much a construction zone, with a considerable part of the interior closed due to construction and with many cranes towering over the unfinished building.

While the façade of the Passion was completed by Josep Maria Subirachs, various other architects have taken over the building's construction since Gaudí's death. The primary architect in charge of the church's construction from 1987 until 2011 has been Jordi Bonet i Armengol.

Gaudí's inscribed works are protected by Spanish historical heritage laws. Overall responsibility for the administration and management of the inscribed properties is the responsibility of the Territorial Commission of the city of Barcelona and the Territorial Commission for the Cultural Heritage of Barcelona.

The death of Gaudí is especially sad and poignant. Taking his usual walk to the church of Sant Felip Neri on 7 June, 1926, he was struck by a streetcar. Dressed in shabby clothing and having no identification on him, he was thought by passersby to be a beggar and received no immediate medical attention. After finally being taken to a hospital, he received only minimal treatment. By the next day when he was finally recognized as being the famous architect, Gaudí's condition had worsened to the extent that he could no longer be saved. Dead at age 73, on

10 June, his funeral was attended by a massive crowd of mourners.

Today, Catalonia's most famous architect and designer lies buried in the crypt of the Sagrada Familia in the chapel of Our Lady of Mount Carmel.

Adapted from:

http://whc.unesco.org/en/list/320

https://en.wikipedia.org/wiki/List_of_Gaud%C3%AD_Buildings

https://www.nationalgeographic.com/travel/world-heritage/antoni-gaudi

http://en.wikipedia.org/wiki/Antoni_Gaudí

SPAIN

Country name: Kingdom of Spain (Spanish: Reino de España)

Site name: Cathedral, Alcázar and Archivo de Indias in Seville

Location: Province of Seville (Spanish; Sevilla), Autonomous Community of Andalusia

UNESCO World Heritage Site: Inscribed 1987, modified, 2010; no. 383

Tour Dates: 1-9 January 2008

SEVILLE'S CATHEDRAL, ALCÁZAR AND ARCHIVO DE INDIAS

Seville, known as Sevilla in Spanish, is Spain's fourth largest city and is the capital and largest city of the province of Sevilla and the autonomous region of Andalusia. The city's Old Town contains three UNESCO World Heritage Sites. Covering four square kilometers (two square miles), the area inscribed by UNESCO includes the Cathedral, the Alcázar, and the Achivo de Indias. Together the monumental group of buildings, often referred to as the Conjunto Monumental, represents Spain's Golden Age.

Founded as Hispalis in Roman times, the city became known as Ishbiliya after its conquest by Muslims in 712 CE and came under the control of the Caliphate of Córdoba. Sevilla was later ruled by the Muslim Almoravids and in 1248 CE became part of the Christian Kingdom of Castile under King Ferdinand III.

With the discovery of the New World, Sevilla became one of the primary centers of the Spanish Empire. As Spain's only river port, its harbor was only eighty kilometers (50 miles) upstream from the Atlantic Ocean. In 1514, it was from Sevilla that Ferdinand Magellan departed for his epic voyage around the world.

Cathedral

With its central nave and four side aisles, Sevilla's Cathedral is Europe's largest Gothic cathedral. Started in the fifteenth

The Giralda (bell tower) of the Cathedral of Seville, Spain

century, it was built over the site of the city's Almorhad Mezquita Mayor or main mosque.

The mosque's minaret, now known as the Giralda, has been preserved as the cathedral's bell tower. Topped with a Renaissance style cupola by Hernán Ruiz, the tower has become one of Spain's most famous and iconic structures.

On my first visit to Sevilla in the 1980s, I found it possible to climb up the broad, winding passageway leading to the top of the tower. Not being the usual spiral stairway, the wide ramp leading up the tower is said to have been constructed so the caliph could ride his horse to the tower's top. Not only was the view of the city from the tower's top impressive, but it was also possible to look down on the cathedral's massive stone vaults. There was also an outstanding view of the cathedral's adjacent courtyard, the Patio de Naranjos, planted with orange trees. Tickets are available for access to both the cathedral and the Giralda.

The massive cathedral also contains the monumental tomb of Christopher Columbus. Whether or not it actually contains any of the remains of the famous explorer is the subject of much dispute, especially since Santo Domingo in the Dominican Republic also has claims of having his remains.

Noteworthy are the cathedral's massive, golden altarpiece, its paintings by Bartolomé Esteban Murillo, and its elliptical Cabildo by Hernán Ruiz, considered to be an outstanding example of the Renaissance style.

Alcázar

Built in the tenth century, the Alcázar was the Muslim governor's palace that later became the Spanish royal family's residence. Originally built as the palace of the Muslim Almohads, it includes various palatial structures, baths, courtyards such as the Patio del Yeso, and large gardens such as the Jardines del Crucero. The complex was built in a wide variety of architectural styles such as Neoclassical and

Renaissance, as well as the Mudejar style as seen in the Palacio de Pedro I.

Archivo General de Indias

Constructed in 1585, the Casa Lonja or the consulate of the Merchants of Seville (Consulado de Mercaderes de Sevilla), became the Archivo General de Indias in 1786. Designed by the same illustrious architect who completed the El Escorial, Juan de Herrera, it is a prime example of Spanish Renaissance architecture. It is reputed to have had much influence on Spanish Andalusian, Neoclassical, and Baroque architecture. Today, it houses 40,000 historical maps and other documents relating to the discovery and exploration of the New World, spanning three centuries, and is renowned as an extraordinary resource collection.

Sevilla's monuments have been declared Properties of Cultural Interest in addition to their UNESCO World Heritage citation. Although there are no ongoing plans for their preservation, consideration is being given to expanding their buffer zone. Cited for possible inclusion are the San Telmo palace and the Atarazanas or shipyard.

The greatest threat to Sevilla's ancient monuments is the construction of a nearly 600-foot-high skyscraper in the midst of its historic buildings. Planned to reach forty stories and a height of 178m (580 feet), it has been designed by the Argentine-American architect, César Pelli. Twelve of its stories have already been built, and so far, all requests to keep the tower at a lower height have been ignored. Built across the Guadalquivir River from Sevilla's historic sites and on the location of the Expo site of 1992, the tower is seen as having a serious impact on Sevilla's three UNESCO inscribed monuments as well as on the nearby riverside Tower of Gold, dating from the twelfth century. Unless the tower's height is lowered, Sevilla's monuments may be listed as endangered by UNESCO or they may lose their World Heritage status.

Sevilla was visited on two separate occasions, in the 1980s as well as on the tour in 2008, and I have found that Sevilla always continues to fascinate.

Adapted from:

http://whc.unesco.org/en/list/383

https://www.theguardian.com/world/2012/jan/20/seville-unesco-heritage-pelli-tower

https://en.wikipedia.org/wiki/Seville

http://www.andalucia.com/travel/world-heritage/seville.htm

SRI LANKA

Country name: Democratic Socialist Republic of Sri Lanka
(known as Ceylon prior to 1972)

Site name: Kandy

Location: Central province of Sri Lanka

UNESCO World Heritage Site: Inscribed 1988; no. 450

Date of Visit: 20-21 October 2010

SRI LANKA'S SACRED CITY OF KANDY

Kandy is the second largest city in the island nation of Sri Lanka after its capital, Colombo. Being smaller in size and having a cooler climate, Kandy is often seen as being the more pleasant and accessible of the two cities. Located in a mountainous area in the center of the island, it is one of the country's eight UNESCO World Heritage Sites. It is regarded as the nation's cultural capital and as possessing some of its most sacred sites. It has a compact central city area surrounded by scenic hills and mountains covered with forests.

The island of Sri Lanka is located in the Indian Ocean and southwest of the Bay of Bengal. It is situated 21 km (19.3 miles) to the southeast of the Indian subcontinent. The present name, Sri Lanka, is derived from the Sanskrit, with "sri" meaning "venerable" and "lanka" meaning "land." It was the Portuguese who gave the island its name of Ceilão, and the island was known as Ceylon while a British colony. In 1948, after independence, it became known as the Dominion of Ceylon until the name was changed to Sri Lanka in 1972.

When the Portuguese arrived in 1505, the island possessed three main kingdoms: Kotte, along the west coast; Yarlpanam, in the north; and Kandy, in the central mountainous region. It was the Kingdom of Kandy in the more remote central region that remained independent until the arrival of the British.

Although much of the island came under the control of Europeans, the interior mountainous region remained largely independent with its capital in Kandy. Known as the sacred

244

Walkway to the entrance of the Temple of
the Sacred Tooth, Kandy, Sri Lanka

Buddhist city of Senkadagalapura, it was the last capital of the kings of Sinhala. Until the arrival of the British, it was the center of the flourishing Dinahala culture. In 1796, the British East India Company took control of the island. In 1802 it was designated a crown colony, but it was not until 1815, with the fall of the Kingdom of Kandy, that the island was unified under the British rule.

Located on the north shore of a lake bordered by white stone parapets is the complex known as the Dalada Maligawa which contains the royal palace and the Temple of the Tooth Relic. Sitting on a granite base said to be inspired by Anuradhapura, Sri Lanka's former capital, the complex of buildings was, in large part, reconstructed in the eighteenth century. Since then the Temple has suffered numerous terrorist bombings but has always been fully restored.

The Temple of the Tooth Relic is one of the country's most sacred places and is a major pilgrimage site. Since it is believed that whoever possesses the sacred tooth of the Buddha is the one who rules the country, special care is taken in protecting it.

At the inner chamber of the Temple, monks conduct daily rituals three times each day: at dawn, noon, and in the evening. In an annual rotation, the rituals are conducted by the two chapters of Malwatte and Asgiriya monks. A symbolic ritual involving the bathing of the sacred relic occurs on Wednesdays. During the rite, a preparation of a fragrant flower called Nanumura Mangallaya and scented water are poured over the relic. Thought to have healing powers, the water is also distributed to worshippers.

On the day of our visit to the Temple, scores of worshippers carrying large lotus blossoms as votive offerings were flocking to the temple complex on the long walkway leading to the temple. We were especially privileged to attend the noon ritual inside the Temple that included a loud, raucous session of drumming. At a long shed-like structure adjacent to the main temple, a large group of worshippers were also seen burning candles. The burning candles were so numerous that their smoke almost obscured the entire scene.

Located approximately 5 km to the west of the city center at Peradeniya is the Royal Botanical Garden. Covering 59 hectares (147 acres), the garden contains more than 4,000 different plant species. On the day of our visit, many local visitors as well as sizable school groups were seen visiting the park. Up to two million people are said to visit the gardens every year. In size, scope, and the beauty of its carefully manicured areas, the gardens were among the best I had ever seen.

In addition to the National Museum of Kandy located in the Royal Palace, there were many other sites in Kandy that it was not possible to visit. Among sites not visited were the Dankatilaka Temple, one of the finest examples of traditional Sihalese temple architecture, the Gadaladeniya Temple, with its South India design, and the Royal Palace Park, also known as the Wace Park.

While both Colombo and Kandy felt more westernized and less exotic than many of the ancient, historic sites elsewhere visited while on the trip, both cities contain sites that must be seen on any trip to Sri Lanka.

We were fortunate to have a most accommodating local guide and driver who was always very agreeable to taking us to see numerous sites that were not always on our tour itinerary. His professional services went far in making the trip to Sri Lanka one of our best trips ever.

Adapted from:

https://wikitravel.org/en/Kandy
http://whc.unesco.org/en/list/450
https://en.wikipedia.org/wiki/
World_Heritage_Sites_of_Sri_Lanka
https://en.wikipedia.org/wiki/Kandy

SRI LANKA

Country Name: Democratic Socialist Republic of Sri Lanka
  (formerly Ceylon)

Site: Polonnaruwa (also called Pulattipura; Tamil:
Polannaruvai or Pulatti nakaram)

Location: Polonnaruwa District in the North Central Province,
  Sri Lanka

UNESCO World Heritage Site: Inscribed 1982; no. 201

Date of Visit: 19 October 2010

SRI LANKA'S ANCIENT CITY OF POLONNARUWA

Polonnaruwa is part of Sri Lanka's "cultural triangle" that also includes the country's first capital, Anuradhapura, and the hill capital of Kandy. Also included are the fortress of Sigiriya, Minhintale, and the cave temples of Dambula.

In 1070 CE, King Vijayabahu I proclaimed Polonnaruwa his new capital. He had defeated the invading Cholas who had destroyed Sri Lanka's first capital, Anuradhapura, in 993 CE. For the second time in its history, Sri Lanka was united under a local ruler.

The golden age of Polonnaruwa came later in the twelfth century under King Parakramabahu I. He is credited with developing the city's extensive irrigation system. One of his most notable creations was the Parakrama Samudra, the country's largest man-made, rainwater reservoir. Measuring 2,500 hectares, the huge lake survives as a major source of water in the region and continues to support the area's agriculture.

Except for Parakramabahu's successor, Nissankamalla I, later kings were primarily concerned with infighting and securing their positions through intermarriages with other members of the local royalty. Then from 1215-1624 CE, the Jaffna kingdom came into power with the invasion in 1241 CE of King Kalinga Magha of the Aryacakravarti dynasty. The capital was moved to

The reclining image of the Buddha
at the Gal Vihara, Polonnaruwa, Sri Lanka

Dambadeniya, and during the brief Pandya period, Polonnaruwa became known as Jananathamangalam.

One of Polonnaruwa's most notable sculptures is located on the eastern bank of the Parakrama Smudra reservoir and about 100 meters (330 feet) from the Potgul Vihara. It is a statue of a standing figure holding a manuscript in its arms. Sometimes identified with King Parakramabahu I, it is also thought that the bearded figure holding a palm-leaf manuscript might represent the sage, Pulasti.

Located in the northern section of the vast archaeological site is the Gal Vihara, meaning "stone shrine." It is also sometimes referred to as the Kalugal Vihara or the Black Stone Shrine. At the site are four colossal, rock-cut Buddhist images. Reputed to have been constructed in the twelfth century by King Parakramabahu I, the four images were carved out of the face of a large outcropping of granite.

The images are said to be part of Parakramabahu I's northern monastery. On the rock face between the rock-cut cave and the image of the standing Buddha is one of ancient Sri Lanka's longest inscriptions. In it, Parakramabahu describes his reforming of the Buddhist religion and outlines a new ethical code for monks.

Two of the colossal figures carved out of the cliff face are images of the Buddha seated in the lotus or meditative pose of *dhyani mudra*. The larger image, measuring 4.6m (15 feet) in height, sits under an arch. Smaller images of the Buddha look down from celestial temples, possibly evidencing Mahayana Buddhist influence, while niches containing lions and the crossed symbols of the *vajra* may evidence Tantric symbolism.

The smaller, seated image of the Buddha, also in *dhyani mudra*, measuring 1.2m in height (4 feet), now sits in a carved recess closed off by a metal grille.

The most famous image at the Gal Vihara is the reclining Buddha, measuring 14m. in length (46 feet), depicting the *parinirvana* of the Buddha. It is one of Sri Lanka's most iconic images and is among the largest images in all of Southeast Asia. Especially notable is the way that the Buddha's head makes a subtle depression on the pillow that has been placed under his head. Lotus blossoms decorate both the end of the pillow and the soles of the feet of the image.

The standing image, measuring nearly 7m in height (23 feet), is the most enigmatic of the four figures. Many scholars maintain that it is not an image of the Buddha at all. With arms crossed across his chest, a highly unusual gesture for an image of the Buddha, it may be an image of Ananda, a disciple of the Buddha, whose sad expression depicts grief at the *parinirvana* or death of the Buddha. Other scholars have discredited the theory and maintain that it is an image of the Buddha, since other Buddha images have been found in a similar pose.

All four images of the Buddha have been admired for the artful way in which the natural strata of the rock has been used to such a great advantage in the carving of the images.

The images at the Gal Vihara are counted as being among Sri Lanka's most photographed and are considered among the supreme masterworks of the ancient Sinhalese stone carvers.

It should also be mentioned that Polonnaruwa was one of Sri Lanka's sites with a large monkey population. For the most part, the toque macaques ignored visitors to the site, although it was obvious that some of them were expecting handouts.

Recently, Polonnaruwa has been undergoing a development project supported by President Maithripala Sirisena. In 1982, the city, considered to be one of Sri Lanka's most scenic ancient sites, became the location for the filming of the music video of Duran Duran's "Save a Prayer."

I strongly recommend visiting Polonnaruwa along with the other sites of the "cultural triangle" when visiting the island nation of Sri Lanka.

Adapted from:

https://en.wikipedia.org/wiki/Gal_Vihara
http://whc.unesco.org/en/list/201
http://www.buddhanet.net/sacred-island/gal-vihara.html
https://lanka.com/about/attractions/gal-vihara-polonnaruwa/

THAILAND

Country name: Kingdom of Thailand (formerly Siam)

Site name: Historic City of Ayutthaya (full name: Phra Nakhon Si Ayutthaya)

Location: Phra Nakhon Si Ayutthaya Province, 85 km north of Bangkok

UNESCO World Heritage Site: Inscribed 1991; no. 576

Date of Visit: 28 March 2000

ANCIENT THAILAND'S SECOND CAPITAL CITY: AYUTTHAYA

Founded in 1351 CE by Ramathibodi I, Ayutthaya was ancient Thailand's second capital city, while Sukhothai is recognized as its first. Located in Thailand's central plains, the city remains the capital city of the province with the same name. Ayutthaya's location at the confluence of three rivers, the Chao Phraya, the Lopburi, and the Pa Sak, gives the city its access to the sea and the Gulf of Siam.

At its height, Ayutthaya was once one of the world's largest cities, with what is believed to have been one million residents. The city was a center of trade and commerce extending even to European countries such as France, Mughal India, and the Far Eastern countries of China and Japan. Within the city, there were foreign traders, giving rise to a cosmopolitan culture as evidenced in much of the city's art and architecture.

The Burmese first invaded Ayutthaya in 1569 and then nearly burned it to the ground in 1767. Thirty-five different kings are reputed to have ruled over the once-great city. Now an archaeological ruin, there are still remains of its many reliquary towers or *prangs* and its immense Buddhist monasteries.

With the inscribed area covering 289 hectares, only certain parts of the Ayutthaya Historical Park have been designated a UNESCO World Heritage Site. First designated a historical park in 1976, Ayutthaya received its World Heritage status in 1991.

View of one of the ruined temples at
Thailand's ancient capital city of Ayutthaya

Currently only the monuments on Ayutthaya Island are included, so extending the inscribed area to cover the entirety of the ancient city is under consideration.

Although in ruins, the city's layout can still be seen in its systematic grid plan of moats, canals, and roads, around which were arranged its primary buildings. Siting in the midst of three rivers, the city also had a sophisticated system of hydraulic engineering which was unique and advanced for its time.

When the capital was moved to Bangkok, much of Ayutthaya's city layout and architecture were used as models for the new capital. Craftsmen and architects were brought from Ayutthaya to work at the new capital. The name "Ayutthaya" is even said to have been retained as part of the official name of Bangkok.

Included in the UNESCO citation are such temples as Wiharn Phra Mongkhon Bopit, Wat Phra Ram, Wat Mahathat, and Wat Ratchaburana. Khmer influence emanating from Angkor is said to be seen in such temples as Wat Maha That, Wat Phra Ram, and Wat Phutthai Sawan. Following the plans of Khmer temples, they have central towers surrounded by four smaller towers which are, in turn, enclosed by galleries and courtyards. At times their galleries are interrupted by such monastic structures as assembly and ordination halls.

Many of Ayutthaya's more important monuments have been repaired, and some have been reconstructed. Ayutthaya is protected under Thailand's Act on Ancient Monuments, Antiques, Objects of Art and National Museums. It also receives the protection of the Fine Arts Ministry of Culture, the Enhancement and Conservation of National Environmental Quality Act of 1992, and the Building Control Act of 1979. The development and conservation of the ancient city receives funds from both Thailand's government as well as from private sources.

Today, Ayutthaya remains a very popular tourist destination. Even in its ruinous state, its ancient remains evoke the grandeur of the once-great city. The vestiges of the images of the Buddha clad in modern, yellow silk robes proclaim that the ancient Theravada Buddhist beliefs retain their validity even in today's Thailand.

With its proximity to Bangkok, Ayutthaya is an easy day trip from Thailand's present capital city. A boat trip from Ayutthaya back down to Bangkok via the Chao Phraya River was an especially enjoyable experience on one of my several trips to Thailand.

Adapted from:

http://whc.unesco.org/en/list/576

https://en.wikipedia.org/wiki/Ayutthaya_Historical_Park

http://www.ayutthaya-history.com/Temples_Ruins_MahaThat.html

THAILAND

Country name: Kingdom of Thailand (formerly Siam)
Site name: Historic Town of Sukhothai and Associated Towns
Location: Sukhothai Province, Lower Northern Thailand
UNESCO World Heritage Site: Inscribed 1991; no. 574
Date of Visit: 30 March 2000

ANCIENT THAILAND'S FIRST CAPITAL CITY: SUKHOTHAI

Sukhothai, meaning "the happiness of Thai," or "dawn of happiness," is regarded as Thailand's first capital city. Flourishing in the thirteenth and fourteenth centuries CE, it is regarded as the cradle of Thailand as a nation and as a distinct culture. Located in northern Thailand, the ancient city site of Sukhothai is located near the present-day city of the same name. Within an area measuring 1.6 km by 2 km, the ancient, ruined city is reputed to have one hundred and ninety-three monuments within a space of seventy square kilometers. In addition to a royal palace, the city is known to have had twenty-six temples, the largest of which was the Wat Mahathat.

Before the thirteenth century, there were numerous Thai kingdoms. As early as 1180, Sukhothai began to exert its own autonomy during the reign of Pho Khun Sri Naw Namthom. In about 1180, it was conquered by the Mons. In 1289, Sukhothai was taken back from the Mons by two brothers, Pho Khun Bangklanghao and Pho Khun Pharmeung. The Sukhothai kingdom was expanded under Pho Khun Ban Muang and Ram Khambaeng, and it was under the latter king that Theravada Buddhism was spread throughout the land and that the Thai system of writing was developed. It is King Ram Khambaeng who is highly regarded as the founding father of the Thai nation.

In 1378 Ayutthaya invaded Sukhothai and forced King Thammaracaha II to submit to its authority. After the battle of 1583 at the Sittaung River, the people of Sukhothai were forced to relocate to Thailand's central plain as a result of an earthquake and war with the Burmese. After only one hundred and twenty years, in 1365 Sukhothai was reduced to a vassal state of Ayutthaya which was on the rise to the south.

Although the city now remains only in ruins, there are many vestiges of canals, lakes, moats, palaces, temples, and gateways. The UNESCO inscribed area includes 11,852 hectares and, in addition to Sukothai, includes the cities of Si Satchanalai and Kamphaeng Phet. Sukothai functioned as the kingdom's administrative capital, while Si Satchanalai was its spiritual center. The three cities were united by a main highway known as the Thanon Phra Ruang, named after the king who commissioned it. United by language and its administrative system, the three cities functioned as a single kingdom.

Wat Mahathat, meaning "temple of the great relic," is Sukothai's most important temple. Founded by King Sri Indraditya, the great temple was built in 1345 to contain relics of the Buddha. The central stupa is in the form of a lotus bud, while the temple base is decorated with 168 sculptures in stucco. In addition to assembly and ordination halls, the temple has 200 smaller stupas surrounding its central stupa, radiating out in eight directions. Also, on either side of the central stupa are images of the Buddha measuring nine meters in height.

The city's royal palace, the None Prasat or Palace Hill, was discovered in 1833. It sits on a base measuring 200m square. Found within the palace is the Manangasila Throne, a gray stone slab measuring 1m by 2.5m by 15 cm and decorated with petals of the lotus.

One of the city's oldest temples is the Wat Si Sawai. Originally built as a Hindu temple dedicated to Vishnu, the temple has three stupas or *prangs* dedicated to the Hindu trinity. The temple was later dedicated to Buddhism in the fourteenth century.

The largest temple within the city is the Wat Phra Phan Luang. Built in the late twelfth century, it functioned as the city's ritual center.

View of the ruined temples of Thailand's
ancient capital city of Sukhothai

Also within the historical park is a branch of Thailand's National Museum, the Ramkhamhaeng National Museum, which opened in 1964. Starting with a collection of more than two thousand objects donated by the abbot of the Ratchathani Temple, the museum's collection has been augmented by *objets d'art* from other local temples.

The historic town of Sukhothai and the two other historic city parks are managed by the Fine Arts Department of the Ministry of Culture. The sites are protected by the Act on Ancient Monuments, Antiques, Objects of Art and National Museums of 1961. In addition, they are recognized as protected areas under the Ratchaphasadu Land Act of 1975, the Building Control Act of 1979, and the Enhancement and Conservation of National Environmental Quality Act of 1992. Funds for the conservation of the historic areas come from both private and government sources. Attention is also being paid to the protection of Sukhothai's historic landscapes and to the maintenance of ancient roads, canals, dams, and dikes which are still in use today.

The kingdom of Sukhothai is regarded as Thailand's golden age and as a time for the codification of the Thai language, literature, religion, and law, resulting in Thailand becoming a distinct nation in its own right.

Today, Sukhothai is among Thailand's most-visited ancient sites. Its park-like setting makes it one of Thailand's most picturesque archaeological sites, with its ancient ruins spread out over grassy areas and among scenic ponds.

Adapted from:

http://whc.unesco.org/en/list/574
https://en.wikipedia.org/wiki/Sukhothai_Historical_Park

TUNISIA

Country name: Republic of Tunisia (French: Tunisie)

Site name: Amphitheater

Location: El Jem (aka El Djem), Mahdia Governorate, Tunisia

UNESCO World Heritage Site: Inscribed 1979; no. 38

Date of Visit: 18 May 2009

NORTH AFRICA'S LARGEST ROMAN AMPHITHEATER AT EL JEM

Two hundred and thirty ancient Roman amphitheaters are reputed to have survived from Antiquity, and one of the largest and best-preserved is not to be found in Italy or any other part of present-day Europe. The size of the amphitheater at El Jem in Tunisia is reputed to be surpassed only by the Colosseum in Rome and by the amphitheater of Capua.

Although it has sometimes been referred to as a "colosseum," that term should only properly be applied to the amphitheater in Rome, since that term, in Latin, refers to the gargantuan amphitheater which was located next to a colossal statue of the emperor Nero in Rome.

Dating from the year 238 CE, the amphitheater, reputed to have held 35,000 spectators, is located in North Africa in what is today the small Tunisian village of El Jem. Also spelled El Djem, the village sits on a plain in central Tunisia in the Mahdia Governorate of Tunisia. In Roman times, the huge amphitheater was located in what was known as the Roman city of Thysdrus located in the Roman province of Bycanena. As with many other Roman cities, it is thought that the ancient Roman city was rebuilt over an earlier Punic settlement. Especially in the second century CE, the city was an important olive oil manufacturing center. Later it became the seat of a Roman Catholic bishopric.

At the time of the amphitheater's construction, the Roman city of Thysdrus was the second most important city after Carthage and rivaled Hadrumetum, modern Sousse. The construction of the amphitheater, starting in 238 CE, was at an inauspicious time, with that year being known as the "Year of Six Emperors" when six rulers were being recognized as emperors of Rome. It is thought that the amphitheater was constructed by the proconsul Gordian I or possibly by his grandson, Gordian III. It was in 238 CE that an uprising in North Africa made the 80-year-old Gordian I the Roman emperor. Constructed at a time of such political turmoil, it is thought by many that the amphitheater may never have been fully completed. After an unsuccessful revolt and the suicide of Gordian I, soldiers loyal to the emperor, Maximinus Thrax, destroyed the city of Thysdrus.

El Jem's amphitheater is thought to have been constructed primarily for gladiatorial performances and chariot races. It was constructed entirely of stone and was entirely freestanding. It was also built without foundations. While it was modeled on the Colosseum in Rome, it was not an exact copy.

As one of the world's largest amphitheaters, its largest axis measures 148m, while its smaller axis measures 122m. Its façade is constructed in three levels and of arcades in the Corinthian style. Especially remarkable is its interior, which remains largely intact. It retains most of its tiers of seats, its podium wall, and many of its underground passageways.

Until the seventeenth century, the great amphitheater remained largely intact, but then its stones began to be used for construction in the nearby village of El Jem. Its stones were also carried off for the construction of the Great Mosque of Kairouan. Later, the Ottomans used canon fire to flush out rebels hiding inside the great amphitheater. In the medieval period, it was used as a fortress and as a place where saltpeter was manufactured. During the eighteenth and nineteenth centuries, it was used to house shops and domestic dwellings and to store grain.

Finally, in 1979 the amphitheater was inscribed as a UNESCO World Heritage Site. More recently it has been used as a site for the filming of such movies as Monty Python's "Life of

View of the interior of the ancient, Roman
amphitheater at El Jem, Tunisia

Brian" and "Gladiator." It has also been used to host the yearly "Festival international de mystique symphonique d'El Jem."

Today, the amphitheater is covered under Law 35-1994, which protects archaeological and other historic sites, and is managed by the National Heritage Institute. Measures are also being taken to create a buffer zone around the amphitheater to protect it against encroachment by contemporary urban development.

Archaeological research in the area of ancient Thysdrus has revealed floor mosaics. Also, aerial photographs have revealed what is believed to be a large, ancient racetrack, but little field archaeology has been conducted in the area.

Few sports fans realize that when they are watching a televised super bowl game, the stadium in which the game is being played has, as its prototype, the ancient form of an amphitheater, an architectural form perfected in large part over 2,000 years ago by ancient Roman builders.

Adapted from:

http://whc.unesco.org/en/list/38

https://en.wikipedia.org/wiki/El_Djem

https://en.wikipedia.org/wiki/Amphitheatre_of_El_Jem

http://www.ancient-origins.net/ancient-places-africa/amphitheatre-el-djem-gladiatorial-arena-tunisia-003321

TUNISIA

Country name: Tunisian Republic (French: Tunisie)
Site name: Kairouan (aka al-Qayrawan)
Location: Kairouan Governorate, Tunisia
UNESCO World Heritage Site: Inscribed 1988; no. 499
Date of Visit: 19 May 2009

TUNISIA'S SACRED CITY: KAIROUAN

Kairouan is regarded as one of Islam's spiritual centers and one of its most sacred cities. Despite a move of the capital of Tunisia to Tunis in the twelfth century, Kairouan, founded by the Umayyads in 670 CE, is still regarded today as the Maghreb's major sacred city. Located on a plain nearly equidistant between the sea and mountains, the city was inscribed as a UNESCO World Heritage Site in 1988. Especially during the reign of Caliph Mu'awiya from 661 to 680 CE, Kairouan became a center of Sunni learning and scholarship.

The city's Great Mosque is among the earliest Islamic places of worship, having been built only thirty-eight years after the Prophet Muhammad's death. Also, the city's Sawiya of Sidi Sahab is said to be the site of the remains of Abu Djama, a companion of the Prophet.

A variety of ancient structures and old city areas are included in the UNESCO-designated areas of Kairouan, but it is primarily the Great Mosque, also known as the Great Mosque of Sidi-Uqba, that is widely regarded as the masterpiece of early Islamic architecture. Founded by the Arab general, Uqba ibn Nafi in 670 CE (50 AH according to the Islamic calendar), most of what is seen today is said to date from the nineth century. Not only important for its very early date, the mosque, measuring 9,000 square meters in area, is widely regarded as being the prototype for most of the later mosques built in North Africa and in Andalusia.

The mosque, with its fortress-like exterior, possesses nine gates: six opening to the courtyard, two opening to the prayer

View of the courtyard and minaret of the
Great Mosque of Kairouan, Tunisia

hall, and one opening to the *maqsura*. Forming a quadrilateral measuring 135ms by 80m, the mosque possesses a massive courtyard of flagstone, with interior dimensions of 57 by 52m, bordered by arcades on all four sides. On the courtyard's shorter north side stands the mosque's three-story minaret.

Located in the massive courtyard is an intricately carved drain or "impluvium" carrying rainwater to a cistern below. The courtyard's white marble sundial, bearing an inscription in *naskhi* script dating it to 1843 (1258 AH), can be viewed by climbing up a small stairway located to one side.

Towering over the courtyard is the great minaret, measuring 31.5m in height. With a base dating from 724-728 CE, the minaret dates primarily from 836 CE. Inside, the minaret contains one hundred and twenty-nine steps arranged around a central column. It is regarded as the world's earliest minaret and the oldest one still surviving.

Unfortunately, the mosque's prayer hall was closed to non-Muslims, but on the day of my visit, two of the ornately carved, wooden doors had been opened so I could peer into the hall's dimly-lit interior. The great hall possesses seventeen aisles of eight bays and 414 columns. The columns and their capitals of granite, marble, and porphyry have been taken from earlier structures for the most part. Many were taken from the ruins of ancient Carthage. As a result, they display a wide variety of styles, including the late Roman, early Christian and Byzantine. The number of columns in the mosque has been considered to be so large that a legend claims that a person would go blind if attempting to count them all.

In the center of the *qibla* wall, is the *mihrab*, or niche pointing the direction toward Mecca, and dating from 862-863 CE.. The *mihrab* is considered one of Islam's most beautiful, with its tile work glazed in iridescent colors, thought to possibly be the work of Baghdad artisans.

The *minbar*, or pulpit, sitting to one side of the *mihrab*, is said to be the world's oldest. Dating from 862 CE, the pulpit possesses eleven steps and measures 3.31m in height. More than three hundred carved wooden panels decorate the *minbar's* exterior.

Among the other sites visited while at Kairouan were the Aghlabid basins, two massive water reservoirs. Dating from the ninth century, the two interconnected basins constitute a hydraulic group that provided water to the city.

The Mausoleum of Sidi Sahib, commonly called the Mosque of the Barber, was also visited. The present building, actually a *zaouia*, is located outside the city and is reputed to date primarily from the seventeenth century. The site immortalizes Abu Zama' al-Balaui, a companion of the Prophet, who is said to have acquired three hairs of the Prophet's beard. The very elaborate and colorful ceramic tiles and stucco work on the courtyard walls were especially impressive.

Only a brief stop was made at the *souk* or marketplace located within the *medina* or old city center of Kairouan. It was also possible to see a section of the old city wall and its ramparts, measuring three kilometers in length.

Among the sites not visited was the Mosque of Three Gates. Named for the three arched doorways on its façade, it was built in 866 CE. Decorating the doorways are verses from the Quran in the Kufic script as well as decorative reliefs and friezes. The Mosque of Ansar, dating from 1650, and the Mosque Al Bey, dating from the late seventeenth century, were also not visited.

In addition to the UNESCO citation, the historic districts of Kairouan are today covered by Law 35 of 1994, providing for the preservation of the city's archaeological heritage and its traditional arts and crafts. Management of the city's ancient heritage is the responsibility of the National Heritage Institute.

For many years and dating back to when I was an art history student, I had known of the great importance of Kairouan's Great Mosque. Finally being able to see it firsthand was one of the highlights of the trip to Tunisia. I also found it remarkable that such an important early Islamic masterwork had remained in such a fine state of preservation after so many centuries.

Adapted from:

http://www.sacred-destinations.com/tunisia/kairouan-great-mosque

http://whc.unesco.org/en/list/499

https://en.wikipedia.org/wiki/Kairouan

https://en.wikipedia.org/wiki/Great_Mosque_of_Kairouan

https://www.khanacademy.org/humanities/art-islam/islamic-art-early/a/the-great-mosque-of-kairouan

http://www.discoverislamicart.org/database_item.php?id=monument;isl;tn;mon01;2;en

TURKEY

Country name: Republic of Turkey (Turkish: Türkiye)

Site name: Aphrodisias

Location: Near the village of Geyre, upper valley of the Morsynus River, southwest coast of Turkey

UNESCO World Heritage Site: Inscribed 2017; no. 1519

Date of Visit: 15 November 2011

DEDICATED TO THE GODDESS OF LOVE: APHRODISIAS

Aphrodisias has been called one of the finest archaeological sites in Asia Minor. It is cited for its remarkable preservation and for its somewhat remote location, making it less crowded than the highly popular site of Ephesus.

As early as 5800 BCE, the Neolithic site of Aphrodisias was known as the center of a local female fertility deity or Mother Goddess cult. The site eventually became associated with the Greek goddess of love, Aphrodite, and was given the name of Aphrodisias. Remaining as only a local shrine for centuries, it flourished and developed into a prosperous artistic and cultural center after Mithridates was defeated by the Romans in 74 BCE. Especially during the Hellenistic and Roman periods, it became wealthy and world-famous for the very fine marble extracted from its nearby quarry. Its marble is said to have been the source for marble throughout the Roman world, including Hadrian's villa at Tivoli. After becoming the seat of a Christian bishopric during the Byzantine era, Aphrodisias was largely abandoned in the early ninth century CE.

Temple of Aphrodite

Completed in the first century CE, the temple was built entirely of marble and dedicated to the goddess of love, Aphrodite, known to the Romans as Venus. It functioned as the central element around which the ancient city was built. Fourteen columns of the ancient temple have been re-erected.

Gateway of the ancient, Roman Temple of
Aphrodite at Aphrodisias, Turkey

The temple was later converted into a Christian church during the Byzantine era by dismantling walls and columns to enlarge and modify the building. Stabilization of the columns and the replacement of corroded iron bands with stainless steel was accomplished in 2004 by the Kress Foundation European Preservation Program of the World Monuments Fund.

Bouleuterion (Council House)

Located in the center of the ancient city and on the north side of the northern agora, this structure resembles a small theater with nine rows of marble seats facing a stage with a multi-story colonnade which was filled with statues of deities and local dignitaries. In 2003, the World Monuments Fund undertook a major conservation project at the Bouleuterion that succeeded in not only stabilizing the structure but also in developing conservation techniques that could be applied to other structures at Aphrodisias.

Tetraphlon

Built in the second century CE, this monumental gateway leading to the Temple of Aphrodite is one of the finest ancient remains of Aphrodisias. It leads from the city's major north-south street to a large plaza in front of the temple. It is estimated that 85% of the original gateway has survived, and, as a result of its reconstruction completed in 1991, it is one of most impressive sights of Aphrodisias.

Hadrianic Baths

Dedicated to the emperor Hadrian and built in the early second century CE, the bath complex was composed of a colonnaded forecourt flanked by various barrel-vaulted bathing rooms. Built of limestone and covered with a veneer of marble, the massive structure was decorated with many sculptures enclosed in niches. Still visible are the remains of the *hypocaust*, the heating system built beneath the floors of the elaborate bathhouse. Despite its relatively good condition, it has not received the repair and reconstruction it deserves.

Stadium

Regarded as one of the best-preserved of ancient stadiums, that at Aphrodisias measures 270m (890 feet) by 60m (200 feet). It has a track measuring 225m (738 feet) by 30m (98 feet) and has thirty rows of seats on each side. It is thought to have been capable of accommodating up to 30,000 spectators.

Theater

Completed in 27 BCE, the theater was modified in 200 CE for gladiatorial contests.

In addition to its remarkably preserved architectural remains, Aphrodisias is notable for having been the site of an active school of sculpture. Many full-length figures have been found in the city's large agora. Numerous sarcophagi have been found decorated with columns and garland. Also, what has been called "peopled scrolls" have been found carved with human figures, birds, and other animals entwined within acanthus leaves.

Nearly two thousand inscriptions have been discovered at Aphrodisias by archaeologists working under the aegis of New York University. Many of the inscriptions have been found on stones reused in the city's walls. Most inscriptions date from the Roman period, but others date from the Hellenistic and Byzantine eras.

The excavation and conservation of Aphrodisias is largely due to the efforts of the Turkish archaeologist, Kenan Erim, who essentially dedicated his adult life to the study of Aphrodisias. Working and living at the site for thirty years, Erim was buried at the site, and today his grave can be found there. Work continues at Aphrodisias by Christopher Ratte of NYU and R.R. Smith of Oxford University under the aegis of New York University

On my trip to western Turkey in 2011, I found Aphrodisias to be as impressive as the archaeological site of Ephesus, if not even more so. Fortunately, our local guide scheduled our visit to Ephesus very early in the morning. By the end of our tour of

Ephesus, the site was filling up with hordes of tourists who had embarked from the cruise ships docked in the Aegean. In marked contrast, our tour group had Aphrodisias almost totally to itself.

Adapted from:

http://en.wikipedia.org/wiki/Aphrodisias

https://whc.unesco.org › Culture › World Heritage Centre › The List

https://www.timetravelturtle.com/aphrodisias-best-ruins-turkey/

https://www.wmf.org/project/aphrodisias-archaeological-site

http://www.aphrodisias.com

TURKEY

Country name: Republic of Turkey (Turkish: Türkiye)

Site name: Göbekli Tepe

Location: 12 km southeast of Sunliurfa, southeastern Anatolia

UNESCO World Heritage Site: Nominated for designation at the 42nd World Heritage Committee Meeting, 2018

Date of Visit: 18 May 2012

EARTH'S OLDEST TEMPLES: GÖBEKLI TEPE

The discovery of Göbekli Tepe is regarded as one of the greatest archaeological finds of the twentieth century. Some archaeologists have said that it is a site that "changes everything" and that proves "all our theories were wrong." It invalidates many previous assumptions about the early development of human settlements and civilization. Other archaeologists have said that it provides evidence that "first came the temple and then the city," rather than the opposite. It is now thought that temples may have been built first and then agriculture developed to feed the temple builders.

What is most impressive is the great age of the site, which has been dated to the tenth to eighth millennia BCE. Another well known Anatolian site, that of Catalhöyük, dates from two thousand years later.

Göbekli Tepe, meaning "pot belly hill" in Turkish, is an artificial hill and once even had a depression at its top resembling a navel. The site measures 15m (49 feet) in height and approximately 300m (980 feet) in diameter. Located on a hill and rising 1000 feet above the valley, the site has a panoramic view of the surrounding mountains and plains. It is believed to have been a gathering place for the region, attracting people from up to 150 km (90 miles) away. Göbekli Tepe is thought to have served almost exclusively as a religious and social gathering site for what was basically a hunter-gatherer society, especially since there is no evidence of any nearby settlements.

Sculptures of animals decorate many of the T-shaped
monoliths of Göbekli Tepe, located in eastern Turkey.

The large quantity of broken animal bones and stone vessels excavated at the site is thought to be evidence of its being a place for feasting. Of the 100,000 bones excavated at the site, up to sixty percent were found to be gazelle bones. Many bones of various birds were also found, including those of vultures, cranes, geese, and ducks. Cut marks on the bones are thought to be evidence that the birds were killed, cooked, and eaten.

Göbekli Tepe was first surveyed by the University of Chicago and Istanbul University in 1963. At that time, an American archaeologist, Peter Benedict, collected objects from the site that he identified as being from the Aceramic Neolithic, but he misinterpreted the site's T-shaped pillars as grave markers from the Byzantine period. Also, since the area had been under cultivation for many decades, some farmers had broken the stones they found, mistaking them for ordinary rocks.

In 1994, after having worked at the Neolithic site of Nevah Çori, a German archaeologist associated with the German Archaeological Institute, Klaus Schmidt, undertook work at Göbekli Tepe. He excavated the first of the site's T-shaped pillars, often weighing up to sixteen tons, in collaboration with the museum at nearby Sanliurfa. Schmidt led the excavations at Göbekli Tepe from 1996 until his death in 2014. Excavations have taken place primarily at the southern side of the site, but it is estimated that less than five percent of the site has been excavated so far.

Human activity at the site is said to go back to the Epipaleolithic era, and evidence points to the site having become a religious center by 11,000 BCE or earlier. Activity at Göbekli Tepe has also been divided into two periods: the Pre-Pottery Neolithic A, dated to the tenth century BCE, and the Pre-Pottery Neolithic B, dated to the ninth century BCE.

The T-shaped pillars found at Göbekli Tepe stand at a height of sixteen feet and may weigh between seven and ten tons. They form circular areas measuring up to sixty-five feet in diameter. Of the many representations of animals found on the pillars, none appear to depict hunting activities, the wounding of animals, or animals used as sacrifices. Examples of animals carved on the pillars by stone blades and hammers include foxes, wild boars, cranes, wild ducks, snakes, spiders, scorpions, and lions. The wide variety of animals depicted do not make for any simple answers as to their intended symbolism. Especially noteworthy is that no evidence of the domestication of animals or plants has been found at Göbekli Tepe. It appears that the site flourished before the beginnings of animal husbandry and agriculture and the invention of the wheel and writing.

Especially mysterious are the carvings on the site's T-shaped pillars which are humanoid in form and appear to depict stylized arms, hands, and loincloths. It is suggested that the carvings may be representations of ancestors which served shamanistic purposes. Although nothing comparable to Göbekli Tepe in its size and significance has been found since its discovery, other T-shaped pillars have been located at such sites as Karahan Tepe, Sefer Tepe, Tase Tepe, and Hamzan Tepe.

Nearby, quarrying activity can be seen in the channels measuring 10m (33 feet) long and 20 cm (7.9 inches) wide located on the southern side of the site's plateau. Three Neolithic T-shaped pillars still lie embedded in the rock on the plateau's northern side, while two unfinished pillars lie on its southern side.

Göbekli Tepe has been included on UNESCO's tentative list of heritage sites for the last five years and is scheduled to be reviewed and approved as a heritage site at the World Heritage committee's meeting in 2018. Its acceptance as a heritage site has been actively promoted by the local government, various tourist agencies, the Turkish government, and by Turkey's private sector. It is stated that it is the strongest nominee to be considered at the meeting in 2018.

A four thousand square meter, steel roof is being constructed to cover and protect the site while it is temporarily closed. The project is reputed to cost some six million euros and to be supported by the Economic Union. A permanent UNESCO delegation is also said to have been sent to the site to oversee the construction.

When I visited the site in 2012, only a small guard house and temporary wood walkways were seen at the excavated site. There were also wooden caps temporarily covering many of the relief sculptures on the T-shaped pillars.

Today, the site is being visited by hundreds of tourists every day, and a parking area and gift shop have been added. Plans are underway for a larger visitors center, and improved fencing and walkways are planned in order to protect the site. Not only is there the increasing impact of tourism, but the site is near the border with Syria and at a crossing point for Syrian refugees.

At best, Göbekli Tepe remains an archaeological enigma. Not known is why every few decades the old temple pillars were covered over and new, smaller temples were then built inside the older, larger ones. Abandoned in about 8000 BCE, Göbekli Tepe was deliberately backfilled with 300 to 500 cubic meters of soil, refuse, and stone fragments, vessels, and tools. In the process, the ancient sites have been preserved as they otherwise would not have been.

As with many other such ancient sites, we will probably never know all the secrets hidden in the prehistory of Göbekli Tepe.

Adapted from:

https://www.dailysabah.com/.../gobeklitepe-expected-to-be-permanently-registered-on...

https://en.wikipedia.org/wiki/Göbekli_Tepe

gobeklitepe.info/

www.ancient-origins.net/.../monumental-cover-why-did-gobekli-tepe-end-dirt-00835...

TURKEY

Country name: Republic of Turkey (Turkish: Türkiye)

Site name: Nemrut Dag (also called Nemrut Dagi)

Location: 9 km from Kahta, 43 km from Adigaman; in the eastern Taurus mountain range, Adiyaman province, Turkey

UNESCO World Heritage Site: Inscribed 1987; no. 448

Date of Visit: 15 May 2012

THE SYNCRETIC MAUSOLEUM OF ANTIOCHUS I: NEMRUT DAG

The Hierotheseion, or temple-tomb, of Antiochus I Theos (69-34 BCE), stands atop one of the highest peaks of the Taurus Mountains in eastern Turkey. Antiochus reigned over a kingdom located north of Syria and the Euphrates River called Commagene. Formed after the fragmentation of the empire of Alexander the Great, the kingdom had dual origins in both Greek and Persian cultures. In Commagene, King Mithridates I had established an independent kingdom that reached its height during the reign of his son, Antiochus. Unfortunately, Commagene soon lost its independence in 72 CE after losing a war with Rome.

The massive funerary monument is a circular tumulus with a diameter of 145m and a height of 50m. It stands within a protected site measuring 13,830 hectares. Some of its stones are estimated to weigh nine tons. On three sides, the north, west and east, are terraces, with processional paths leading off to the west and east. On both its east and west sides are located five giant, seated figures of limestone. Guardian animals representing lions and eagles were placed at either side of the rows of images. Only the bodies of the images, measuring up to seven meters high, remain on the upper levels of the tumulus with their heads now sitting at a lower level where two rows of sandstone stelae with inscriptions mounted on pedestals are located. One row of stelae contains relief sculptures representing the paternal, Persian ancestry of Antiochus, while other stelae bear depictions of his maternal, Macedonian lineage. The king is represented as a descendant of Darius by means of Mithridates, his father, and as a descendent of Alexander the Great through his mother, Laodice.

Attesting to the very syncretic pantheon of deities seen at Nemrut Dag is the association of the Greek god, Zeus, with Oromasdes (the Persian deity, Ahuramazda) and the blending of the Greek, Heracles, with Artagnes (the Persian god, Verathragna).

While the stelae on the north terrace have no inscriptions or relief sculptures, on the western terrace there are rows of stelae, sitting to one side of the main altar areas, which contain scenes of handshaking (dexiosius) with Antiochus shaking hands with a deity. Also, a stele said to represent a lion horoscope is thought to be indicative of the date of the monument's construction.

While it is assumed that the enormous tumulus harbors the ashes or bones of Antiochus in an underground chamber later covered over with rubble, excavations undertaken in the mid-twentieth century resulted in locating no burial chamber.

The massive tumulus is estimated to have originally measured an estimated height of 60m, but its height is believed to have been diminished over the centuries by weathering, exposure to the sun, snow accumulation, and by visitors who used to be allowed to climb atop it. Located near the East Anatolian Fault, the monument is also vulnerable to earthquakes.

In addition to the UNESCO World Heritage Site designation in 1987, the site is protected under the National Conservation Law no. 2863. In 1988 it was declared a national park and is protected under National Parks Law no. 2873. In 2008 the site was designated an Interaction Transition Zone by the Sanliufga Regional Council for Conservation of Cultural Property. A study of the site was also initiated in 2002 by the Commagene Nemrut Conservation Development Program (CNCDP). In 2009 plans were made for the construction of visitor centers located outside

Head of a deity from the mountaintop
mausoleum of Nemrut Dag, eastern Turkey

the protected site area on the routes to the site from both Malatya and Adiyaman.

The monument has been called a unique artistic masterwork and, with its complicated design and massive scale, has been heralded as a monument unparalleled in the history of antiquity. It is also seen as one of the most ambitious constructions of the Hellenistic world.

The site is best reached by car with a local guide, since it is located in a very high, remote, mountainous area reached only by a long, twisting mountain road. The car park ends at a distance from the site itself, so there is a very long, rocky path to be climbed before one even catches a glimpse of the monument at the very top of the mountain. The stone steps winding up the mountainside are particularly treacherous due to all the small, loose stones on the path. Rather than making the very chilly climb up the mountain on foot, one tour member chose to ride one of the donkeys available for hire at the parking area.

While the very arduous climb up the mountainside is worthwhile to see one of eastern Turkey's most important and famous ancient monuments, it sits atop a mountain that rises 2,000 meters over the surrounding area, providing spectacular views overlooking the Firat River and the plains below.

Adapted from:

http://whc.unesco.org/en/list/448

http://www.kultur.gov.tr/EN,99770/adiyaman---nemrut-dagi-national-park.html

https://www.atlasobscura.com/places/nemrut-dagi

UNITED STATES OF AMERICA

Country name: United States of America (USA)
Site name: Everglades National Park
Location: southern tip of the state of Florida
UNESCO World Heritage Site: Inscribed 1979; no. 76

AMERICA'S ENDANGERED HERITAGE SITE: FLORIDA'S EVERGLADES

The Everglades National Park is the only American UNESCO heritage site listed as being endangered. As a result, it is one of the fifty-four sites on the worldwide heritage list cited as endangered. Of the 1,073 sites on UNESCO's, list twenty-three are within the borders of the USA.

The Everglades include one and a half million acres of wetlands on the southernmost tip of the state of Florida. It is the USA's largest park in the lower forty-eight states after Death Valley and Yellowstone National Park and attracts more than a million visitors every year. It is the world's only area to be included on three international lists: the International Biosphere Reserve, the list of Wetlands of International Importance and the UNESCO World Heritage List.

In 1976, the Everglades, along with the Dry Tortugas National Park, were cited as an International Biosphere Reserve, a project of the Man and Biosphere program of UNESCO. On 26 October, 1979, the Everglades were cited as a UNESCO World Heritage Site. In June of 1987, they were listed as a Wetland of International Importance. In 1971, at a convention in Ramsar, Iran, an international treaty had been signed protecting wetlands and their resources. The Ramsar List of Wetlands of Importance lists 1,929 sites, including the Everglades.

The Everglades were first inscribed on the List of World Heritage in Danger in 1993 after Hurricane Andrew and after suffering damage caused by urban and agricultural development. In 2007 it was removed from the list after efforts toward restoration had been made. In July of 2010, at the USA's request, they were again listed as being endangered. Water flow had been reduced by sixty percent. Nutrient pollution had increased, and there had been a decline in marine habitat. Also at the request of the USA, scientists from the UNESCO World Heritage Center and the International Union for the Conservation of Nature (IUCN) were invited to assist in conservation and restoration plans to remove the Everglades from the endangered list.

The park contains the Western hemisphere's largest area of mangroves, the largest region of sawgrass prairie, and one of North America's most important breeding areas for wading birds. The Everglades are also North America's largest subtropical area and a region where temperate and subtropical climates meet, where fresh water mixes with saltwater, and where a complex habitat has formed supporting a high diversity of fauna and flora. South Florida has been described as having both a tropical savanna and tropical monsoon climate and as having two primary seasons, wet and dry.

As home to a wide variety of plant life, the Everglades are especially notable for their epiphytic orchids and bromeliads. In addition to the twenty-five known varieties of orchids identified as living in the park are 120 tree species and more than a thousand seed-bearing plants.

The area is the home of thirty-six endangered or threatened animal species. The Florida Panther is one of its most endangered. It is estimated that only about fifty panthers live in the park and in the Big Cypress Swamp. The Atlantic green sea turtle, the Atlantic hawksbill, and the Atlantic loggerhead turtles are also all at risk. As for the Cape Sable seaside sparrows, 6,656 were reported as being found in 1981, but only 2,624 of the birds could be located in 2002. The West Indian manatee also continues to be threatened by loss of habitat and by collisions with boats.

One thousand American crocodiles are said to live in southern Florida, which is their only habitat in the USA. While they have increased in numbers and have been classified as threatened rather than endangered, they continue to be threatened by loss of habitat and by collisions with vehicles.

The Everglades are also threatened by exotic or non-native species, accounting for twenty-six percent of the mammals, fish, birds and reptiles found in south Florida. The park also has one of the world's largest numbers of non-native plant species, such as the melaleuca tree, the Brazilian pepper, and the Old World climbing fern. Invasive insects include the Bromeliad beetle, while the Burmese python is undoubtedly its most invasive reptile. The U.S. Fish and Wildlife Service has been compiling statistics on such species, and it is estimated that their control costs some five hundred million dollars per year, while 6,900 square km (1,700,000 acres) of land in south Florida continue to be infested.

Two major highways crossing the state, the Tamiami Trail and the so-called "Alligator Alley," have been built and have inhibited the flow of water southwest from Lake Okeechobee. Replacing much of the highways with bridges will cost millions of dollars. The Everglades are also endangered by global warming. As an example, water levels at Florida's Key West have been shown to have recently risen by 0.2 meters (0.7 feet).

Conservation and restoration of the Everglades has been an especially politically-charged issue in south Florida. In 1882 it was proposed that the wetlands be drained and converted to urban development and agricultural use. Water flowing from Lake Okeechobee was diverted and controlled. In the 1880s the first canals were built but succeeded in draining little of the land. From 1905 to 1910, Broward County succeeded in draining sufficient land to sell it off at $30 per acre, to establish the city of Davie, and to develop parts of Lee and Dade counties. Land was also cleared to make way for fields growing sugarcane. With the economic boom of the 1920s, a four-story wall was built around Lake Okeechobe. Canals were upgraded, while water levels dropped dramatically. Especially during the 1950s and 1960s, 2,300 km (1,400 miles) of levees and sixteen pumping stations were constructed to direct water away from the Everglades.

In 1947 a reporter for the *Miami Herald*, Marjory Stoneman Douglas, succeeded in publishing her book, *The Everglades: River of Grass*. The book sold five hundred thousand copies, and Douglas became known as the "Grand Dame of the Everglades." As founder of the Friends of the Everglades, she continued to advocate for the preservation of the wetlands of the Everglades until her death in 1998 at the age of 108.

In 1923, a proposal to form a national park was initiated, primarily under the leadership of Ernest F. Coe, often called the "Father of the Everglades." On 30 May, 1947, the Everglades became the first national park to protect a region that was not noted for its geological and scenic beauty but as a protected area for its ecological uniqueness and its diverse flora and fauna. The U.S. House of Representative passed the bill creating the national park, but only after a rider was added that no money be allocated for the park for the next five years.

In 1949, the Central and Southern Florida Flood Control Plan, managed by the Army Corps of Engineers, was was established, allowing the construction of thousands of miles of flood control structures and canals and basically cutting off the Everglades' supply of water. Then in 1989, President George W. Bush approved the Everglades National Park Protection and Expansion Act. It closed the park to airboats and added 109,506 acres to the park. It also directed the Department of the Army to restore water to the park in order to improve its ecology. In 2000, Congress formed the Comprehensive Everglades Restoration Plan (CERP). The controversial plan was supported by the National Audubon Society but criticized by the Friends of the Everglades and the Biodiversity Legal Foundation as reflecting primarily business and agricultural interests.

Today the Everglades National Park covers 6,110 square km (1,509,000 acres) and parts of Florida's Collier, Dade and Monroe counties. It sits, on average, from sea level to 2.4m (8 feet) in height, while some areas may rise as high as 20 feet above sea level. Essentially a very flat wetland, the park's underlying limestone has contributed much to its diverse ecosystems. With no springs feeding into the Everglades, it is rainwater that essentially continues to supply its underground reservoir called the "Florida Aquifer." Lying about 300m (1,000 feet) under south Florida, the permeable limestone has a great ability to store water. Water evaporating from the Everglades rains over the region, providing fresh water eventually flowing from such watershed areas as the Kissimmee River and Lake Okeechobee. It finally becomes a shallow, slow moving river measuring forty to seventy miles in width flowing to the south.

The park continues to be encroached upon by the growth of such cities as Cape Coral, Naples and Fort Myers to the west. In an evaluation of protected areas carried out by National Geographic, the park received the low score of thirty-two out of one hundred points, based on a system rating park management and sustainable tourism.

The state of Florida has set aside more than $2 billion for restoration of the Everglades, but relatively few federal funds have been forthcoming. As of 2008, the federal government had spent only $400 million of the $7.8 billion that it had originally appropriated for upgrading the park.

It is estimated that only fifty percent of what originally was part of the Everglades survives intact to this day.

Adapted from:

http://en.wikipedia.org/wiki/Everglades_National_Park
www.southfloridaparks.org/Find_Your_Park/Everglades
http://whc.unesco.org/en/news/638/
http://whc.unesco.org/en/list/76
https://www.nps.gov/ever/learn/news/international designations.htm

UZBEKISTAN

Country name: Republic of Uzbekistan (Uzbek: O'zbekiston Respublikasi)

Site name: Shakhrisabz (also spelled Shakhrisyabz)

Location: Qashqadaryo region, southern Uzbekistan; located approximately 80 km south of Samarkand

UNESCO World Heritage Site: Inscribed 2000; no. 885

Date of Visit: 10 October 2013

TAMERLANE'S HOME TOWN: SHAKHRISABZ

Most visitors to Uzbekistan will visit Samarkand and will see the famous Gur Emir, the tomb of Timur the Lame, best known in the West as Tamerlane. But they should also visit the city of Shakhrisabz, located to the south to see the remains of what was Tamerlane's most grandiose architectural project, the Ak-Saray.

Amir Timur is undoubtedly one of Central Asia's best-known rulers. Born on April 9, 1336, into the family of a local chief in Shakhrisabz, he considered the city his home town. It appears that he originally planned to have his tomb built there until Samarkand became the larger and more important city, leaving Shakhrisabz somewhat of a backwater town.

Shakhrisabz, meaning "Green City" and known as Kesh in Tamerlane's day, is regarded as being more than 2000 years old. Located on one of the ancient Silk Roads, it was the primary center of the Kesh area in the fourteenth and fifteenth centuries. It then reached its height in the fifteenth and sixteenth centuries under the rule of Tamerlane.

The ruins of Timur's summer palace are the primary attraction in Shakhrisabz. Known as the Ak-Saray, meaning "white palace," the huge palace's construction was started in 1380 and lasted twenty-four years. Records show that the palace

Statue of Tamerlane, located at his palace,
the Ak-Saray, at Shakhrisabz, Uzbekistan

was constructed by architects and craftsmen from Khwarezm, an area recently conquered by Timur. An inscription gives the date of the completion of the palace as 798 AH (1395-6 CE), but completing the decoration of the palace probably took much longer. Another inscription gives the name of Muhammad Yusuf Tebrizi from the city of Tabriz as one of the craftsmen working on the palace.

Today, all that remains of the grandiose palace are the enormous pylons of a *pishtaq*, the projecting elements of an *iwan* or a large, formal gateway. It is estimated that the portal must have originally stood at a height of 70m. Topped by arched pinnacles it had corner towers some 80m high set on multifaceted pedestals. The immense entryway is thought to have measured 50m in width, while its archway is thought to have been Central Asia's largest, spanning 22.5m.

Fortunately, a Spanish ambassador, Ruy Gonzalez de Clavijo, visited Shakhrisabz in 1404 and left a detailed description of the magnificent palace. He described it as having a large courtyard around which many living and service quarters were grouped. The main courtyard is estimated to have measured 120-124m wide and 240-250m long. He also described the palace as having meadows and shady gardens filled with fruit trees and formal pools. Today, climbing the 116 steps to the top of the surviving ruins not only provides visitors with views of the surrounding countryside but will give them more of an appreciation of the immensity of the palace's size.

Tradition credits Abdullakhan as having destroyed the immense palace and killing Timur's descendants in his sieges to conquer Shahrisabz. By the 18th century only the pillars and the arch of the palace's primary entrance remained.

Today, the palace ruins have, in large part, not received the dubious Russian reconstructions and restorations seen elsewhere in Central Asia. One cannot help but be impressed by the refinement of the tile designs and the sophistication of the colors of blue, white, and gold, glazed decoration, even as fragments. In addition to the complex geometric ornament and exquisite foliate designs are inscriptions from the Koran.

Today, a modern statue of Timur stands at a distance from the surviving ruins of the palace portal in what was once the huge palace's central courtyard. The day of our visit, the statue was the crowded scene of wedding parties taking photographs.

Although the tomb of Tamerlane, the Gur Emir, is located in Samarkand, in 1943 archaeologists discovered an underground chamber containing a single tomb in Shakhrisabz. The ruler's name inscribed on it has led some to believe that it was originally intended for Tamerlane. Mysteriously, the tomb contained only the remains of two unidentified bodies.

In addition to the Ak-Saray, there are other notable monuments, especially those dating from the Timurid period, that have led to UNESCO's inscribing the old parts of the city as a World Heritage site. Enclosed within the old city walls, parts of which still remain, is a group of quite exceptional ancient areas. Built at two cross streets is the roofed, octagonal-shaped Chur-su bazaar. There is a bathhouse, built in the fifteenth century, still in use today. The large complex, the Dorus Saodat, is not only a burial ground but also contains a mosque, accommodations for pilgrims, and a religious community. In addition to numerous historic houses, Shakhrisabz possesses notable mosques of a more recent date, including the Kunchibar, Kunduzar, Chubin, and Mirhamid mosques.

Of special note is the Kok-Gumbaz Mosque, dated 1435, located in the Donut-Tilavat memorial complex. With a name meaning "blue dome," it is the largest Friday mosque in Shakhrisabz. The mosque bears a portal inscription stating that it was built by Ulugbek in honor of his father, Shakhruh. The square mosque, with its four niches oriented towards the four directions, is recognizable due to its very prominent dome covered in blue, ceramic tiles.

In July of 2016, Shakhrisabz's historic center was placed on the List of World Heritage in Danger. There was concern that the historic center of the city had been adversely affected by overdevelopment and by the construction of visitor facilities such as hotels. It was feared that irreversible changes were being made to the city's old center and that its ancient appearance was being compromised. As a result, a joint mission of UNESCO's World Heritage Center and the International Council of Monuments and Sites (ICOMOS) was proposed to assess what damage to the city had occurred and what corrective measures should be taken.

Even in its highly ruinous state, it is the Ak-Saray that makes a trip to Shakhrisabz especially worthwhile. Even in ruins, it impresses with its extraordinary scale, its exceptionally refined ornament and the grandeur of Timur's architectural conception.

Adapted from:

https://en.wikipedia.org/wiki/Shahrisabz
http://whc.unesco.org/en/list/885
http://www.advantour.com/uzbekistan/shakhrisabz/ak_saray.htm

VIETNAM

Country name: Socialist Republic of Vietnam (Vietnamese: Viet Nam)

Site name: My Son

Location: Duy Xuyen District, Quang Nam Province, central Vietnam; 69 km southwest of Da Nang

UNESCO World Heritage Site: Inscribed 1999, no. 949

Tour Dates: 4-17 December 2009

BOMBED INTO OBLIVION: MY SON

In one week in August of 1969, American B52 airplanes extensively carpet-bombed Vietnam's historic site of My Son. It had been targeted as a hideout of the Vietcong. Only after protests sent in January of 1971 to President Richard Nixon by Philippe Stern, an expert on Vietnam's Cham art, were measures finally taken to preserve what remained of My Son. Today much of the surrounding area remains dangerous due to unexploded ordnance, and much de-mining work in the area has yet to be accomplished.

In the early twentieth century, the French archaeologist Henriy Parmentier had identified seventy-one ancient temples at My Son and had divided them into fourteen basic groups. Today, only the ruins of eighteen temples are known to have survived. With aid from UNESCO, archaeologists are now struggling to piece together what remains at My Son, but much has been lost forever.

My Son, meaning "beautiful mountain" in Vietnamese, is thought to be one of the longest-inhabited sites and the most important site of its type in Vietnam. It is cited as having been the religious and cultural center of the Champa kingdom, lasting for a millennium from the fourth to the fourteenth centuries CE.

Since I found myself with a free afternoon after a drive from Hoi An, I felt fortunate that our tour director found it possible to locate a local guide who would take me out to the archaeological site. It became an almost magical trip back in time to the ancient kingdom of Champa. As I walked through the site on my own, the ruined, ancient Hindu temples slowly emerged from the lush, green jungle vegetation almost like a mirage when I finally arrived at the archaeological site itself. I had only half a day at the site, but my recommendation is that My Son is best visited as a day trip from either Danang or Hoi An.

The site, measuring approximately 2 km in width, is exceptionally picturesque, set in a valley covered in a dense, verdant jungle with the mountain, Hon Quap (Cat Tooth Mountain) overlooking the area. Surrounded by a ring of mountains, it sits in a basin that is the source of the Thu Bon River which eventually flows into the South China Sea at the port city of Hoi An.

Built by the kings of Champa (Chiem Thanh in Vietnamese), My Son's earliest records date from the time period of King Fanhuda (Vietnamese: Phom Ho Dat). Reigning from 380 to 413 CE, his name meant "blessed armor" or is thought to possibly be a reference to the Jasminum sambac flower.

My Son was dedicated to the worship of the Hindu deity Shiva, known locally under various names, the most important of which was Bhadreshvara. Its temples, regarded as among the most important of their kind, were also constructed to symbolize the great Hindu mountain, Mount Meru. Two hundred years after its foundation My Son was rebuilt by King Sambhuvarman (Vietnamese: Pham Phan Chi, reigning 577 to 629 CE) and dedicated to Bhadreshvara under the name of Sambhu-Bhadreshvara. After central Vietnam was conquered by the Viet and the slow decline of the Champa kingdom, My Son became almost totally forgotten.

The French archaeologist M. C. Paris is credited with discovering My Son in 1898. In the following year, the site came under the study of the École française d'Extrême Orient (EFEO). In 1904 the discoveries at My Son were published in the

One of the few remaining temples remaining
after the bombing of My Son, Vietnam

society's bulletin, and My Son's inscriptions were published by M. L. Finot.

While none of the inscriptions in Sanskrit and old Cham written on perishable materials have survived, many inscriptions on stone have been found at My Son. Thirty-two inscriptions on stone stelae, primarily dealing with political and religious matters, have been located, transcribed, and translated.

Much about the construction of My Son's temples is not fully understood. Most of its temples were constructed of red brick. Only the temple given the number "B1," has been identified as being of stone. Decorative motifs or reliefs were cut directly into the brick rather than being made on slabs of sandstone later inserted into the fabric of the temples. Still not fully understood are how the bricks were fired and what type of mortar was used.

Although many pieces of Cham art have been sent to France or have been relocated in local museums, two temporary museums have been set up at the site. I felt especially fortunate in that the next day after visiting My Son, our tour itinerary included a visit to the Museum of Cham Sculpture or "Bao Tang Cham" in Danang, founded by the École française d'Extrême Orient in 1915. The museum is well known as housing the world's finest collection of Cham art.

While My Son continues to be at risk due to such climatic conditions as high humidity and flooding, one of the most pressing concerns is the unexploded ordnance remaining in the site's buffer zones. Land mines have hindered the exploration of new areas and the upgrading of the site for visitors. In addition to the UNESCO World Heritage Site inscription in 1999, My Son has been cited by the Culture Ministry as a National Site in 1979 and is protected under the Cultural Heritage Law of 2001.

Having visited My Son nearly fifty years after it was nearly bombed into oblivion, I could only be very deeply saddened when thinking about what the site possibly may have looked like before the advent of the so-called "American War." I couldn't help but feel that the devastation at My Son was not only that of Vietnam's legacy but was the destruction of the legacy of all of us as humans.

Adapted from:

https://en.wikipedia.org/wiki/Mỹ_Sơn
http://whc.unesco.org/en/list/949
https://wikitravel.org/en/My_Son

GEOTOURISM AND THE FUTURE

GEOTOURISM

As defined by Jonathan B. Tourtellot, director of the National Geographic Society's Sustainable Tourism, geotourim is "tourism that sustains or enhances the geographical character of the place being visited … its environment, its heritage, its aesthetics, its culture and the well-being of its citizens."

Ecotourism is said to be exclusively concerned with preserving nature, while geotourim is said to include "everything that goes into making a place a place" and to focus on "recognizing that there are opportunities to build on character of place, and so enrich both the travel experience and the quality of the locale."

Tourtellot goes on to identify three types of tourism:

• "Touring" that depends both on the physical and natural characteristics of a location

• "R and R tourism" that is concerned with only the physical properties of a place, such as beaches, lakes and ski slopes

• "Entertainment tourism" that depends on neither, such as theme parks

In addition, Tourtellot says that geotourism draws "attention, in a holistic way, to all of the natural and human attributes that make a place worth visiting that … includes flora and fauna, historic structures and archaeological sites, scenic landscapes, traditional architecture, and all of the things that contribute to culture."

He also states that over half of those who travel believe that unspoiled locations are becoming harder to find. Seventy-five percent say they don't want to harm the sites they visit. Eighty percent want to see scenic locations.

As a result, National Geographic has established its Sustainable Tourism Research Center, a "TravelWatch" column in its *National Geographic Traveler* magazine, and World Legacy Awards in cooperation with Conservation International.

The thirteen principles that have been outlined by the Center for governments and travel organizations are:

1. Maintaining the integrity of a place
2. Adhering to international codes
3. Encouraging community involvement
4. Maximizing community benefit
5. Insuring tourist satisfaction
6. Conservation of resources
7. Protection of a destination's appeal
8. Sustainable planning
9. Appropriate land use
10. Maintaining market diversity
11. Interactive interpretation
12. Market selectivity
13. Continued evaluation

Adapted from:

http://www.traveldailynews.asia/columns/article/20790

https://www.linkedin.com/in/jonathan-tourtellot-a6a589

https://www.nationalgeographic.com/maps/geotourism/geotourism-principles.html

https://www.nationalgeographic.com/maps/geotourism/about/

OVERTOURISM

One of the primary concerns often heard when UNESCO World Heritage site status is mentioned is the possibility of its significantly increasing tourism. On the other hand, one wonders if the UNESCO World Heritage status of such tourist destinations as Italy's Florence, Rome, and Venice is a factor in tourists' decisions to visit such sites plagued by overtourim. Since few, if any, studies or surveys appear to have been conducted, it still remains to be seen if tourism at a particular site has actually increased significantly once UNESCO status has been given to the site.

The piazza, crowded with tourists, in front of St. Mark's, Venice

Some tour itineraries mention the UNESCO status of a site or list the number of such sites on a tour, but whether or not such factors cause potential travelers to book a particular tour or not remains to be determined. Also, how many travelers conduct research prior to their trips and determine the UNESCO status of sites is also largely unknown. It appears that travelers usually visit a site without knowing of its UNESCO status and that even many experienced travers may be unaware of UNESCO's World Heritage site program.

Yet overtourism, for whatever reason, is becoming an ever increasing problem at many sites around the world.

Overtourism and the need for what was called "destination councils" were the topics discussed at a meeting of the Global Sustainable Tourism Council (GSTC) in September of 2017. While the travel industry provides essential services at travel destinations, it was noted that it usually has provided no oversight of the destinations themselves. The council type of organization called for at the meeting would be "an effective

The Erechtheion atop Athen's Acropolis is often the backdrop for many tourists' photos and selfies.

organization, department, group, or committee responsible for a coordinated approach to sustainable tourism, with involvement by the private sector and public sector." It would also have "defined responsibilities, oversight, and implementation capability for the management of environmental, economic, social, and cultural issues."

It was noted that very few such "holistic, council-type arrangements exist," and the call was made to gather information on agencies or organizations that already meet some of the GSTC's criteria.

Examples of travel destinations where overtourism has already created many problems include Florence, Barcelona, and Venice.

Adapted from:

http://destinationcenter.org/author/jbtourtellot/

UNESCO

As with any human endeavor, UNESCO's World Heritage Site program may have a serious downside. Site designation could very well stimulate overtourism and create the development of nearby infrastructure supporting tourism that results in the downgrading of the site. The inscription of UNESCO sites has, in numerous instances, already been used for political purposes. A prime example is the withdrawal the United States from UNESCO on the grounds that it will not recognize Palestine as an independent state or as a valid UNESCO member and will not accept the inscription of the Palestinian city of Hebron as a UNESCO site.

Politics also enters the picture in the lobbying that is often done by countries to have their nominated sites approved by the UNESCO committee that meets annually. The UNESCO inscription of a site may be more about national pride than concern about the preservation of a site. It may also be seen as a means of increasing tourism and the revenue it generates rather than any intent of conserving or restoring a site. Politics also plays a role in which sites receive UNESCO funding for restoration projects. Often larger countries with the most international clout and visibility receive funding while smaller countries may be largely ignored.

Overtourism often includes the tourist who is primarily interested in getting a selfie in front of a popular site without any actual intent of learning much about the site being visited. Information given by licensed, local guides may become geared to the most common level. It may also trivialize the true nature of the site and may even encourage misinformation.

Overblown bureaucracy and red tape to be overcome to get things accomplished often becomes inbred with such a large, multinational organization as UNESCO. In addition, UNESCO often has little authority in the oversight of a designated site and can only recommend needed improvements. So far, it has deleted sites from its list in only two instances.

NEW TECHNOLOGIES

In our fast-changing world, many new technologies have had profound influences on such fields as archaeology and historic preservation.

LIDAR is an acronym for "light detection and ranging." It is also often called "laser scanning" and "3-D scanning." It is a method of surveying that measures the distances to targets with pulses of laser light and then measures the pulses of light reflected back to a sensor. It has been found to be very useful in making high resolution maps and to have had applications in such fields as archaeology, geography, geology, seismology, and forestry.

LIDAR has been found to be especially useful in locating archaeological remains hidden under dense vegetation and jungle canopies. It has also been useful for identifying large archaeological features that are often not identifiable at the ground level. It has become a relatively inexpensive and efficient means of integrating data into a Geographic Information System (GIS) for later analysis.

An example of the use of LIDAR in archaeology is the discovery of more than 60,000 man-made structures in the Maya Biosphere Reserve, revealing that Mayan civilization was much more widespread than archaeologists have originally believed it to be.

GPR is the acronym for "ground penetrating radar," which uses pulses of radar to map images beneath a surface. It uses electromagnetic radiation to reflect signals from subsurface structures and objects. It can be used to detect not only subsurface objects but also changes in the properties of materials, as well as cracks and voids. It can be applied to such various media as soil, rock, pavements, structures, and fresh water. Since the time needed to receive reflected signals can be measured, GPR can also be used to determine the depths at which objects are located. It has proved to be especially useful in making maps of subterranean structures and in the making of three-dimensional models of archaeological sites. It has also proven to be a method of identifying subsurface artifacts without the time and expense needed for systematic excavations.

Advances in aerial photography have also been found to be highly useful in the field of archaeology and especially in the mapping of large archaeological sites.

Digitalization has made it possible to bring together vast amounts of data on archaeological and historic sites and objects. The International Dunhuang Project (IDP) is an example of bringing together data on objects that once were priceless treasures stored in Cave 17 at the Mogao Caves in western China but which have since become scattered in public and private collections throughout the world.

Open Heritage is a project of Google that has formed a platform of highly-detailed, three-dimensional, digitized models of locations in danger around the world. For seven years, Google's Arts and Culture site has collaborated with CyArk, a non-profit organization. Thus far, sites covered by the digitized models include Mexico's Mayan site of Chichén Itzá and the Ananda Ok Kyaung temple in Bagan, Myanmar. In the case of the temple at Bagan, images have been made before and after the damaging earthquake of 2016. The Google project intends to make the scanned images available to a larger audience, whereas such detailed images have previously been available only to scholars, archaeologists, and three-dimensional scanning experts. While the project has, as its intent, the drawing of attention to imperiled sites and the aiding in their preservation, the project has come under criticism for lacking any sense of a human presence and not giving supporting interpretation of the sites recorded. Nevertheless, the project has been praised for the very impressive amount of data which it has gathered.

Sketchfab has also been cited as another project with an even larger online database of 3-D images. A cursory investigation of the *sketchfab.com* website's "Cultural Heritage and History" section revealed three-dimensional models of such well-known historic sites as the Al-Khazneh, or Treasury, at Jordan's Petra, the Colosseum in Rome, and the Sainte-Chapelle in Paris.

Still remaining to be seen is the extent to which virtual reality (VR) will develop and be able to give someone wearing a VR visor a close approximation of having actually visited a historic site.

Adapted from:

https://hyperallergic.com/438821/google-arts-culture-open-heritage/?utm_source=Breakfast+with+ARTnews&utm_campaign=81c06bb158

https://en.wikipedia.org/wiki/Lidar

https://en.wikipedia.org/wiki/Ground-penetrating_radar

THE FUTURE

What will happen to UNESCO's World Heritage Sites program in the future remains to be seen. Such a large, multinational organization is not likely to disappear anytime soon, and it can be assumed that sites meeting its criteria for inscription will continue to be added to its list every year. But its effectiveness may become increasingly threatened by political power plays among its various members. Scarcity of funds may also threaten its effectiveness if member nations continue to withhold membership dues. Conservation and restoration projects overseen and funded by UNESCO may become fewer.

Instability and warfare in many parts of the world will almost undoubtedly continue to threaten and cause the destruction of highly important heritage sites. Religious radicalism and zeal may also increasingly endanger many sites. With the recent rise in nationalism, protectionism, and the fears of globalization, many more sites may very well not receive the attention they deserve. Expanding populations and industrialization may continue to encroach upon designated sites and may continue to cause their degradation.

Human beings must be among the most contentious of species if past history is any indication. Cities, nations, and ethnic and religious groups have pitted themselves against each other in warfare and in ethnic cleansing. Warfare on local, regional, national, and international levels may continue to devastate important heritage sites. Wars may also greatly curtail conservation and restoration efforts.

Winners in conflicts have often assumed that they have the right to rewrite history and have proceeded to attempt to destroy, replace, or modify what has gone before. Examples are the hieroglyphics of Egyptian pharaohs being replaced by their successors and ancient temples being allowed to survive and modified as Christian churches such as seen in the Parthenon in Athens and the Pantheon in Rome. Mayan and Incan temples have been in large part destroyed, and Christian cathedrals have often been built over the sites as seen in Mexico City and in Cuzco, Peru.

Also taking their toll on historic sites are the rise, flourishing, and fall of various nations and empires. Often the fall of cities and empires has been the result of natural disasters. Volcanic eruptions destroyed ancient Pompeii, while it is thought that drought may have been part of the causes for the abandonment of Mayan cities and the downfall of the Khmer empire in Southeast Asia. The overextension and hubris of the Roman Empire is often regarded as being among the causes for its downfall. It is also seen that, after locations have been abandoned, nature very soon overtakes almost anything built by humans.

UNESCO often comes under criticism for not being as effective as many feel it should have been in the preservation of both natural and archaeological sites. In such an imperfect world as ours, it would seem quite unreasonable to expect anything near perfection from such a multinational agency. Instead, perhaps we should be amazed at what UNESCO has managed to accomplish in saving many historic sites from oblivion or from further degradation. Perhaps we should be thankful for all the many restoration projects it has seen fit to undertake and fund.

Seen from outer space, planet Earth has often been described as looking like a "blue marble" sitting in isolation in the blackness of space. When seen from space, one sees no political boundaries. One sees only one lonely planet where we human beings live. From outer space we can see that we all share one common heritage as human beings.

By not preserving Planet Earth's cultural legacy, we humans must be reminded, as the comic strip character Pogo has said, "We have met the enemy, and he is us."

Made in the USA
San Bernardino, CA
07 July 2018